# KS3 HISTORY
## Third Edition

# Invasion, Plague and Murder

# Britain 1066–1509

Aaron Wilkes
Katrina Shearman

# Teacher Handbook

OXFORD
UNIVERSITY PRESS

# OXFORD
UNIVERSITY PRESS

Great Clarendon Street, Oxford, OX2 6DP, United Kingdom

Oxford University Press is a department of the University of Oxford.
It furthers the University's objective of excellence in research,
scholarship, and education by publishing worldwide. Oxford is a
registered trade mark of Oxford University Press in the UK and in
certain other countries

British Library Cataloguing in Publication Data
Data available

978-0-19-839322-1

10 9 8 7 6 5 4 3 2 1

Paper used in the production of this book is a natural, recyclable
product made from wood grown in sustainable forests.
The manufacturing process conforms to the environmental
regulations of the country of origin.

Printed in Great Britain by Bell and Bain Ltd., Glasgow

**Acknowledgements**
The publishers would like to thank the following for permissions to
use their photographs:

Cover illustration by Matthew Hollings

Although we have made every effort to trace and contact all
copyright holders before publication this has not been possible in all
cases. If notified, the publisher will rectify any errors or omissions at
the earliest opportunity.

Links to third party websites are provided by Oxford in good faith
and for information only. Oxford disclaims any responsibility for
the materials contained in any third party website referenced in
this work.

# Contents

# Scheme of Work

This table shows all the lessons available in the *Invasion, Plague and Murder Student Book*, in the *Key Stage 3 History* series, so that you can easily navigate through the book and supporting digital material on Kerboodle to select the key themes and topics that you might use to inform your own scheme of work.

**Key to resources**

SB – Student Book

TH – Teacher Handbook

K – Kerboodle

| Lesson title | Key Question | Resources |
|---|---|---|
| What is chronology? | What is chronology? | • SB pp.6–7<br>• K Baseline Auto-Marked Test<br>• K Baseline Assessment Task<br>• K Chronology Worksheet |
| A journey through the Middle Ages | What will we be learning this year in History? | • SB pp.8–9 |
| **Chapter 1: 1066 and all that** | | **1 Source Bank, 1 Auto-Marked Test on Kerboodle** |
| 1.1A The story of Britain… up to 1066 | What was Britain's early history? | • SB pp.10–11<br>• TH p.24<br>• K 1.1A Using Evidence History Skills Activity<br>• K 1.1A True or False Worksheet |
| 1.1B The story of Britain… up to 1066 | What was the Bronze Age like in Britain? | • SB pp.12–13<br>• TH p.25<br>• K 1.1B Significance History Skills Activity<br>• K 1.1B Immigrants Worksheet |
| 1.1C The story of Britain… up to 1066 | What happened after the Romans left Britain? | • SB pp.14–15<br>• TH p.26<br>• K 1.1C Using Evidence History Skills Activity<br>• K 1.1C Alfred Jewel Worksheet |
| 1.2A England before 1066: what was it like? | Who ruled England in the years up to 1066? | • SB pp.16–17<br>• TH p.27<br>• K 1.2A Using Evidence History Skills Activity<br>• K 1.2A Source Worksheet |
| 1.2B England before 1066: what was it like? | How do we know what happened in England before 1066? | • SB pp.18–19<br>• TH p.28<br>• K 1.2B Enquiry History Skills Activity<br>• K 1.2B Changes Worksheet |
| 1.3 Who will be the next King of England? | Who had the best claim to the throne? | • SB pp.20–21<br>• TH p.29<br>• K 1.3 Enquiry History Skills Activity<br>• K 1.3 Vote Worksheet 1<br>• K 1.3 Vote Worksheet 2 |
| 1.4 Round 1: the Battle of Stamford Bridge | Who fought at the Battle of Stamford Bridge? | • SB pp.22–23<br>• TH p.30<br>• K 1.4 Using Evidence History Skills Activity<br>• K 1.4 First Encounter Worksheet 1<br>• K 1.4 First Encounter Worksheet 2 |
| 1.5 Match of the day! | What weapons and tactics were used at the Battle of Hastings? | • SB pp.24–25<br>• TH p.31<br>• K 1.5 Enquiry History Skills Activity<br>• K 1.5 Warriors Worksheet 1<br>• K 1.5 Warriors Worksheet 2 |
| 1.6 Round 2: the Battle of Hastings – the morning | Where and how did the armies fight in the early stages of the battle? | • SB pp.26–27<br>• TH p.32<br>• K 1.6 Chronology History Skills Activity<br>• K 1.6 Diary Worksheet<br>• K 1.6 Build-Up Film Clip<br>• K 1.6 Film Worksheet<br>• K 1.56 Map Mini-Movie |
| 1.7 Round 2: the Battle of Hastings – the afternoon | How did William win the Battle of Hastings? | • SB pp.28–29<br>• TH p.33<br>• K 1.7 Using Evidence History Skills Activity<br>• K 1.7 Commentary Worksheet<br>• K 1.7 Tactics Film Clip<br>• K 1.7 Film Worksheet |
| 1.8 History Mystery: how did King Harold die? pp30-31 | How did King Harold die at the Battle of Hastings? | • SB pp.30–31<br>• TH p.34<br>• K 1.8 Using Evidence History Skills Activity 1<br>• K 1.8 Using Evidence History Skills Activity 2<br>• K 1.8 Investigation Worksheet 1<br>• K 1.8 Investigation Worksheet 2 |

| Chapter 2: The Norman Conquest | | 2 Source Bank, 2 Auto-Marked Test on Kerboodle |
| --- | --- | --- |
| 2.1A The conquest of England | As the king of England, how did William deal with problems? | • SB pp.32–33<br>• TH p.37<br>• K 2.1A Using Evidence History Skills Activity<br>• K 2.1A William Worksheet 1<br>• K 2.1A William Worksheet 2 |
| 2.1B The conquest of England | How did King William control the areas he conquered? | • SB pp.34–35<br>• TH p.38<br>• K 2.1B Using Evidence History Skills Activity<br>• K 2.1B Castles Worksheet |
| 2.2 William the castle-builder | How did King William use castles to control his new kingdom? | • SB pp.36–37<br>• TH p.39<br>• K 2.2 Significance History Skills Activity<br>• K 2.2 Motte and Bailey Worksheet<br>• K 2.2 Castles Film Clip<br>• K 2.2 Film Worksheet |
| 2.3 The Domesday Book | How did King William use the Domesday Book to control his new kingdom? | • SB pp.38–39<br>• TH p.40<br>• K 2.3 Using Evidence History Skills Activity<br>• K 2.3 Survey Worksheet 1<br>• K 2.3 Survey Worksheet 2<br>• K 2.3 Domesday Film Clip<br>• K 2.3 Film Worksheet |
| 2.4 The feudal system: who's the boss? | How did King William use barons to control his new kingdom? | • SB pp.40–41<br>• TH p.41<br>• K 2.4 Significance History Skills Activity<br>• K 2.4 Feudalism Worksheet 1<br>• K 2.4 Feudalism Worksheet 2<br>• K 2.4 Feudalism Worksheet 3<br>• K 2.4 Clever William Film Clip<br>• K 2.4 Film Worksheet |
| Chapter 3: Castles | | 3 Source Bank, 3 Auto-Marked Test on Kerboodle |
| 3.1A How did castles develop? | How did castles change after 1066? | • SB pp.42–43<br>• TH p.44<br>• K 3.1A Change and Continuity History Skills Activity<br>• K 3.1A Labelling Worksheet<br>• K 3.1A Tour Film Clip<br>• K 3.1A Film Worksheet |
| 3.1B How did castles develop? | Why did castles change after 1066? | • SB pp.44–45<br>• TH p.45<br>• K 3.1B Using Evidence History Skills Activity<br>• K 3.1B Letter Worksheet |
| 3.2A The siege of Rochester Castle | What tactics and weapons were used to get into a castle under siege? | • SB pp.46–47<br>• TH p.46<br>• K 3.2A Significance History Skills Activity<br>• K 3.2A Game Worksheet<br>• K 3.2A Interview Mini-Movie |
| 3.2B The siege of Rochester Castle | How did these tactics and weapons work? | • SB pp.48–49<br>• TH p.47<br>• K 3.2B Using Evidence History Skills Activity<br>• K 3.2B Diary Worksheet |
| 3.3A Who's who in a castle? | What was day-to-day life like in a castle? | • SB pp.50–51<br>• TH p.48<br>• K 3.3A Using Evidence History Skills Activity<br>• K 3.3A Roles Worksheet<br>• K 3.3A Inhabitants Film Clip<br>• K 3.3A Film Worksheet |
| 3.3B Who's who in a castle? | What were the names and jobs of the people who lived in castles? | • SB pp.52–53<br>• TH p.49<br>• K 3.3B Using Evidence History Skills Activity<br>• K 3.3B Application Worksheet |
| 3.4 Where have all our castles gone? | Why did the golden age of castle building end and how do we protect castles today? | • SB pp.54–55<br>• TH p.50<br>• K Assessment Task Presentation 1<br>• K 3.4 Estate Agent Worksheet |
| Assessing Your Learning 1 | What do we need to know about castles? | • SB pp.56–57<br>• TH pp.51–52<br>• K Assessment Task Presentation 1<br>• K Assessment Worksheet 1<br>• K Success Criteria Teacher Grid 1 |
| Chapter 4: How religious were people in the Middle Ages? | | 4 Source Bank, 4 Auto-Marked Test on Kerboodle |
| 4.1 Religious beliefs | What role did religion play in the lives of medieval people? | • SB pp.58–59<br>• TH p.53<br>• K 4.1 Using Evidence History Skills Activity<br>• K 4.1 Church Worksheet 1<br>• K 4.1 Church Worksheet 2 |

| 4.2 A day in the life of a monk | What did monks do and how did they contribute to medieval society? | • SB pp.60–61<br>• TH p.54<br>• K 4.2 Significance History Skills Activity<br>• K 4.2 Routine Worksheet<br>• K 4.2 Monastery Film Clip<br>• K 4.2 Film Worksheet |
|---|---|---|
| 4.3 Was it fun to be a nun? | What did nuns do and how did they help people in medieval society? | • SB pp.62–63<br>• TH p.55<br>• K 4.3 Using Evidence History Skills Activity<br>• K 4.3 Letter Worksheet 1<br>• K 4.3 Letter Worksheet 2 |
| 4.4 What were the Wars of the Cross? | Why was Jerusalem an important city for Christians, Muslims and Jews? | • SB pp.64–65<br>• TH p.56<br>• K 4.4 Using Evidence History Skills Activity<br>• K 4.4 Understanding Diversity History Skills Activity<br>• K 4.4 Jerusalem Worksheet |
| 4.5 Cuthbert the Crusader | What reasons did people have for going on Crusades? | • SB pp.66–67<br>• TH p.57<br>• K 4.5 Understanding Diversity History Skills Activity<br>• K 4.5 Postcard Worksheet |
| 4.6 Chronicles of the Crusades | What were the main events that happened during the Crusades? | • SB pp.68–69<br>• TH p.58<br>• K 4.6 Using Evidence History Skills Activity<br>• K 4.6 Timeline Worksheet<br>• K 4.6 New Ideas Mini-Movie |
| 4.7 What did the Crusades do for us? | How and why did life in Europe change after the Crusades? | • SB pp.70–71<br>• TH p.59<br>• K 4.7 Cause and Consequence History Skills Activity<br>• K 4.7 New Ideas Worksheet 1<br>• K 4.7 New Ideas Worksheet 2 |
| **Chapter 5: Life in the Middle Ages** | | **5 Source Bank, 5 Auto-Marked Test on Kerboodle** |
| 5.1A What was life like in a medieval village? | What were medieval villages like? | • SB pp.72–73<br>• TH p.62<br>• K 5.1A Change and Continuity History Skills Activity<br>• K 5.1A Map Worksheet<br>• K 5.1A Rosie Film Clip<br>• K 5.1A Film Worksheet |
| 5.1B What was life like in a medieval village? | How would a typical medieval villager spend his day? | • SB pp.74–75<br>• TH p.63<br>• K 5.1B Using Evidence History Skills Activity<br>• K 5.1B Peasants Worksheet<br>• K 5.1B Gong Farmer Film Clip<br>• K 5.1B Film Worksheet |
| 5.2A What was life like in a medieval town? | What were medieval towns like and how did they grow? | • SB pp.76–77<br>• TH p.64<br>• K 5.2A Enquiry History Skills Activity<br>• K 5.2A Labelling Worksheet |
| 5.2B What was life like in a medieval town? | What kinds of trades took place in medieval towns? | • SB pp.78–79<br>• TH p.65<br>• K 5.2B Change and Continuity History Skills Activity<br>• K 5.2B Using Evidence History Skills Activity<br>• K 5.2B Trades Worksheet |
| 5.3 How smelly were the Middle Ages? | How important was personal hygiene and cleanliness in the Middle Ages? | • SB pp.80–81<br>• TH p.66<br>• K 5.3 Using Evidence History Skills Activity<br>• K 5.3 Hygiene Worksheet 1<br>• K 5.3 Hygiene Worksheet 2 |
| 5.4 Could you have fun in the Middle Ages? | What kinds of hobbies and sports did people do in the Middle Ages? | • SB pp.82–83<br>• TH p.67<br>• K 5.4 Change and Continuity History Skills Activity<br>• K 5.4 Games Worksheet<br>• K 5.4 Holy Day Mini-Movie |
| 5.5 Has football changed much since the Middle Ages? | What are the origins of the game of football? | • SB pp.84–85<br>• TH p.68<br>• K 5.5 Using Evidence History Skills Activity<br>• K 5.5 Mob Football Worksheet |
| 5.6 Let me entertain you | Was music important to medieval people? | • SB pp.86–87<br>• TH p.69<br>• K 5.6 Significance History Skills Activity<br>• K 5.6 Miracle Play Worksheet<br>• K 5.6 Dancing Film Clip<br>• K 5.6 Film Worksheet |
| 5.7 Keeping in fashion | Was fashion important to medieval people? | • SB pp.88–89<br>• TH p.70<br>• K 5.7 Using Evidence History Skills Activity<br>• K 5.7 Clothing Worksheet<br>• K 5.7 Styles Film Clip<br>• K 5.7 Film Worksheet |

| | | |
|---|---|---|
| 5.8 The story of the English language | What are the origins of the main language spoken in Britain today? | • SB pp.90–91<br>• TH p.71<br>• K 5.8 Enquiry History Skills Activity<br>• K 5.8 Understanding Diversity History Skills Activity<br>• K 5.8 Origins Worksheet 1<br>• K 5.8 Origins Worksheet 2 |
| 5.9 Come dine with me! | What did medieval people eat, and was it healthy? | • SB pp.92–93<br>• TH p.72<br>• K 5.9 Using Evidence History Skills Activity<br>• K 5.9 Meals Worksheet |
| 5.10 Knight life | What role did knights play in medieval society? | • SB pp.94–95<br>• TH p.73<br>• K 5.10 Significance History Skills Activity<br>• K 5.10 Ceremony Worksheet |
| 5.11 Welcome to the tournament | What kinds of activities took place at medieval tournaments? | • SB pp.96–97<br>• TH p.74<br>• K 5.11 Significance History Skills Activity<br>• K 5.11 Jousting Worksheet 1<br>• K 5.11 Jousting Worksheet 2<br>• K 5.11 Tournament Mini-Movie |
| 5.12 What was heraldry? | What were the rules of heraldry and why was it important in the Middle Ages? | • SB pp.98–99<br>• TH p.75<br>• K 5.12 Significance History Skills Activity<br>• K 5.12 Shield Worksheet |
| 5.13 Enough of history: what about herstory? | What was life like for medieval women? | • SB pp.100–101<br>• TH p.76<br>• K 5.13 Using Evidence History Skills Activity<br>• K 5.13 Roles Worksheet |
| 5.14 Matilda: the forgotten queen | What were Matilda's claims to the throne? | • SB pp.102–103<br>• TH p.77<br>• K 5.14 Using Evidence History Skills Activity<br>• K 5.14 Rivals Worksheet 1<br>• K 5.14 Rivals Worksheet 2<br>• K 5.14 Rivals Worksheet 3 |
| **Chapter 6: Who rules?** | | **6 Source Bank, 6 Auto-Marked Test on Kerboodle** |
| 6.1 Crown versus Church: the story of Henry II and Thomas Becket | Why did Henry II and Thomas Becket become enemies? | • SB pp.104–105<br>• TH p80<br>• K 6.1 Enquiry History Skills Activity<br>• K 6.1 Factors Worksheet<br>• K 6.1 Friends Film Clip<br>• K 6.1 Film Worksheet |
| 6.2A Newsflash: murder in the cathedral | Why, and by whom, was Thomas Becket murdered? | • SB pp.106–107<br>• TH p.81<br>• K 6.2A Interpretations History Skills Activity<br>• K 6.2A Feud Worksheet 1<br>• K 6.2A Feud Worksheet 2<br>• K 6.2A Knight's Tale Film Clip<br>• K 6.2A Film Worksheet |
| 6.2B Newsflash: murder in the cathedral | What were the consequences of Thomas Becket's murder? | • SB pp.108–109<br>• TH p.84<br>• K 6.2B Using Evidence History Skills Activity 1<br>• K 6.2B Using Evidence History Skills Activity 2<br>• K 6.2B Ranking Worksheet |
| 6.3 King John: Magna Carta man | What happened when King John lost control? | • SB pp.110–111<br>• TH p.85<br>• K 6.3 Cause and Consequence History Skills Activity<br>• K 6.3 Barons Worksheet |
| 6.4A Where did our Parliament come from? | Why did King Henry III argue with the barons? | • SB pp.112–113<br>• TH p.86<br>• K 6.4A Interpretations History Skills Activity<br>• K 6.4A Mistakes Worksheet |
| 6.4B Where did our Parliament come from? | What are the origins of Britain's Parliament? | • SB pp.114–115<br>• TH p.87<br>• K 6.4B Using Evidence History Skills Activity<br>• K 6.4B Origins Worksheet 1<br>• K 6.4B Origins Worksheet 2 |
| 6.5 Why were peasants so angry in 1381? | What caused the peasants to be so angry? | • SB pp.116–117<br>• TH p.88<br>• K 6.5 Enquiry History Skills Activity<br>• K 6.5 Speech Worksheet |
| 6.6A Power to the people | What happened during the Peasant's Revolt? | • SB pp.118–119<br>• TH p.89<br>• K 6.6A Chronology History Skills Activity<br>• K 6.6A Revolt Worksheet |

| 6.6B Power to the people | What effect did the Peasant's Revolt have? | • SB pp.120–121<br>• TH p.90<br>• K 6.6B Using Evidence History Skills Activity<br>• K 6.6B Cause and Consequence History Skills Activity<br>• K 6.6B Accounts Worksheet<br>• K 6.6B Executioner Film Clip<br>• K 6.6B Film Worksheet |
|---|---|---|
| Assessing Your Learning 2 | Was King John really such a bad king? | • SB pp.122–123<br>• TH pp.91–93<br>• K Assessment Task Presentation 2<br>• K Assessment Worksheet 2<br>• K Success Criteria Teacher Grid 2 |
| **Chapter 7: Health and medicine** | | **7 Source Bank, 7 Auto-Marked Test on Kerboodle** |
| 7.1A We're all going to die! | What were the main symptoms of the Black Death? | • SB pp.124–125<br>• TH p.94<br>• K 7.1A Cause and Consequence History Skills Activity<br>• K 7.1A Villagers Worksheet |
| 7.1B We're all going to die! | How did people try to prevent or cure the Black Death? | • SB pp.126–127<br>• TH p.95<br>• K 7.1B Using Evidence History Skills Activity<br>• K 7.1B Plagues Worksheet |
| 7.2 How deadly was Black Death? | What was the impact of the Black Death across the world? | • SB pp.128–129<br>• TH p.96<br>• K 7.2 Using Evidence History Skills Activity 1<br>• K 7.2 Using Evidence History Skills Activity 2<br>• K 7.2 Spread Worksheet<br>• K 7.2 Plague Film Clip 1<br>• K 7.2 Plague Film Clip 2<br>• K 7.2 Film Worksheet |
| 7.3A Who healed the sick in the Middle Ages? | How were illnesses treated in the Middle Ages? | • SB pp.130–131<br>• TH p.97<br>• K 7.3A Enquiry History Skills Activity<br>• K 7.3A Diagnosis Worksheet<br>• K 7.3A Doctor Film Clip<br>• K 7.3A Film Worksheet |
| 7.3B Who healed the sick in the Middle Ages? | How were illnesses diagnosed in the Middle Ages? | • SB pp.132–133<br>• TH p.98<br>• K 7.3B Using Evidence History Skills Activity<br>• K 7.3B Change and Continuity History Skills Activity<br>• K 7.3B Cures Worksheet |
| 7.4 Was it dangerous to be the king? | How healthy were medieval monarchs? | • SB pp.134–135<br>• TH p.99<br>• K 7.4 Enquiry History Skills Activity<br>• K 7.4 Chronology History Skills Activity<br>• K 7.4 Royal Deaths Worksheet 1<br>• K 7.4 Royal Deaths Worksheet 2 |
| Assessing Your Learning 3 | What were the consequences of Black Death? | • SB pp.136–137<br>• TH pp.100-102<br>• K Assessment Task Presentation 3<br>• K Assessment Worksheet 3<br>• K Success Criteria Teacher Grid 3 |
| **Chapter 8: Could you get justice in the Middle Ages?** | | **8 Source Bank, 8 Auto-Marked Test on Kerboodle** |
| 8.1 Keeping law and order | How did society keep law and order in the Middle Ages? | • SB pp.138–139<br>• TH p.105<br>• K 8.1 Change and Continuity History Skills Activity<br>• K 8.1 Crimes Worksheet 1<br>• K 8.1 Crimes Worksheet 2 |
| 8.2 Trial and punishment | How were people tried and what punishments did people receive? | • SB pp.140–141<br>• TH p.106<br>• K 8.2 Using Evidence History Skills Activity<br>• K 8.2 Stories Worksheet<br>• K 8.2 Hangman Film Clip<br>• K 8.2 Film Worksheet<br>• K 8.2 Criminals Mini-Movie |
| **Chapter 9: England at war** | | **9 Source Bank, 9 Auto-Marked Test on Kerboodle** |
| 9.1 England and its neighbours: Wales | How and why did England try to conquer Wales? | • SB pp.142–143<br>• TH p.109<br>• K 9.1 Significance History Skills Activity<br>• K 9.1 Invasion Worksheet<br>• K 9.1 Iron Ring Mini-Movie |
| 9.2 England and its neighbours: Scotland | How and why did England try to conquer Scotland? | • SB pp.144–145<br>• TH p.110<br>• K 9.2 Using Evidence History Skills Activity<br>• K 9.2 Fact File Worksheet |

| 9.3 England and its neighbours: Ireland | How and why did England try to conquer Ireland? | • SB pp.146–147<br>• TH p.111<br>• K 9.3 Using Evidence History Skills Activity<br>• K 9.3 Puzzle Worksheet |
| --- | --- | --- |
| 9.4A Why do we give the 'V sign' as an insult? | What were the key events of the Hundred Years War? | • SB pp.148–149<br>• TH p.112<br>• K 9.4A Cause and Consequence History Skills Activity<br>• K 9.4A Importance Worksheet<br>• K 9.4A Archer Film Clip<br>• K 9.4A Film Worksheet |
| 9.4B Why do we give the 'V sign' as an insult? | What weapons and tactics were used in the Hundred Years War? | • SB pp.150–151<br>• TH p.113<br>• K 9.4B Using Evidence History Skills Activity<br>• K 9.4B Roller Coaster Worksheet |
| 9.5 Joan of Arc – the teenage girl who led an army | Who was Joan of Arc and what did she do? | • SB pp.152–153<br>• TH p.114<br>• K 9.5 Using Evidence History Skills Activity<br>• K 9.5 Joan Worksheet 1<br>• K 9.5 Joan Worksheet 2<br>• K 9.5 Saint Joan Film Clip<br>• K 9.5 Film Worksheet |
| 9.6 Choose your weapons! | Which were the most effective weapons in medieval warfare? | • SB pp.154–155<br>• TH p.115<br>• K 9.6 Enquiry History Skills Activity<br>• K 9.6 Equipment Worksheet<br>• K 9.6 Display Film Clip<br>• K 9.6 Film Worksheet |
| 9.7A What were the Wars of the Roses? | Why did the House of York and the House of Lancaster fight for the throne of England? | • SB pp.156–157<br>• TH p.116<br>• K 9.7A Enquiry History Skills Activity<br>• K 9.7A Battles Worksheet |
| 9.7B What were the Wars of the Roses? | How did Henry Tudor become king? | • SB pp.158–159<br>• TH p.117<br>• K 9.7B Using Evidence History Skills Activity<br>• K 9.7B Bosworth Worksheet |
| 9.8A History Mystery: the Princes in the Tower | Why was Edward V never crowned king? | • ] SB pp.160–161<br>• TH p.118<br>• K 9.8A Using Evidence History Skills Activity<br>• K 9.8A Evidence Worksheet |
| 9.8B History Mystery: the Princes in the Tower | What happened to Edward and his brother? | • SB pp.162–163<br>• TH p.119<br>• K 9.8B Enquiry History Skills Activity<br>• K 9.8B Investigation Worksheet 1<br>• K 9.8B Investigation Worksheet 2<br>• K 9.8B Investigation Worksheet 3 |
| 9.9 Was King Henry VII a gangster? | How did King Henry VII keep control? | • SB pp.164–165<br>• TH p.120<br>• K 9.9 Enquiry History Skills Activity<br>• K 9.9 Problems Worksheet 1<br>• K 9.9 Problems Worksheet 2 |
| **Chapter 10: Medieval Britain: what changed?** | | **10 Source Bank, 10 Auto-Marked Test on Kerboodle** |
| 10.1A What does John know that Edwin didn't? | How did Britain change during the Middle Ages? | • SB pp.166–167<br>• TH p.123<br>• K 10.1A Change and Continuity History Skills Activity<br>• K 10.1A Changes Worksheet |
| 10.1B What does John know that Edwin didn't? | How did these changes affect people? | • SB pp.168–169<br>• TH p.124<br>• K 10.1B Change and Continuity History Skills Activity<br>• K 10.1B Essay Worksheet<br>• K 10.1B John and Edwin Film Clip<br>• K 10.1B Film Worksheet |

# Introduction

## A unique approach

The *KS3 History* series by Aaron Wilkes has become one of the best-selling secondary school History series in recent years. This is its Third Edition, published in line with the new National Curriculum for 2014.

*KS3 History* is not just a series of textbooks. The materials which accompany them make up a complete scheme of work for a comprehensive Key Stage 3 History course. However, the scheme is not meant to be prescriptive. Experienced teachers may want to plunder the materials for suitable resources and ideas, whilst supply teachers, non-specialists or those just starting out in the profession will soon realise that *KS3 History* is a proven scheme of work that has proven effective with the students in the classroom.

The series itself sticks rigidly to the idea that any resources used with students should be as entertaining, accessible and relevant as possible because children learn best when they are interested and engaged in activities that they think are both challenging and worthwhile. If a group of students are hooked early on in a lesson by a disgusting picture, a curious title or a thought-provoking objective, a highly proactive learning environment can be created. Each topic in the book aims to get the students involved, and keep them involved, through imaginatively presented double-page spreads with a clear route through them, headed by progressive learning objectives and finished off with a work section that aims to make the written part of any lesson as much fun and as challenging as possible. Great emphasis has been placed on designing tasks and activities that help students understand the key concepts relating to the study of History and develop the skills needed to become a top historian.

The *Student Books* contain quirky facts, extension and assessment opportunities, and the correct historical vocabulary. The *Kerboodle Lessons, Resources and Assessment* material provides starters, summative and formative assessment opportunities, customizable worksheets, interactive activities, lesson plans, and short films on the key topics.

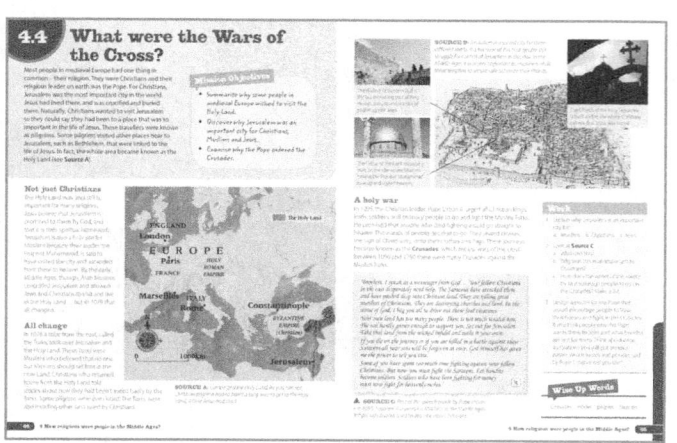

## Developing Skills

In recent years, greater emphasis has been placed on developing students' chronological understanding. *KS3 History* provides an effective base from which to do this throughout the whole of Key Stage 3. The books are written in chronological order, starting in the medieval period and going through to the twenty-first century. With each book and accompanying Kerboodle package, students are encouraged to develop their understanding of the relevant historical conventions by using precise dates, correct vocabulary and chronological terms. A student's sense of chronology, sequence and duration is developed through the use of overviews, summative tasks, enquiry-based topics and concept-specific work sections.

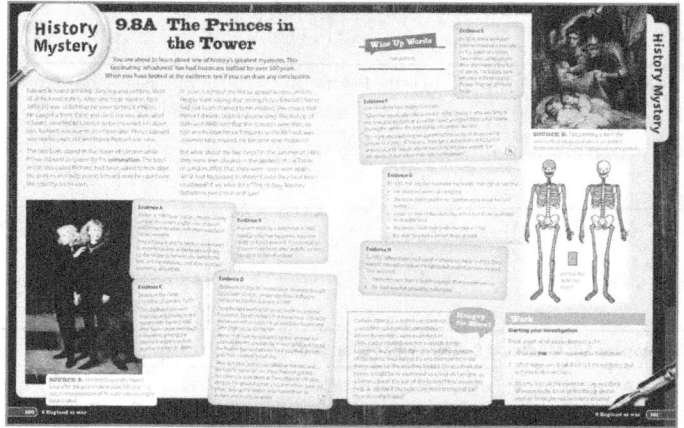

The series also provides a stimulating backdrop for promoting students' knowledge, encouraging their communication skills and their understanding of historical evidence. Some topics, such as *9.8 The Princes in the Tower*, are presented as a History Mystery for students to weigh evidence and analyse sources. They are required to use strategies and enquiry techniques to arrive at effective and reasoned conclusions. In each book, there are specific spreads that are designed to help students develop insights into values, beliefs and culture as well as encouraging their understanding of key processes. For example, lessons such as *3.1 How did castles develop?* focus on the idea of change and continuity. The key concept of cause and consequence forms the central focus of topics such as *4.4 What were the Wars of the Cross?* In the complete chapter entitled *2 The Norman Conquest* students are encouraged to identify and assess significance, whilst in the *Assessing Your Learning*

task on King John students get the chance to analyse and explain different types of historical interpretation. The skills are mapped by lesson onto grids in this book e.g. page 22.

### Literacy in History

Each spread contains a small selection of vital 'Wise Up Words'. Students should be encouraged to look up their meanings in a dictionary and/or use the glossary and index at the back of the book. They should be able to spell, understand and use the words correctly, and the tasks will ask the students to define and deploy these words with precision.

Students are asked to cover basic literacy competencies in the Work sections. They are instructed to 'write in full sentences', 'use capital letters and full stops', and back up their views 'with evidence from the sources'. They are taught to construct a proper paragraph, make a point, 'evidence it', and explain what they mean in preparation for GCSE. There is also a range of activities that employ a variety of creative literacy strategies.

### kerboodle

*Invasion Plague and Murder Britain 1066–1509 Kerboodle Lessons, Resources and Assessment* provides hundreds of lively digital resources, including:

- unique specially commissioned films from The History Squad and film worksheets
- History skills activities
- source banks/collections
- worksheets and self-assessments
- ready-to-go lesson presentations
- supported assessment tasks with success criteria and marking guidance.

You can adapt many of these resources to suit you and your students' individual needs and upload your existing resources so everything can be accessed from one location to help bring History to life in your classroom.

### Assessment and progression

Each book, and its accompanying Kerboodle package, includes a ready-made set of formative and summative assessment tasks.

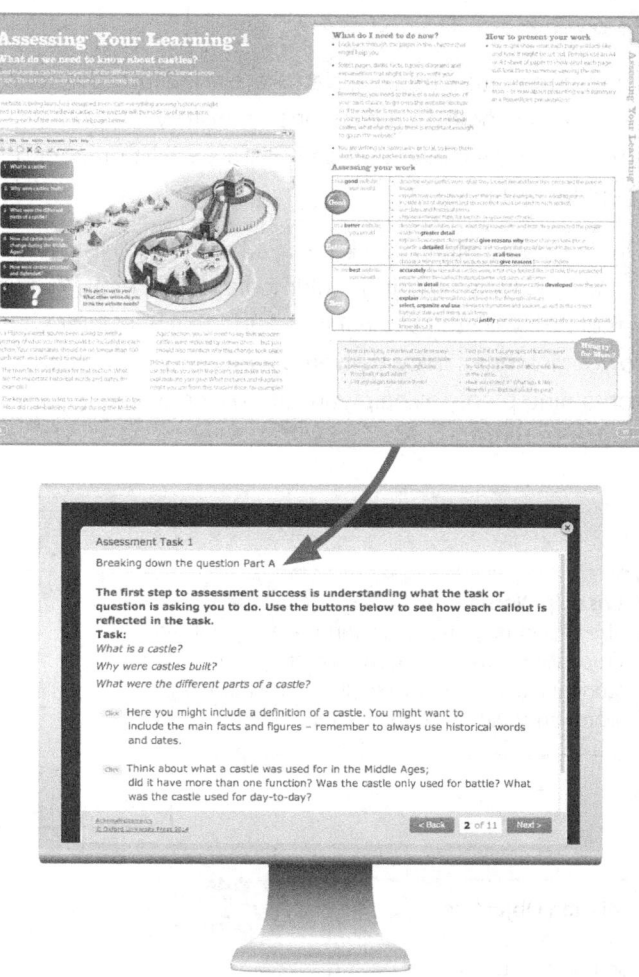

- Learning objectives for each spread are written in student-friendly language. These can be referred to easily throughout any lesson.
- In 'Assessing your Learning' spreads within each book, students' understanding of skills and concepts is tested. Students are made aware of the standards they are aiming for, using the 'good, better, best' model.
- The assessment support package on *Kerboodle* includes: step-by-step task presentations for front-of-class use, self- and peer-assessment worksheets, and auto-marked tests.
- Two baseline tests and a mark scheme are included to help teachers try to establish the level of knowledge and learning that students have acquired in primary school.

We sincerely hope that *KS3 History* helps you deliver the outstanding lessons that we all aspire to, and that the history package we've developed helps inspire and engage a new generation of learners.

With best wishes

Aaron Wilkes    Katrina Shearman

# About this series

**Invasion, Plague and Murder: Britain 1066–1509** is one of four Third Edition *Student Books* in the popular **Key Stage 3 History** series by experienced Head of History, Aaron Wilkes.

Written to match the 2014 National Curriculum, this series uses a fresh angle on great stories in history to hook students' interest in Key Stage 3 History whilst preparing them for GCSE.

On Kerboodle, films from British Pathé and the History Squad and other exciting multimedia resources are fully integrated with the *Student Books* and Teacher Guides, so your lessons can be delivered easily and seamlessly, containing plenty to help you stir, challenge and inspire your young historians!

## The series components

The series consists of:

For students
- Four *Student Books* (and/or four *Kerboodle Books*)
- Four Kerboodle *Lessons, Resources and Assessments*.

For teachers
- Four *Teacher Handbooks*
- Four Kerboodle *Lessons, Resources and Assessment* packages (includes teacher access to the accompanying *Kerboodle Book*).

## Student Book

The **Key Stage 3 History: Invasion, Plague and Murder: Britain 1066–1509 Student Book** uses an entertaining narrative to hook interest and make stories memorable. Throughout the book, lessons and tasks are designed to develop key skills and processes and understand historical terms and concepts, including making connections.

## Key to icons

Source bank | Film | Worksheet | History skills activity | Literacy | Numeracy

**Wise Up Words**
The important phrases and terms are highlighted. Emphasis should be placed on getting the students to learn how to spell and use these words and phrases correctly.

**Mission Objectives**
All sections start by setting the students some 'Mission Objectives'. Generally speaking, they are progressive, which means they often begin with a lower order concept such as comprehension or application (define, recall, relate, identify etc.) leading to higher order concepts such as analysis and evaluation (justify, assess, judge, predict etc.).

**Fact!**
Funny, fascinating and amazing little stories and snippets of history are dotted throughout the books. They are often the piece of information in the spread that gest most student reaction!

**Work**
The tasks in the Work section aim to develop the key skills and concepts that all good History students should focus on. Generally speaking, the tasks are progressive in terms of difficulty and there is often a 'creative' element to one or more of the tasks. The tasks in the Work section also encourage students to develop all sorts of literacy skills relating to speaking, listening, reading and writing. They are often asked to use writing as a tool for their thoughts and encouraged to record, develop and evaluate their ideas as well as read for meaning and complete tasks related to the text in the spread.

# Depth Study

In each book, there is a mini depth study that focuses in more detail on an important and significant event or concept of the period. These sections give students the chance to extend and deepen their understanding of key moments in history.

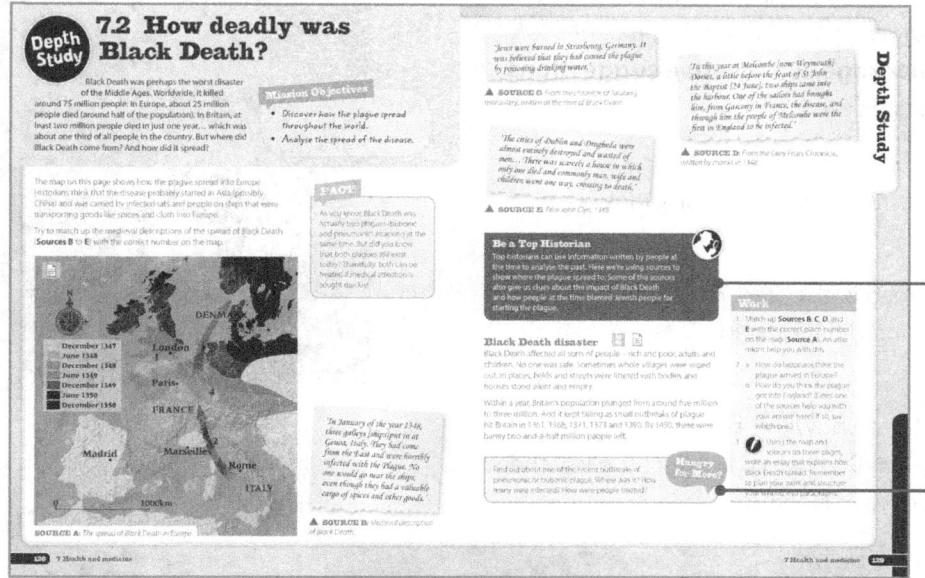

### Be a Top Historian
This highlights some of the key concepts and processes that students will have been working on in the spread. Causes and consequences, change over time, significance, using sources etc. are specifically mentioned here.

### Hungry for More?
This is a chance to extend your students beyond the classroom. These activities can be set as homework tasks and/or extension work, and allow you to try and get students to take responsibility for their own learning and work independently.

# History Mystery

Some of the period's more intriguing, interesting or more controversial topics are covered as History Mystery. A step-by-step approach is used so students can evaluate evidence, consider interpretations and come to their own conclusions.

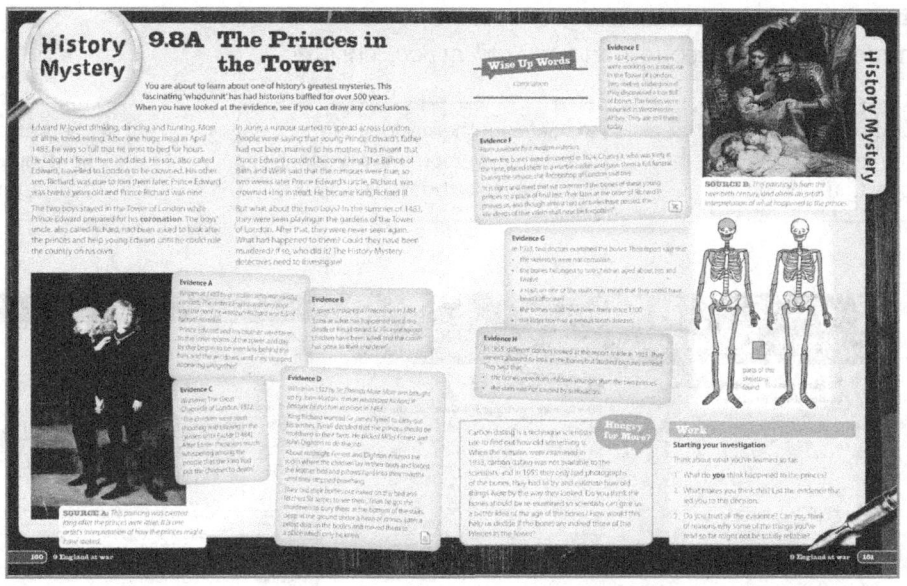

# Assessing Your Learning

In the book, there are three extended assessments. These are opportunities for students to showcase what they have learned about the topic and assess their research and analysis skills. Some are more creative, while others will focus on extended writing or looking at sources. Full marking support is provided in this handbook and on Kerboodle.

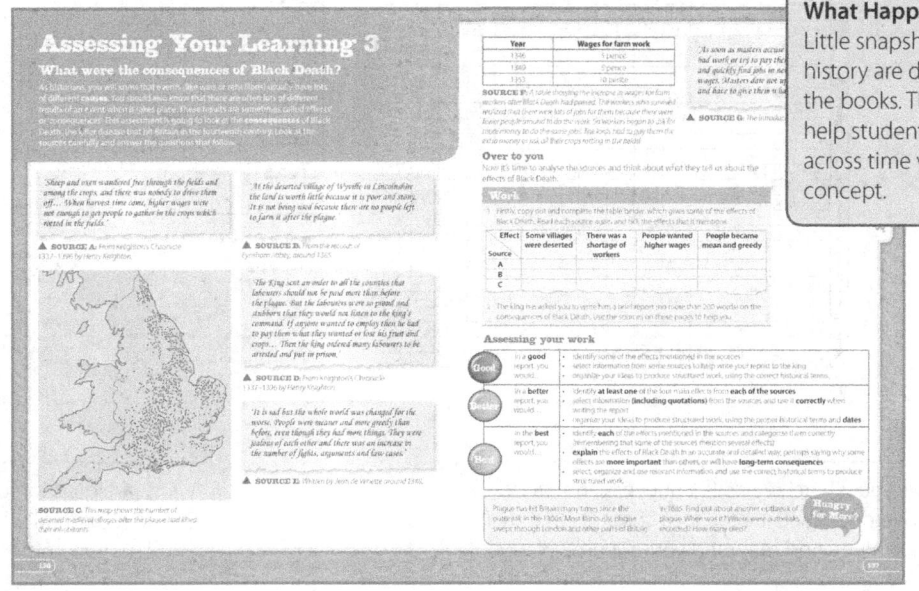

### What Happened When?
Little snapshots of world history are dotted throughout the books. These can also help students make links across time via a common concept.

# Using this book

## Teacher Handbook

The *Key Stage 3 History: Invasion, Plague and Murder: Britain 1066–1509 Teacher Handbook* aims to save you time and effort! It provides **full support** and guidance for the *Invasion, Plague and Murder: Britain 1066–1509 Student Book*, including **practical tasks**, an **assessment package** and **creative suggestions** for incorporating differentiation into your teaching.

### What it provides

Closely matched to each chapter of the *Student Book*, this book provides:

1  a chapter overview
2  help at a glance for each double-page spread in the *Student Book*
3  further suggestions for starters, plenaries and differentiation
4  an assessment overview.

Please turn to the **Contents List** on page 3 to see how this book is structured.
**A Scheme of Work** is also provided on pages 4–9 to help you select the key themes and topics that you might use to inform your own planning.

Find out more about the four main components below.

### 1 The chapter overview

This is your introduction to the corresponding *Student Book* chapter.

- Shows how the *Student Book* chapter relates to the 2014 National Curriculum

- Sets out the key ideas and skills development within the chapter in the *Student Book*

- Sets out the objectives and outcomes for the chapter, and the corresponding lesson numbers

- Shows you where key skills, concepts and processes are covered in the *Student Book* chapter. It will help you with planning and mapping your scheme of work

- Ideas for further learning outside the normal school environment – class trips, or recommended documentaries, for example

## 2 Help at a glance for each lesson

These pages give comprehensive help for each lesson in the *Invasion, Plague and Murder: Britain 1066–1509 Student Book*.

- Starts with a brief walk through the lesson, to show you how it develops and what the expected outcomes are
- A list of all the resources available on Kerboodle for the lesson
- This section provides clarification and extra information for some activities in the *Student Book*, and potential assessment opportunities
- Offers alternative activities and suggestions to support and extend your students
- Suggestion for a possible starter

**1.2B England before 1066: what was it like?**

kerboodle
1.2B Enquiry History Skills Activity
1.2B Changes Worksheets
1 Source Bank

Invasion, Plague and Murder pages 18–19

**Lesson summary**
Students will complete source analysis tasks to understand what life was like in the eleventh century.

***What are the lesson outcomes?***
**All** students will know how England got its name and who ruled England in 1065.
**Most** students will be able to describe in detail what life was like in England in 1065.
**Some** students will be able to use information from sources to support their writing.

**Starter suggestion**
- Students should look back at what they learned last lesson and share the questions they came up with as part of last lesson's plenary exercise. Can other students help them answer their questions?

**Main learning suggestions and assessment**
***What activities will take place?***
**Task 1:** Students should read the information across pages 18–19 and use the prompt questions (the 'NOSY' questions from last lesson) to discuss the sources in this spread.
**Task 2:** Students should complete 1.2B Enquiry History Skills Activity, which asks students to debate whether England was a civilized place to live in 1066.

***How will students demonstrate their understanding?***
**Task 3:** Students should complete Work activities **1–3** on page 19. Activity **3** requires students to complete a fact file. You could look at page 21 of the *Student Book* to model the conventions of a good fact file.

**Task 4**: Students can also complete the table describing how life has changed since 1066 on 1.2B Changes Worksheet. Students should make notes under the following headings: Who is in charge?; How is the country run?; Religion; Jobs; Towns and Cities; Rich and Poor. They can use these notes to show what life was like in 1066 and how life has changed today.

**Plenary suggestions**
- Thumbs up!. Students could answer the question 'Would you like to live in the Middle Ages?' with a 'thumbs up' or a 'thumbs down'. Can they come up with a reason to explain their choice?

**Differentiation suggestions**
*Support*
- You can use 1.2B Changes Worksheet to help support weaker students as they complete the Work activities on page 19.

*Extension: Hungry for more?*
- 'Why do you think life in 1066 was different from today? Would you prefer to live now or then? Can you say why?'
  - Students can be set these questions either as a discussion point or as a written response for homework. If this is structured as a classroom discussion, you may wish to use the same topics as in **Task 4** and allocate each topic to a group/pair of students. Students often reach very different conclusions, leading to excellent class discussions.

28

**1.3 Who will be the next King of England?**

kerboodle
1.3 Enquiry History Skills Activity
1.3 Vote Worksheet 1
1.3 Vote Worksheet 2
1 Source Bank

Invasion, Plague and Murder pages 20–21

**Lesson summary**
Students will complete a research task to find out about the three men who wished to be King of England in 1066.

***What are the lesson outcomes?***
**All** students will know the identities of the three contenders who wished to become the new King of England.
**Most** students will know reasons why each contender believed they should be king.
**Some** students will be able to explain who had the best claim to the throne.

**Starter suggestion**
- Think, pair, share: Students should be given 30 seconds to consider what characteristics the new King of England should have. They should then be given one minute to discuss their ideas with a neighbour. This should feed into a class discussion where each pair shares their ideas with the class in order to create a list of characteristics the new King of England should have.

**Main learning suggestions and assessment**
***What activities will take place?***
**Task 1:** Students should read pages 20–21 and complete 1.3 Vote Worksheet 1 or 1.3 Vote Worksheet 2, researching reasons why each contender should or should not be king. Students should be able to identify, for each contender: Who am I? What's my job? Where am I from? Why should I be king? Why shouldn't I be king?

***How will students demonstrate their understanding?***
**Task 2:** Students can assess their own knowledge by completing 1.3 Enquiry History Skills Activity, identifying contenders by various facts.

**Plenary suggestions**
- Students should complete the voting slip on their worksheet giving a reason why they have placed each contender in each position. The results could be compiled into a class vote to see who the class have decided should become the new king.

**Differentiation suggestions**
*Support*
- Lower ability students can use 1.3 Vote Worksheet 2, which includes sentences starters to support their writing.

*Extension: Hungry for more?*
- Hot seating activity: To develop and assess understanding, students could take part in a hot seating activity. Each student is given the role of one of the contenders, and they should plan their responses to the following questions: Why should you be king? Why would you make a good king? Who is the strongest contender to the throne? What is your biggest weakness?
  - This can be run as a class discussion with students being invited to the front to give their answers to the questions. The class can then respond by offering individual thoughts or questions, or by working in small groups to discuss each response in turn.

29

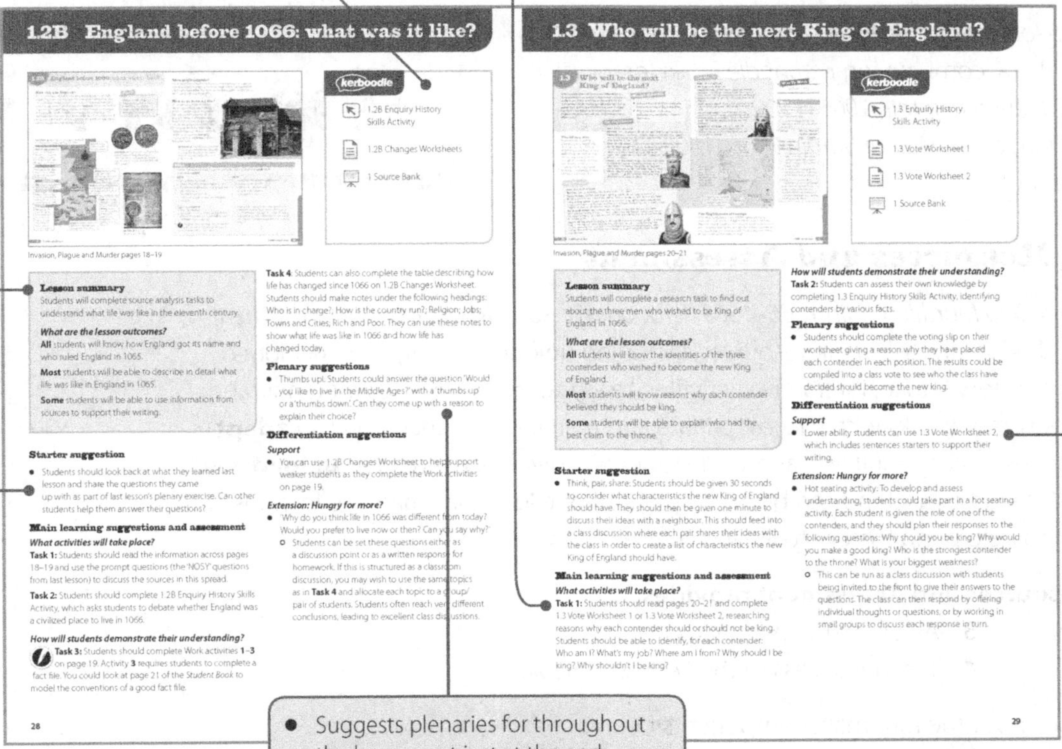

- Suggests plenaries for throughout the lesson, not just at the end

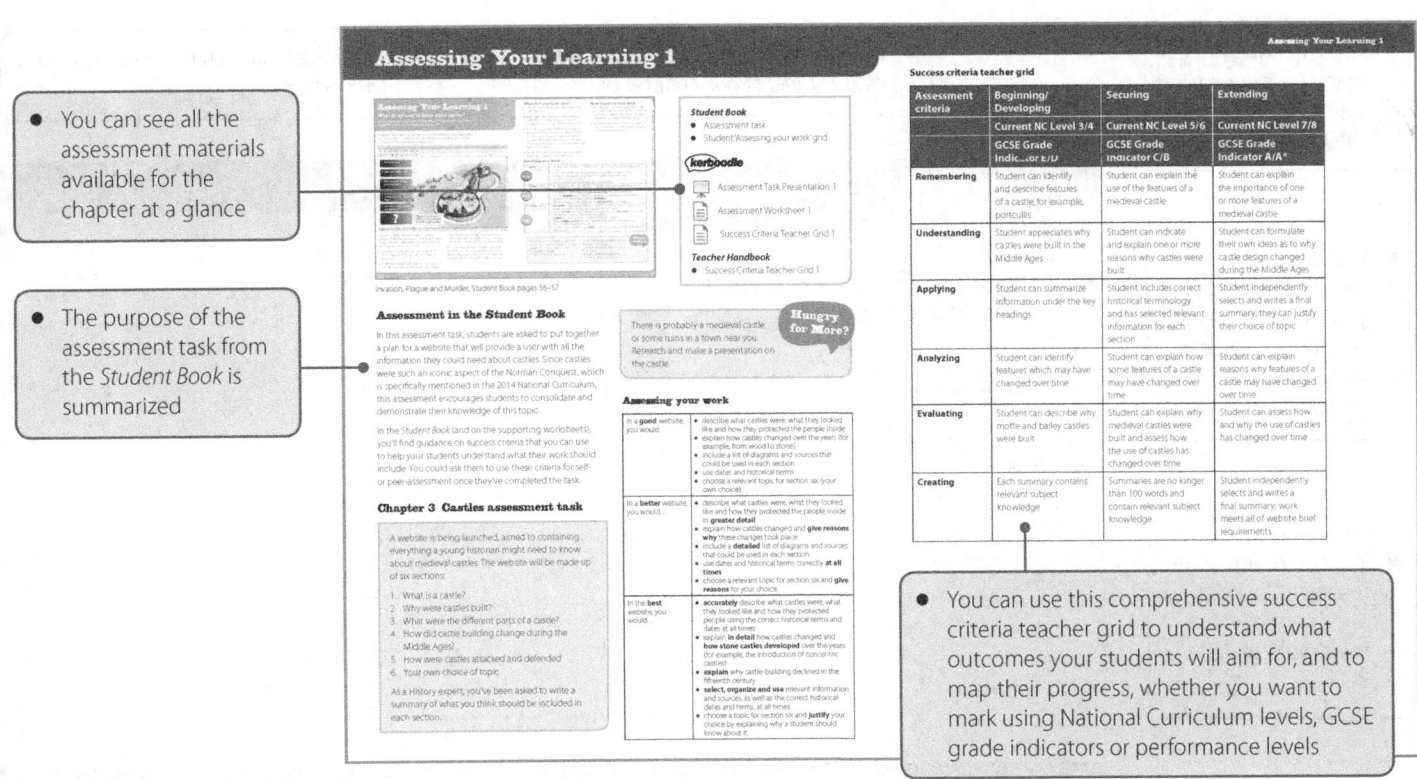

### Assessment

This section introduces you to the end-of-chapter assessment task from the *Student Book*, and describes the support materials available for the chapter.

- You can see all the assessment materials available for the chapter at a glance
- The purpose of the assessment task from the *Student Book* is summarized

**Assessing Your Learning 1**

Invasion, Plague and Murder, Student Book pages 56–57

*Student Book*
- Assessment task
- Student 'Assessing your work' grid

kerboodle
Assessment Task Presentation 1
Assessment Worksheet 1
Success Criteria Teacher Grid 1

*Teacher Handbook*
- Success Criteria Teacher Grid 1

**Assessment in the Student Book**

In this assessment task, students are asked to put together a plan for a website that will provide a user with all the information they could need about castles. Since castles were such an iconic aspect of the Norman Conquest, which is specifically mentioned in the 2014 National Curriculum, this assessment encourages students to consolidate and demonstrate their knowledge of this topic.

In the *Student Book* (and on the supporting worksheets), you'll find guidance on success criteria that you can use to help your students understand what their work should include. You could ask them to use these criteria for self- or peer-assessment once they've completed the task.

**Chapter 3 Castles assessment task**

A website is being launched, aimed to containing everything a young historian might need to know about medieval castles. The website will be made up of six sections:

1. What is a castle?
2. Why were castles built?
3. What were the different parts of a castle?
4. How did castle building change during the Middle Ages?
5. How were castles attacked and defended
6. Your own choice of topic

As a History expert, you've been asked to write a summary of what you think should be included in each section.

**Hungry for More?**
There is probably a medieval castle or some ruins in a town near you. Research and make a presentation on the castle.

**Assessing your work**

| | |
|---|---|
| In a **good** website, you would... | • describe what castles were, what they looked like and how they protected the people inside<br>• explain how castles changed over the years (for example, from wood to stone)<br>• include a list of diagrams and sources that could be used in each section<br>• use dates and historical terms<br>• choose a relevant topic for section six (your own choice) |
| In a **better** website, you would... | • describe what castles were, what they looked like and how they protected the people inside in **greater detail**<br>• explain how castles changed and **give reasons why** these changes took place<br>• include a **detailed** list of diagrams and sources that could be used in each section<br>• use dates and historical terms correctly **at all times**<br>• choose a relevant topic for section six and **give reasons** for your choice |
| In the **best** website, you would... | • **accurately** describe what castles were, what they looked like and how they protected people using the correct historical terms and dates at all times<br>• explain **in detail** how castles changed and **how stone castles developed** over the years (for example, the introduction of concentric castles)<br>• **explain** why castle-building declined in the fifteenth century<br>• **select, organize and use** relevant information and sources, as well as the correct historical dates and terms, at all times<br>• choose a topic for section six and **justify** your choice by explaining why a student should know about it |

**Assessing Your Learning 1**

**Success criteria teacher grid**

| Assessment criteria | Beginning/ Developing | Securing | Extending |
|---|---|---|---|
| | Current NC Level 3/4 | Current NC Level 5/6 | Current NC Level 7/8 |
| | GCSE Grade Indicator E/D | GCSE Grade Indicator C/B | GCSE Grade Indicator A/A* |
| **Remembering** | Student can identify and describe features of a castle, for example, portcullis | Student can explain the use of the features of a medieval castle | Student can explain the importance of one or more features of a medieval castle |
| **Understanding** | Student appreciates why castles were built in the Middle Ages | Student can indicate and explain one or more reasons why castles were built | Student can formulate their own ideas as to why castle design changed during the Middle Ages |
| **Applying** | Student can summarize information under the key headings | Student includes correct historical terminology and has selected relevant information for each section | Student independently selects and writes a final summary; they can justify their choice of topic |
| **Analyzing** | Student can identify features which may have changed over time | Student can explain how some features of a castle may have changed over time | Student can explain reasons why features of a castle may have changed over time |
| **Evaluating** | Student can describe why motte and bailey castles were built | Student can explain why medieval castles were built and assess how the use of castles has changed over time | Student can assess how and why the use of castles has changed over time |
| **Creating** | Each summary contains relevant subject knowledge | Summaries are no longer than 100 words and contain relevant subject knowledge | Student independently selects and writes a final summary; work meets all of website brief requirements |

- You can use this comprehensive success criteria teacher grid to understand what outcomes your students will aim for, and to map their progress, whether you want to mark using National Curriculum levels, GCSE grade indicators or performance levels

# Kerboodle

*Key Stage 3 History: Invasion Plague and Murder:*
*Britain 1066–1509 Kerboodle* is packed full of guided
support and ideas for running and creating effective History
lessons. It's intuitive to use, customizable, and can be
accessed online.

## Kerboodle consists of:

● *Lessons*, *Resources and Assessment* (includes teacher
access to the accompanying *Kerboodle Book*) for *Invasion
Plague and Murder: Britain 1066–1509*

● *Invasion Plague and Murder Britain 1066–1509*
*Kerboodle Book*.

## Lessons, Resources and Assessment

*Invasion Plague and Murder Britain 1066–1509 Kerboodle Lessons, Resources and Assessment*
provides hundreds of lively built-in resources, including unique specially commissioned
films from The History Squad, interactive activities, ready-to-go lesson presentations, and
supported assessment tasks with success criteria and marking guidance. You can **adapt**
many of these resources to suit you and your students' individual needs, and **upload** your
existing resources so everything can be accessed from one location. Image collections are
also included to help bring History to life in your classroom.

### Lessons, Resources and Assessment provides:

1 Resources
2 Lessons
3 Assessment and Markbook
4 Teacher access to the *Kerboodle Book*.

Find out more about the four main components below.

### Resources

Click on the **Resources** tab at the top of the screen to access the full list of
resources for *Invasion Plague and Murder: Britain 1066–1509*.

● You can bring in
many of your own
resources by clicking
the Upload button

● Find all the resources associated with
every *Student Book* chapter or lesson

● Click here to launch the corresponding
*Kerboodle Book* pages

● Lots of content can
be customized and
you can even create
your own resources
using the Create
button

● You can navigate the
resources by book
and chapter, or use
the simple search
bar

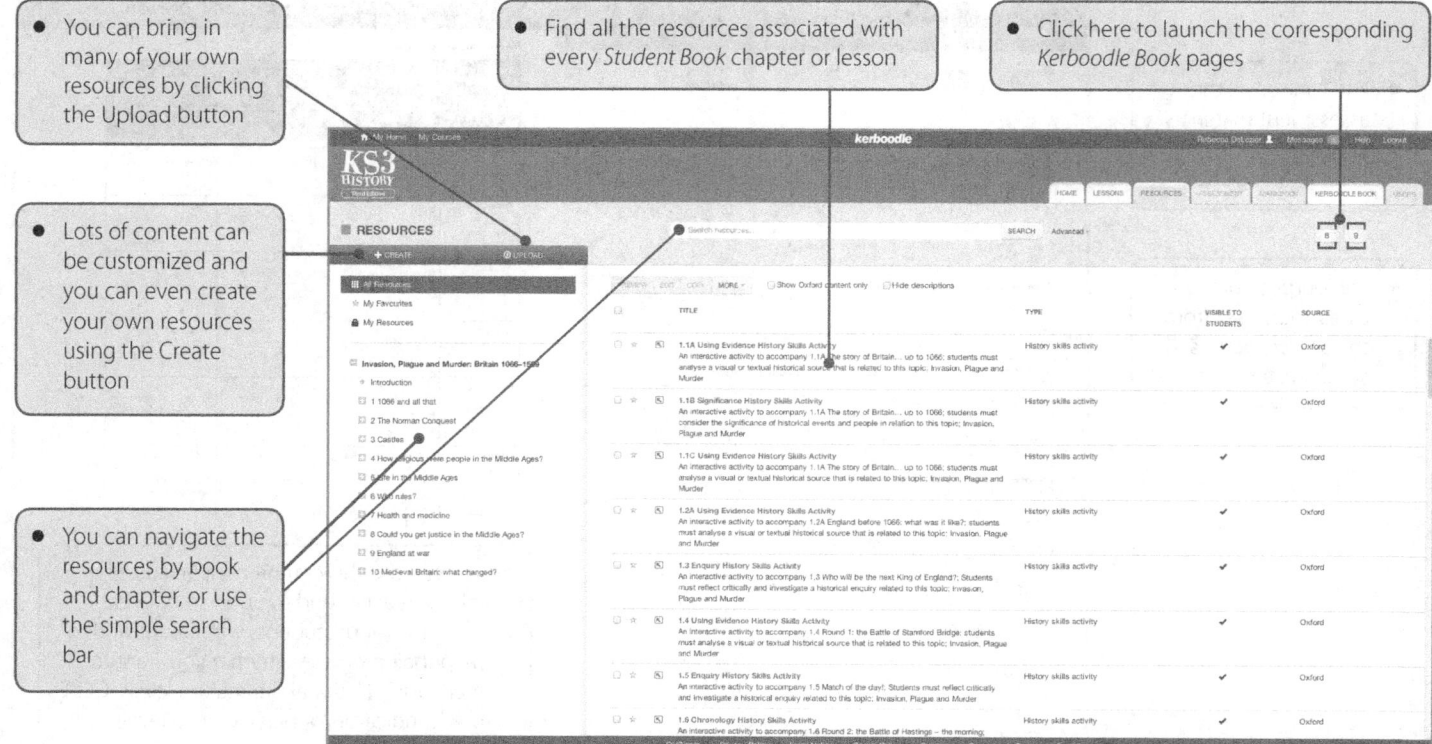

*Invasion Plague and Murder: Britain 1066–1509 Kerboodle*

## The Resources section has more than:

 **20 Film clips:** Specially-commissioned film clips produced at a stunning English Heritage location to bring History to life in your classroom.
**5 Mini-movies:** Short animated clips that cover topics in a visually stimulating and easy to understand way.

 **75 Worksheets:** Worksheets include creative worksheets that help provide differentiation/extension material for each lesson, and film worksheets to help students analyse the History Squad films and link ideas back to the *Student Book* lesson. Worksheets are provided as PDFs, which you can print off and photocopy, and as Word files, which you can customize to suit your students' needs.

 **75 History skills activities:** A range of interactive activities for use on your whiteboard are available for each lesson. They target a number of history skills, concepts and processes: historical enquiry, chronological understanding, cultural, ethnic and religious diversity, change and continuity, cause and consequence, significance, interpretation, and using evidence.

They can also be used for independent study.

 **10 Source banks:** A source bank with captions for each chapter is provided so you can easily enlarge any photo or written source from the *Student Book* on screen and use it as a discussion starter, use them in your own worksheets, or give them to students to use in class or homework activities.

### Teacher support resources

Aaron Wilkes' professional development film clip for each chapter offers ideas and teaching tips to make history memorable for all your students. In these short films, he explains his rationale behind his approach to the *Student Books* and includes suggestions for practical delivery and assessment of the new 2014 National Curriculum.

### *Kerboodle* Resources are fully integrated with the *Student Book*:

All the resources and assessments are completely matched to the *Invasion Plague and Murder Britain 1066–1509 Student Book*.

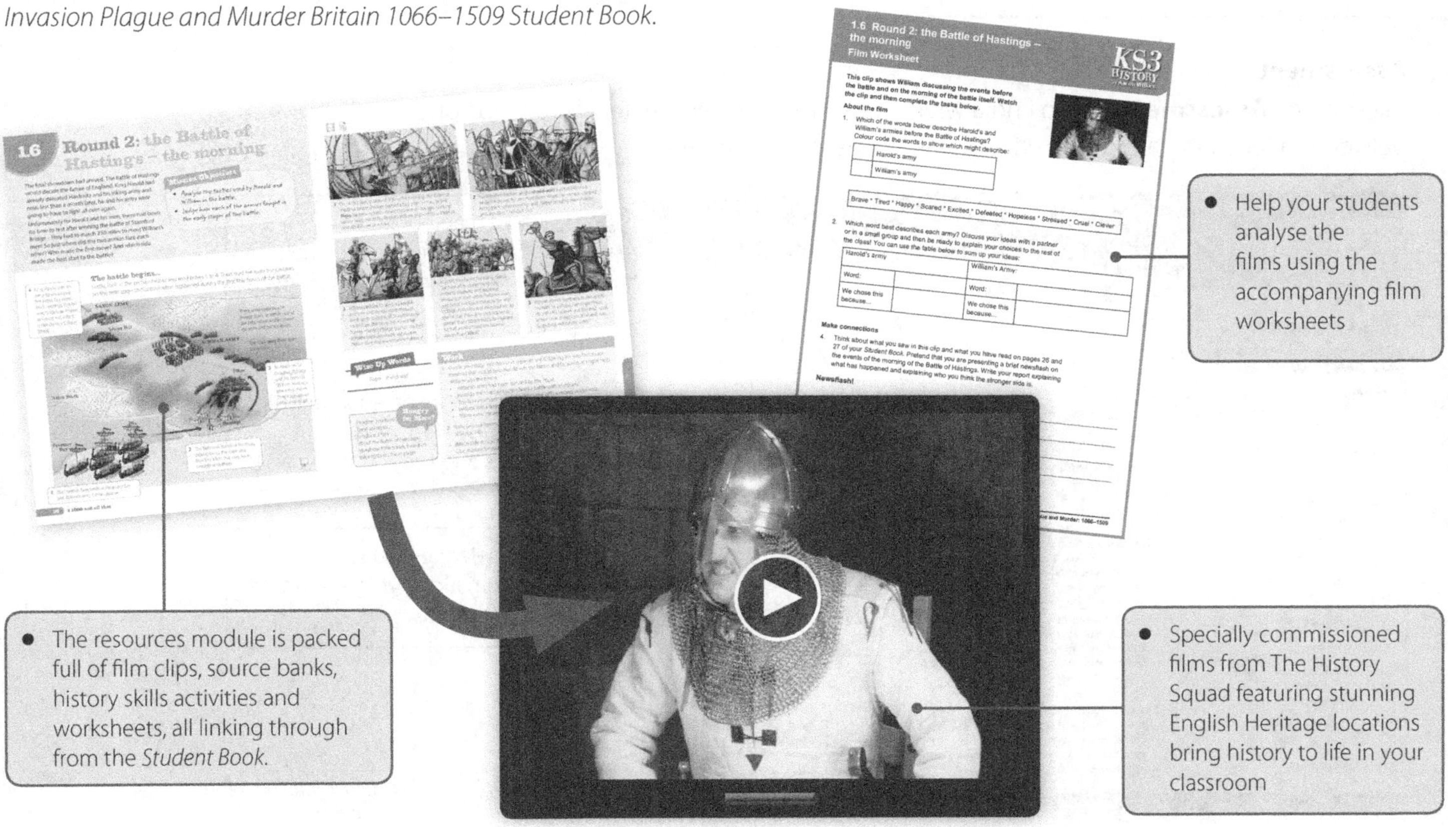

- Help your students analyse the films using the accompanying film worksheets

- The resources module is packed full of film clips, source banks, history skills activities and worksheets, all linking through from the *Student Book*.

- Specially commissioned films from The History Squad featuring stunning English Heritage locations bring history to life in your classroom

## Lessons

Click on the **Lessons tab** to access the full list of lesson presentations and plans for *Invasion Plague and Murder: Britain 1066–1509.*

**Ready-to-play lesson presentations** complement every lesson in the book. Each lesson presentation is easy to launch, and features unit objectives, the related starters, worksheets, film and interactive resources, and closes with a plenary activity. You can further personalize the lessons by adding in your own resources and notes. Your lessons and notes can be accessed by your whole department, and they are a great time-saver and **ideal for non-specialist** teachers and cover lessons.

- Every lesson is accompanied by teacher notes to fully support your lesson delivery

The Lessons module contains ready-to-play lesson presentations and plans that complement every double-page spread in the book

**2.3 Lesson Presentation and Plan**

**'We know where you live!'**

Did you know that the Domesday Book is considered to be a legal document, still valid today as proof of land ownership?

**2.3 Domesday Film Clip**
You are about to watch a clip of King William describing the Domesday Book.

**2.3 Film Worksheet**
What can we learn from this clip? This worksheet contains questions on what is covered in the film.

2.3 Domesday Film Clip

2.3 Domesday Film Worksheet

**Screen 4:**
**Main learning suggestions and assessment:** What activities will take place? Students can watch 2.3 Domesday Film Clip in which William describes the Domesday Book.
How will students demonstrate their understanding? Students can complete 2.3 Film Worksheet.

**Screen 5:**
**Main learning suggestions and assessment:** What activities will take place? Students can complete the source comparison in 2.3 Using Evidence History Skills Activity to compare Source A with Source C.

LESSON   NOTES          Tools   Digital Book   Back   4 of 6   Next

- Resources are built into each presentation so all the relevant activities, films and worksheets are ready to launch

The resources you want to use can also be rearranged and launched in sequence to suit your classroom needs

- For each lesson, a printable set of teacher notes are also available as a guide to support your lesson delivery, and provide further ideas or tips that only teachers can see.

*Invasion Plague and Murder Britain 1066-1509 Lesson Presentation and Plan*

## Assessment

Click on the **Assessment tab** to find a wide range of assessment materials to help you deliver a varied, motivating, and effective assessment programme.

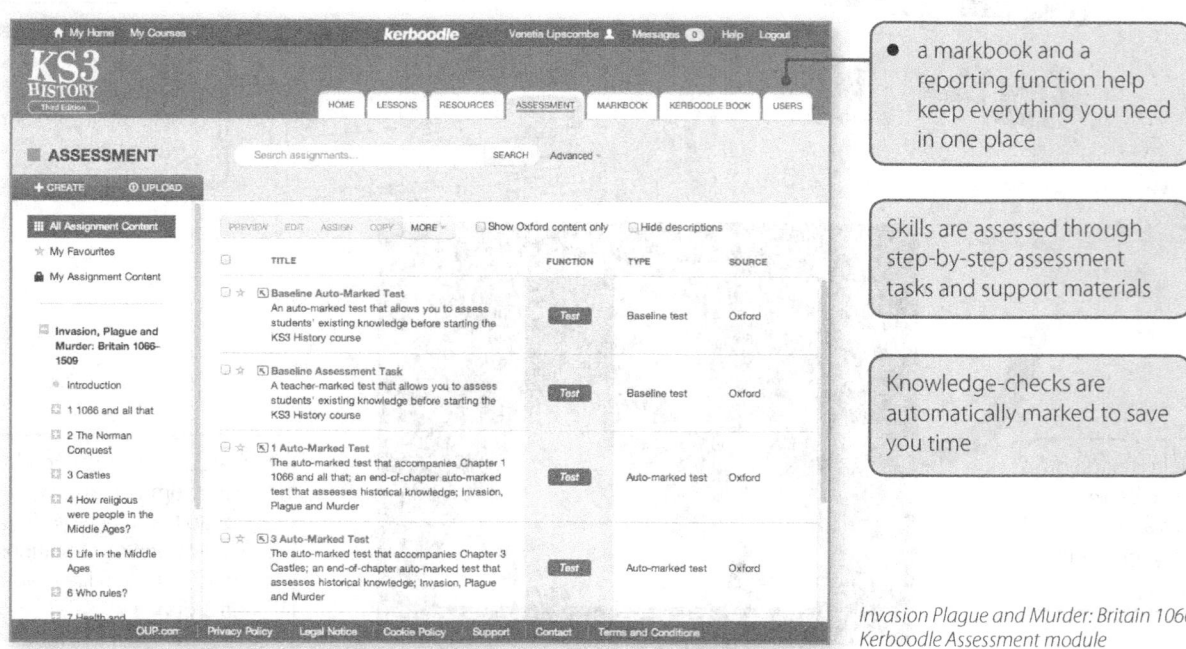

- a markbook and a reporting function help keep everything you need in one place

Skills are assessed through step-by-step assessment tasks and support materials

Knowledge-checks are automatically marked to save you time

*Invasion Plague and Murder: Britain 1066–1509 Kerboodle Assessment module*

**To cover every chapter, the Assessment section provides:**

- 📐 **10 auto-marked tests:** Each end-of-chapter auto-marked test is a knowledge-check. The marks are automatically reported in the **Markbook tab** to help save time setting questions and marking.

- 📄 **75 self-assessment worksheets:** Self- and peer-assessment, opportunities are provided via 'I can…' checklists for each chapter, which encourage students to consider how far they and their peers have understood the concepts and developed skills relevant to that chapter.

**In addition, there are also materials to cover transition from KS2 and bespoke Assessing Your Learning tasks:**

- 📐 **2 baseline tests:** These tests cover basic historical terminology and chronological understanding, as well as an introductory approach to source analysis. They can help you to quickly assess the prior historical knowledge that your new KS3 students may have.

- 🖥 **3 assessment task presentations:** Each assessment task in the *Student Book*, which assesses history **skills**, has a front-of-class presentation for you to use to help guide students towards unpacking the task and understanding what it is asking of them. You can lead students through this step-by-step presentation and help them decide how to prepare to complete the task.

- 📄 **3 success criteria teacher grids:** A grid accompanies each assessment task in the *Student Book*, which helps teachers mark the tasks in relation to such skills as evaluation, analysis, and understanding.

- 📄 **3 sets of assessment worksheets:** These worksheets cvomplement the assessment tasks in the *Student Book* and the assessment task presentations. They recap the task, provide a self-evaluation chart, and space for students to prepare their work.

A **Markbook** with reporting function completes the *Kerboodle* assessment package, so you can keep track of all your students' test results and assessment scores. This includes both the auto-marked tests and work that needs to be marked by you. It is also easy to import class registers and create user accounts for all your students.

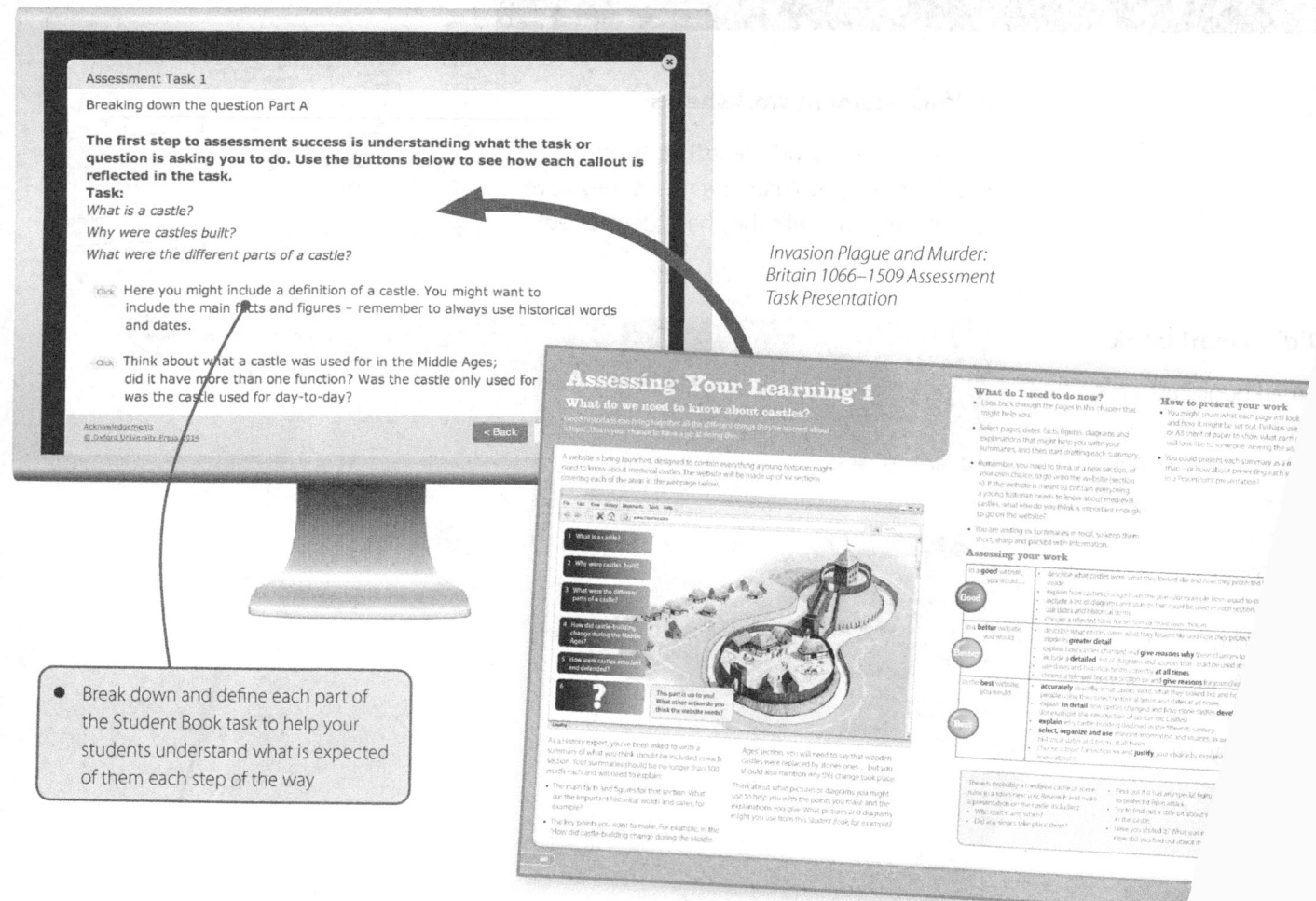

*Invasion Plague and Murder: Britain 1066–1509 Assessment Task Presentation*

- Break down and define each part of the Student Book task to help your students understand what is expected of them each step of the way

**To cover every chapter, the Assessment section provides:**

- 🔼 **10 auto-marked tests:** Each end-of-chapter auto-marked test is a knowledge-check. The marks are automatically reported in the **Markbook tab** to help save time setting questions and marking.

- 📄 **75 self-assessment worksheets:** Self- and peer-assessment, opportunities are provided via 'I can…' checklists for each chapter, which encourage students to consider how far they and their peers have understood the concepts and developed skills relevant to that chapter.

**In addition, there are also materials to cover transition from KS2 and bespoke Assessing Your Learning tasks:**

- 🔼 **2 baseline tests:** These tests cover basic historical terminology and chronological understanding, as well as an introductory approach to source analysis. They can help you to quickly assess the prior historical knowledge that your new KS3 students may have.

- 🖥 **3 assessment task presentations:** Each assessment task in the *Student Book*, which assesses history **skills**, has a front-of-class presentation for you to use to help guide students towards unpacking the task and understanding what it is asking of them. You can lead students through this step-by-step presentation and help them decide how to prepare to complete the task.

- 📄 **3 success criteria teacher grids:** A grid accompanies each assessment task in the *Student Book*, which helps teachers mark the tasks in relation to such skills as evaluation, analysis, and understanding.

- 📄 **3 sets of assessment worksheets:** These worksheets cvomplement the assessment tasks in the *Student Book* and the assessment task presentations. They recap the task, provide a self-evaluation chart, and space for students to prepare their work.

A **Markbook** with reporting function completes the *Kerboodle* assessment package, so you can keep track of all your students' test results and assessment scores. This includes both the auto-marked tests and work that needs to be marked by you. It is also easy to import class registers and create user accounts for all your students.

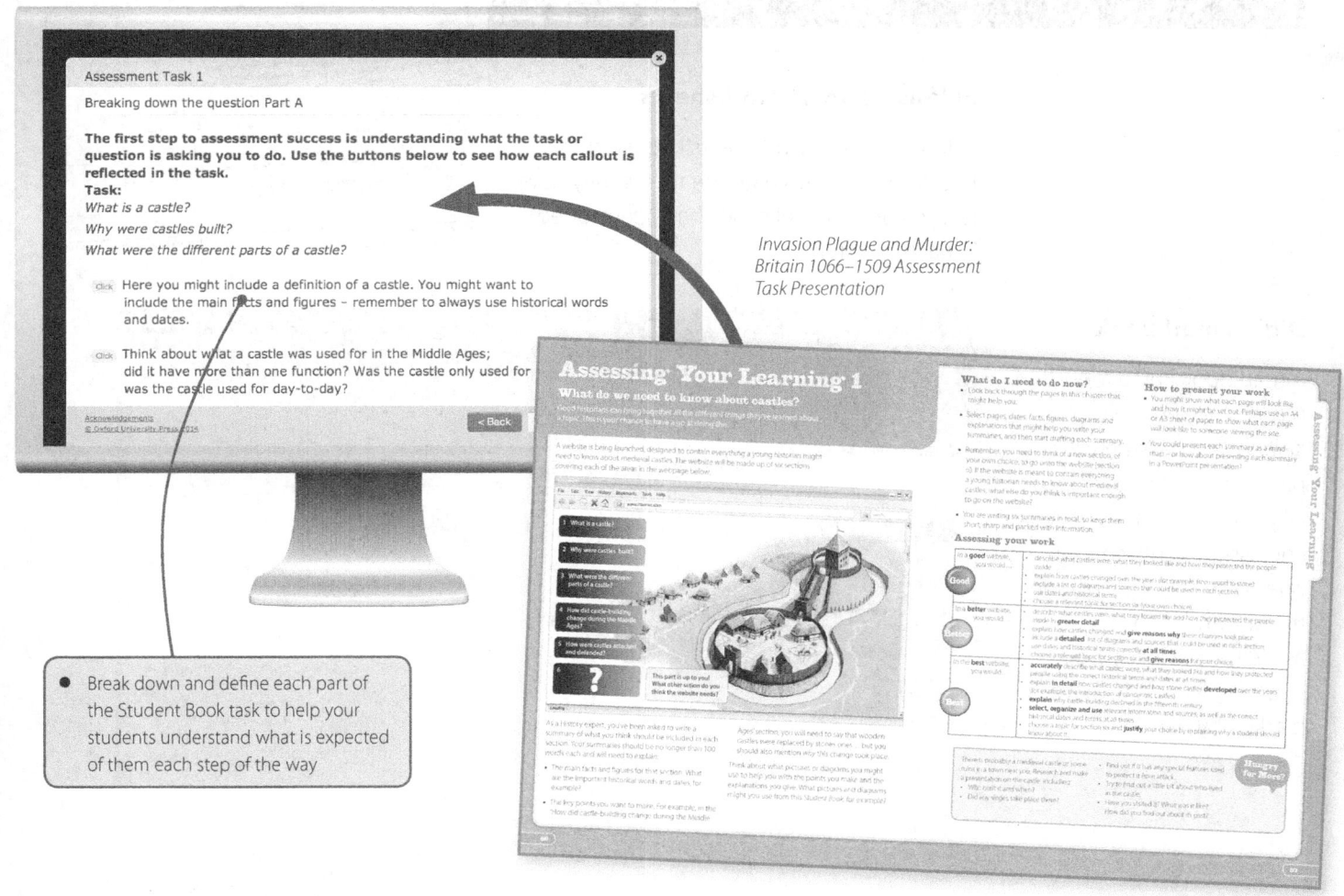

*Invasion Plague and Murder: Britain 1066–1509 Assessment Task Presentation*

- Break down and define each part of the Student Book task to help your students understand what is expected of them each step of the way

# Assessment

## Auto-marked tests

The *Invasion, Plague and Murder Kerboodle* contains auto-marked tests for each chapter to help save you time setting questions and marking for historical knowledge and understanding. Each test contains between 10 and 15 questions and should take most students no more than half an hour. Test results are automatically stored in the markbook.

## Baseline tests

The two baseline tests and a mark scheme are included to help teachers try to establish the level of knowledge and learning that students have acquired in primary school.

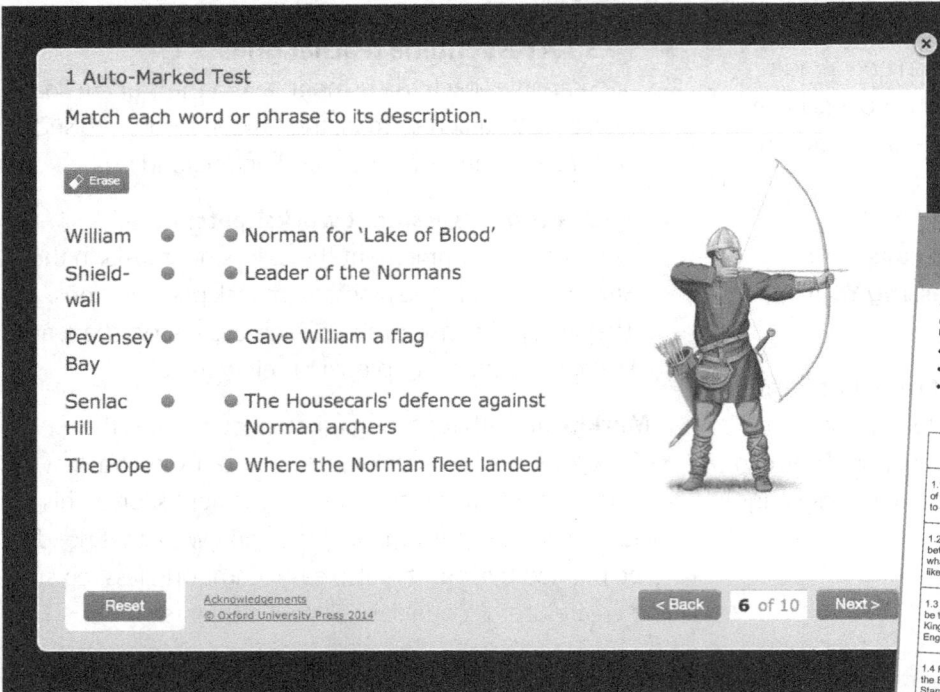

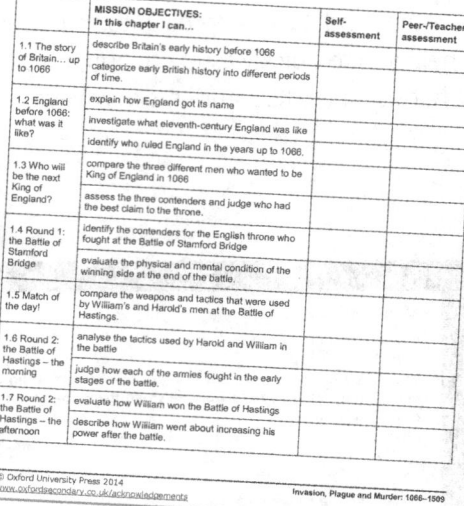

## Self-assessment worksheets

Self-assessment worksheets help students to self- or peer-evaluate the topics they have learned and the skills they have developed in each chapter.

## Digital markbook

A markbook and a reporting function complete the *Kerboodle* assessment package, so you can keep all your students' test results and assessment scores in one place. This can include the auto-marked tests as well as pieces of work you or the students have marked by hand.

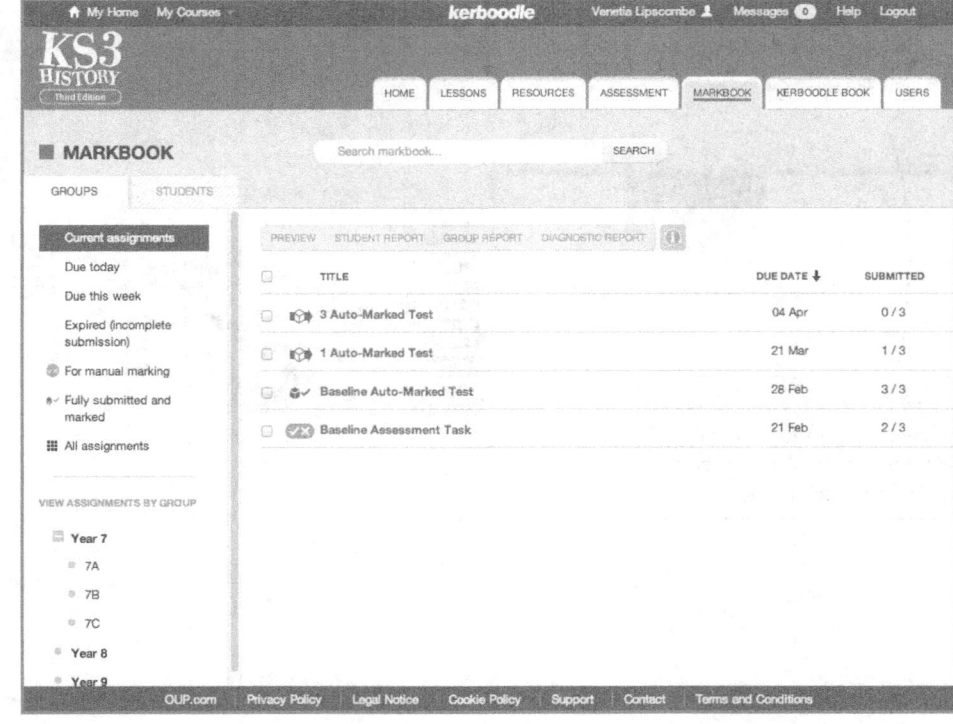

# Overview:
# Chapter 1 1066 and all that

## Helping you deliver KS3 History National Curriculum

This chapter begins by exploring Britain's story up to the eleventh century. Written chronologically, the first three lessons lead from the Stone Age into the Bronze Age and Iron Age. They also look at the Roman conquest and subsequent tribal invasions up to 1066.

Moving on to the momentous events of 1066, students will be challenged throughout by work sections that include extension opportunities and support material. They will create their own structured accounts and investigate historical problems. They will begin to ask their own questions, analyse sources, and compare and contrast why events happened.

## The Big Picture

### Why are we teaching '1066 and all that'?

The events of that year were remarkable! To grasp their significance, students first need to understand what Britain was like before the Norman Invasion, so we have included a broad outline of Anglo-Saxon Britain. Furthermore, in order to put Anglo-Saxon Britain in context, we have decided to go back further to chart our island story.

Students then examine the power struggle that followed the death of Edward the Confessor. Students often reach very different conclusions about the various contenders, leading to excellent class discussions on the nature of debate in history.

At the end, the students are required to pull all the information together in a chronology task and make an overall judgement on the reasons for William's victory. The possible

## Skills and processes covered in this chapter

| | | 1.1A | 1.1B | 1.1C | 1.2A | 1.2B | 1.3 | 1.4 | 1.5 | 1.6 | 1.7 | 1.8 |
|---|---|---|---|---|---|---|---|---|---|---|---|---|
| **History Skills** | Historical enquiry | ✓ | ✓ | ✓ | ✓ | ✓ | ✓ | ✓ | ✓ | ✓ | ✓ | ✓ |
| | Using evidence and source work | | | | ✓ | ✓ | | | | | ✓ | ✓ |
| | Chronological understanding | ✓ | ✓ | ✓ | | | | | | ✓ | ✓ | |
| | Understanding cultural, ethnic and religious diversity | ✓ | ✓ | ✓ | ✓ | ✓ | | | | | | |
| | Change and continuity | ✓ | ✓ | ✓ | ✓ | ✓ | | | | | | |
| | Cause and consequence | | | | | | | ✓ | | | ✓ | ✓ |
| | Significance | | | | | | | | | | ✓ | ✓ |
| | Interpretations | | | | | | | | | | | ✓ |
| | Making links/connections | | ✓ | ✓ | | | | | | ✓ | | |
| | Explores similarities and differences | ✓ | ✓ | ✓ | ✓ | ✓ | | | | | | |
| **Literacy and Numeracy** | Key words identified/deployed | ✓ | | | | | | | | ✓ | | |
| | Extended writing | | | | | | | | | ✓ | ✓ | ✓ |
| | Encourages reading for meaning | | | | | ✓ | | | | | ✓ | ✓ |
| | Focuses on structuring writing | | | | | | | | | ✓ | ✓ | ✓ |
| | Asks students to use writing to explore and develop ideas | | | | | | | | | | ✓ | ✓ |
| | Learn through talk/discussion | | | | ✓ | ✓ | | | | ✓ | | |
| | Numeracy opportunities | | | | | | | | | ✓ | | |
| **Activity types** | Creative task | | | | | | | ✓ | ✓ | | | |
| | Emphasizes role of individual | | | | | ✓ | | | | | | |
| | Group work | | | | | | | | | ✓ | | |
| | Independent research | ✓ | ✓ | | | | | | | | | ✓ |
| | Develops study skills | | | ✓ | ✓ | | | | | | | |

fate of Harold is an ideal way to conclude the study. By looking at one of history's greatest mysteries, the children learn about the nature of evidence and the fact that history very rarely delivers a consensus – even on the most significant events.

## Lesson sequence

| Lesson title | NC references | Objectives | Outcomes |
|---|---|---|---|
| 1.1A The story of Britain... up to 1066 pp10–11<br><br>1.1B The story of Britain... up to 1066 pp12–13<br><br>1.1C The story of Britain... up to 1066 pp14–15 | The study of an aspect or theme in British history that consolidates and extends students' chronological knowledge from before 1066 | • Explore Britain's early history before 1066.<br>• Categorize early British history into different periods of time. | **All** students will know at least four groups of people who lived in or invaded England up to 1066.<br>**Most** students will be able to categorize early British history into different periods of time.<br>**Some** students will be able to identify three ways in which each group improved or changed life in early Britain. |
| 1.2A England before 1066: what was it like? pp16–17<br><br>1.2B England before 1066: what was it like? pp18–19 | The Norman Conquest | • Find out how England got its name.<br>• Investigate what eleventh century England was like.<br>• Identify who ruled England in the years up to 1066. | **All** students will know how England got its name and who ruled England in 1065.<br>**Most** students will be able to describe in detail what life was like in England in 1065.<br>**Some** students will be able to use information from sources to support their writing. |
| 1.3 Who will be the next King of England? pp20–21 | The Norman Conquest | • Compare the three different men who wanted to be King of England in 1066.<br>• Assess the three contenders and judge who had the best claim to the throne. | **All** students will know the identities of the three contenders who wished to become the new King of England.<br>**Most** students will know reasons why each contender believed they should be king.<br>**Some** students will be able to explain who had the best claim to the throne. |
| 1.4 Round 1: the Battle of Stamford Bridge pp22–23 | The Norman Conquest | • Identify the contenders for the English throne who fought at the Battle of Stamford Bridge.<br>• Evaluate the physical and mental condition of the winning side at the end of the battle. | **All** students will know the events of the Battle of Stamford Bridge.<br>**Most** students will know the events of the Battle of Stamford Bridge and be able to identify reasons why Harold won.<br>**Some** students will know the events of the Battle of Stamford Bridge and be able to explain which was the most important reason for Harold's victory. |
| 1.5 Match of the day! pp24–25 | The Norman Conquest | • Compare the weapons and tactics that were used by William's and Harold's men at the Battle of Hastings. | **All** students will be able to identify the weapons and tactics used by the soldiers at the Battle of Hastings.<br>**Most** students will be able to describe in detail the weapons and tactics used by the different soldiers at the Battle of Hastings.<br>**Some** students will be able to explain whether Harold or William had the strongest army. |
| 1.6 Round 2: the Battle of Hastings – the morning pp26–27 | The Norman Conquest | • Analyse the tactics used in the battle by Harold and William.<br>• Judge how each of the armies fought in the early stages of the battle. | **All** students will be able to describe what happened at the Battle of Hastings.<br>**Most** students will be able to explain Harold's tactics at the Battle of Hastings.<br>**Some** students will be able to evaluate who is more likely to win the battle. |
| 1.7 Round 2: the Battle of Hastings – the afternoon pp28–29 | The Norman Conquest | • Evaluate how William won the Battle of Hastings.<br>• Discover how William went about increasing his power after the battle. | **All** students will be able to describe what happened at the Battle of Hastings.<br>**Most** students will be able to describe at least one reason why William won the Battle of Hastings.<br>**Some** students will be able to explain and link together reasons why William won the Battle of Hastings. |
| 1.8 History Mystery: how did King Harold die? pp30–31 | The Norman Conquest | • Come to your own conclusion as to how King Harold died. | **All** students will know the events of Harold Godwinson's death and be able to say how they think he died.<br>**Most** students will be able to justify their explanation of how King Harold died with support from evidence.<br>**Some** students will be able to justify their explanation with support from evidence and question the reliability of each source. |

## Ideas for enrichment

You could try some 'contender role play' with students. Ask them to break into groups and prepare a speech for one of the contenders for the throne in 1066. They could mount a campaign in support of their contender, creating posters and leaflets. You could host an election debate where each group puts forward their persuasive ideas.

It may be possible for you to set up a Battle of Hastings re-enactment! This not only delivers drama through the curriculum and appeals to kinaesthetic learners, it also enables the students to grasp the importance of William's tactics. On a smaller scale, groups of students could act out individual scenes from the story of 1066.

There are a few TV programmes that you could show, for example the BBC's *Battlefield Britain: Medieval Warfare at the Battle of Hastings*, presented by Peter and Dan Snow, and *War Walk: Hastings*, presented by Richard Holmes. There are also a few online class clips about Normans on the BBC's learning zone.

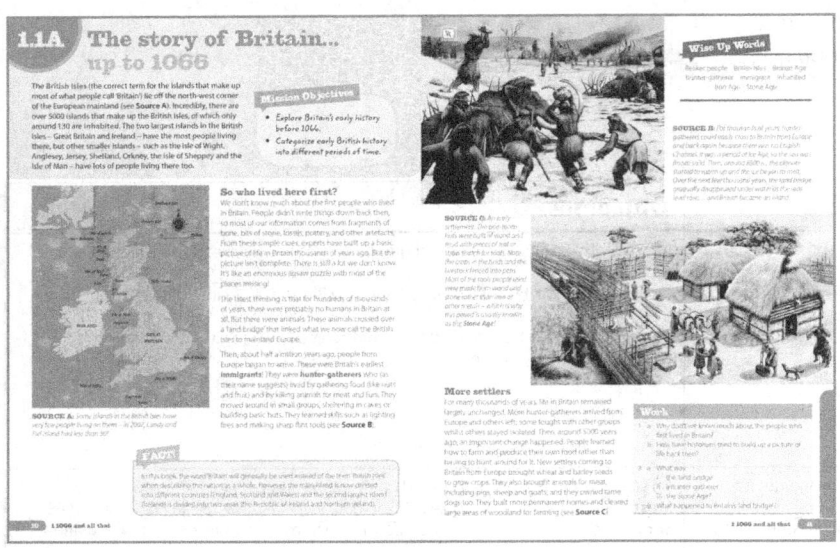

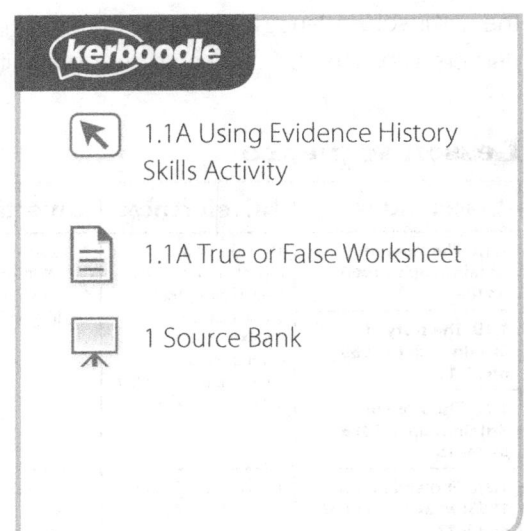

Invasion, Plague and Murder pages 10–11

## Lesson summary

Students will develop an understanding of Britain's early history up to 1066.

### What are the lesson outcomes?

**All** students will know at least four groups of people who lived in or invaded England up to 1066.

**Most** students will be able to categorize early British history into different periods of time.

**Some** students will be able to identify three ways in which each group improved or changed life in early Britain.

## Starter suggestion

- Wise up!: Students should be allocated one of the Wise Up Words. They should then research its meaning using the glossary in the *Student Book* and explain what their word means to the class.

## Main learning suggestions and assessment

### What activities will take place?

**Task 1:** Students should read the information across pages 10 and 11 and complete Work activities **1** and **2**.

### How will students demonstrate their understanding?

**Task 2:** Students should complete 1.1A Using Evidence History Skills Activity to gain a greater understanding of **Source B**.

**Task 3:** Students should complete 1.1A True or False Worksheet and decide which statements are correct for Britain's early settlers and their way of life.

## Plenary suggestions

- Show me the question!: Ask students to look at these four answers: land bridge; hunter–gatherer; 5000 years ago; Stone Age. Can they come up with their own questions for each of them using what they have learned from this lesson?

## Differentiation suggestions

### Support

- Students can write up the false statements in 1.1A True or False Worksheet correctly, using accurate spelling, punctuation, and grammar.

### Extension: Hungry for more?

- Students could research the history of Stonehenge. Where is it? When might it have been built and why? What can it tell us about life in the Bronze Age?

# 1.1B The story of Britain... up to 1066

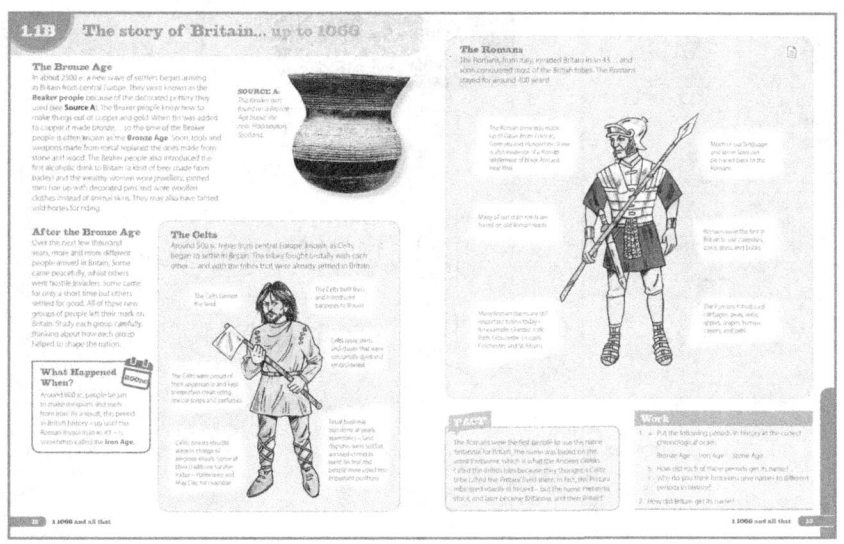

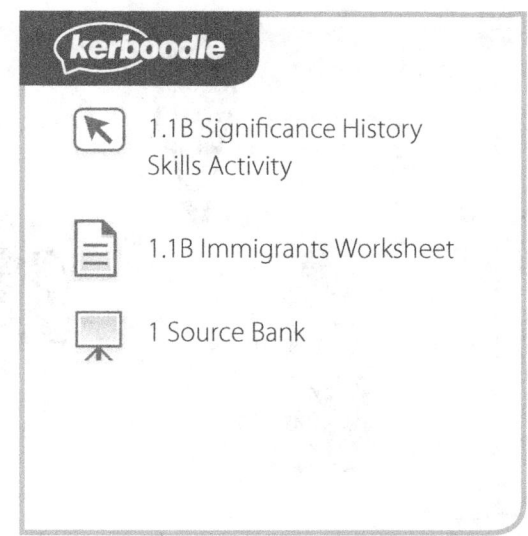

Invasion, Plague and Murder pages 12–13

## Lesson summary

Students will develop an understanding of Britain's early history up to 1066.

### What are the lesson outcomes?

**All** students will know at least four groups of people who lived in or invaded England up to 1066.

**Most** students will be able to categorize early British history into different periods of time.

**Some** students will be able to identify three ways in which each group improved or changed life in early Britain.

## Starter suggestion

● Flash recall!: Nominate students to give the class five facts about life in early Britain from the last lesson.

## Main learning suggestions and assessment

### What activities will take place?

**Task 1:** Students should read the information and complete 1.1B Significance History Skills Activity. Students should sort the positive and negative consequences of being invaded by the Celts, Romans, Vikings, and Anglo-Saxons.

## How will students demonstrate their understanding?

**Task 2:** Students should complete Work activities **1** and **2**.

**Task 3:** Students should complete the mind-map activity on 1.1B Immigrants Worksheet. Each branch of the mind-map should outline the contribution and impact of each of the different groups of invaders and settlers. In this lesson students can complete the Celts and Romans.

## Plenary suggestions

● Hands up!: Ask students to come up with three new ideas or things that the Celts brought to Britain and then three ideas or things that the Romans brought to Britain. Ask them to consider whether these things improved the lives of the people already living in Britain.

## Differentiation suggestions

### Support

● Students might benefit from briefly recapping any early history they may have studied in primary school. Ask students to put their hands up and tell the class one fact about either the Celts or the Romans.

### Extension: Hungry for more?

● Students could research the town of Droitwich Spa and why the Romans chose to settle there. They should research the settlement's Roman name, 'Salinae'.

● Higher ability students can use colour to identify themes on their mind-map from the worksheet for this lesson. They could use the following codes: blue (new technology); green (weapons and warfare); yellow (new foods).

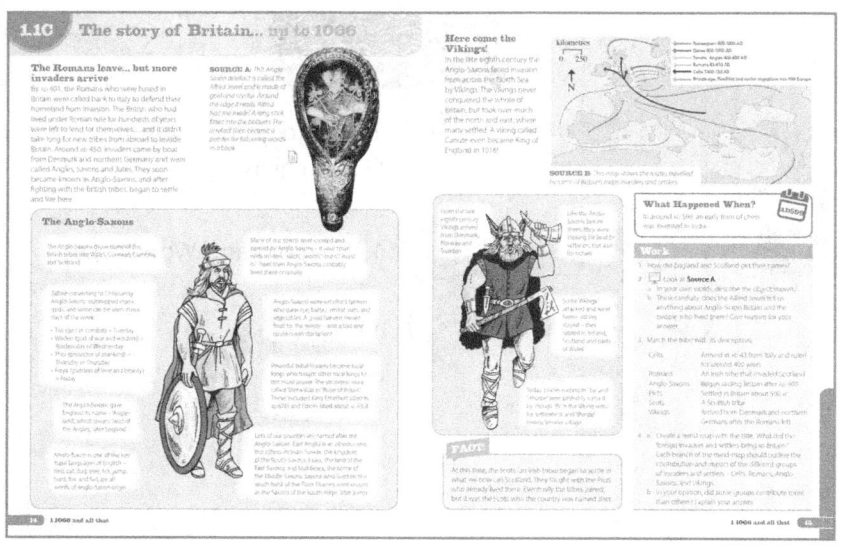

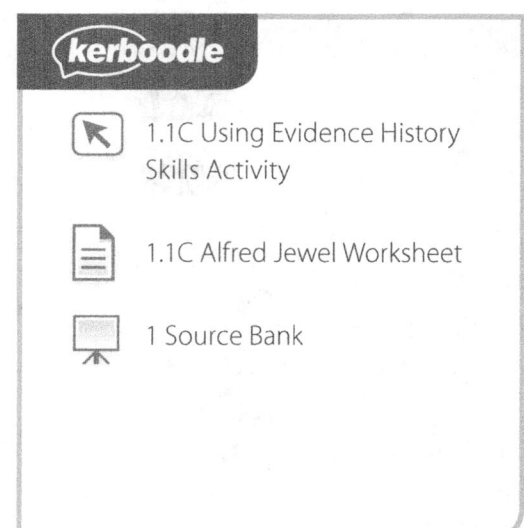

Invasion, Plague and Murder pages 14–15

## Lesson summary

Students will develop an understanding of Britain's early history up to 1066.

### What are the lesson outcomes?

**All** students will know at least four groups of people who lived in or invaded England up to 1066.

**Most** students will be able to categorize early British history into different periods of time.

**Some** students will be able to identify three ways in which each group improved or changed life in early Britain.

## Starter suggestion

- Think, pair, share: What did the Romans and Celts do for us? Pupils should be given 30 seconds to think about one thing the Romans and Celts each brought to Britain. They should then be given one minute to discuss their ideas with their neighbour. This should feed into a class discussion where each pair shares their ideas with the class in order to create a list of examples.

## Main learning suggestions and assessment

### What activities will take place?

**Task 1:** Students should complete 1.1C Using Evidence History Skills Activity or 1.1C Alfred Jewel Worksheet to understand the Alfred Jewel.

### How will students demonstrate their understanding?

**Task 2:** Students should complete Work activities 1–3.

**Task 3:** Students should complete a mind-map with the title 'What did the foreign invaders and settlers bring to Britain?' Each branch of the mind-map should outline the contribution and impact of the different groups of invaders

and settlers. Today, students can complete the Anglo-Saxons and Vikings. Students may wish to complete the mind-map from the last lesson's worksheet.

**Task 4:** Students should consider which group of invaders contributed the most to Britain, explaining their answer.

## Plenary suggestions

- Hands up!: Ask students to come up the three things that the Anglo-Saxons did for us and then three things the Vikings did for us. Ask them to consider whether these were improvements for the people living in Britain.

## Differentiation suggestions

### Support

- Students can use 1.1B Immigrants Worksheet from the previous lesson to help create their mind-map.

### Extension: Hungry for more?

- Students could research the Staffordshire Hoard.

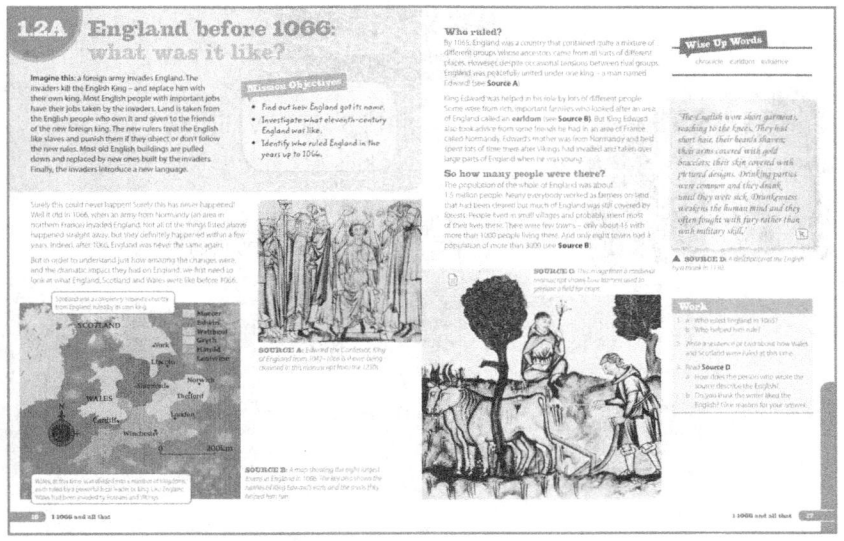

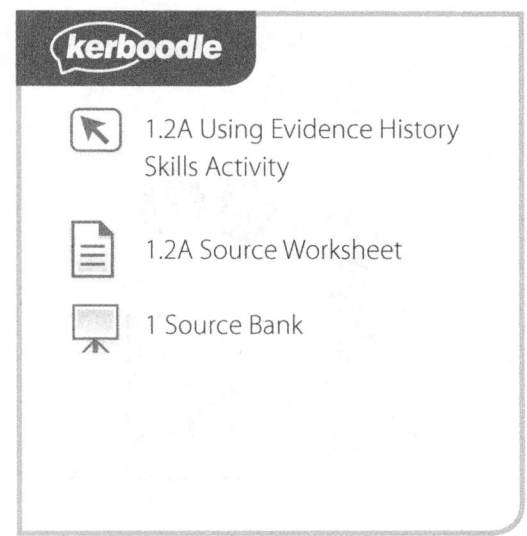

- 1.2A Using Evidence History Skills Activity

- 1.2A Source Worksheet

- 1 Source Bank

Invasion, Plague and Murder pages 16–17

## Lesson summary

Students will complete source analysis tasks to understand what life was like in the eleventh century.

### What are the lesson outcomes?

**All** students will know how England got its name and who ruled England in 1065.

**Most** students will be able to describe in detail what life was like in England in 1065.

**Some** students will be able to use information from sources to support their writing.

## Starter suggestion

- Students should be split into groups and allocated either Source A, C or D. Students should then try to answer the following 'NOSY' questions: WHO is the source talking about? WHEN was it made? WHAT does it tell us about life in England? WHERE is this source talking about? WHY do you think it was made? Students should feed back to the rest of the class about what they have learned.

## Main learning suggestions and assessment

### What activities will take place?

**Task 1:** Students should read the information on pages 16–17. They should then complete 1.2A Using Evidence History Skills Activity to sort the different types of sources that historians can use to help them learn about the past.

### How will students demonstrate their understanding?

**Task 2**: Students should complete Work activities **1** and **2** on page 17. Lower ability students can complete the source analysis task for **Source D** using 1.2A Source Worksheet. Students should read the information and complete the questions around the source. This will help them to understand more about medieval life, and to develop their ability to use sources.

## Plenary suggestions

- Students could write down one thing they have learned today and one question they would like to ask about the topic.

## Differentiation suggestions

### Support

- Lower ability students can use 1.2A Source Worksheet to help support them in the source analysis task in Work activity **2**.

### Extension: Hungry for more?

- Students could read and research the poems by William Langland or John Lydgate about what life was like for English people, especially medieval peasants, at this time.

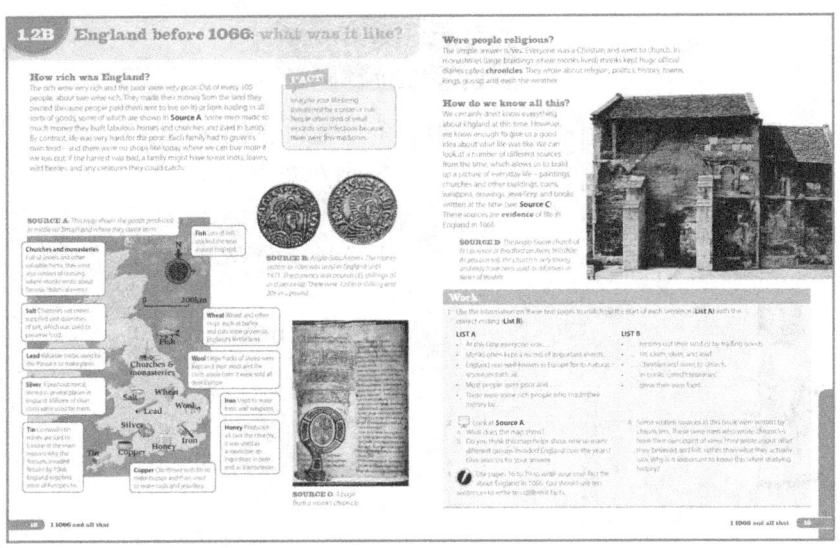

Invasion, Plague and Murder pages 18–19

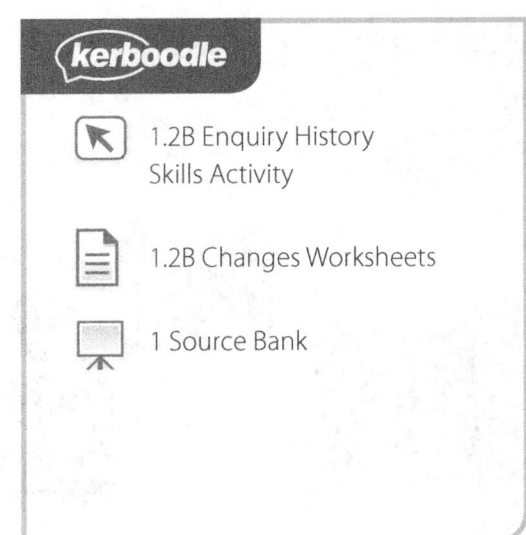

kerboodle

- 1.2B Enquiry History Skills Activity
- 1.2B Changes Worksheets
- 1 Source Bank

## Lesson summary

Students will complete source analysis tasks to understand what life was like in the eleventh century.

### What are the lesson outcomes?

**All** students will know how England got its name and who ruled England in 1065.

**Most** students will be able to describe in detail what life was like in England in 1065.

**Some** students will be able to use information from sources to support their writing.

## Starter suggestion

- Students should look back at what they learned last lesson and share the questions they came up with as part of last lesson's plenary exercise. Can other students help them answer their questions?

## Main learning suggestions and assessment

### What activities will take place?

**Task 1:** Students should read the information across pages 18–19 and use the prompt questions (the 'NOSY' questions from last lesson) to discuss the sources in this spread.

**Task 2:** Students should complete 1.2B Enquiry History Skills Activity, which asks students to debate whether England was a civilized place to live in 1066.

### How will students demonstrate their understanding?

**Task 3:** Students should complete Work activities **1–3** on page 19. Activity **3** requires students to complete a fact file. You could look at page 21 of the *Student Book* to model the conventions of a good fact file.

**Task 4**: Students can also complete the table describing how life has changed since 1066 on 1.2B Changes Worksheet. Students should make notes under the following headings: Who is in charge?; How is the country run?; Religion; Jobs; Towns and Cities; Rich and Poor. They can use these notes to show what life was like in 1066 and how life has changed today.

## Plenary suggestions

- Thumbs up!: Students could answer the question 'Would you like to live in the Middle Ages?' with a 'thumbs up' or a 'thumbs down'. Can they come up with a reason to explain their choice?

## Differentiation suggestions

### Support

- You can use 1.2B Changes Worksheet to help support weaker students as they complete the Work activities on page 19.

### Extension: Hungry for more?

- 'Why do you think life in 1066 was different from today? Would you prefer to live now or then? Can you say why?'
  - Students can be set these questions either as a discussion point or as a written response for homework. If this is structured as a classroom discussion, you may wish to use the same topics as in **Task 4** and allocate each topic to a group/pair of students. Students often reach very different conclusions, leading to excellent class discussions.

# 1.3 Who will be the next King of England?

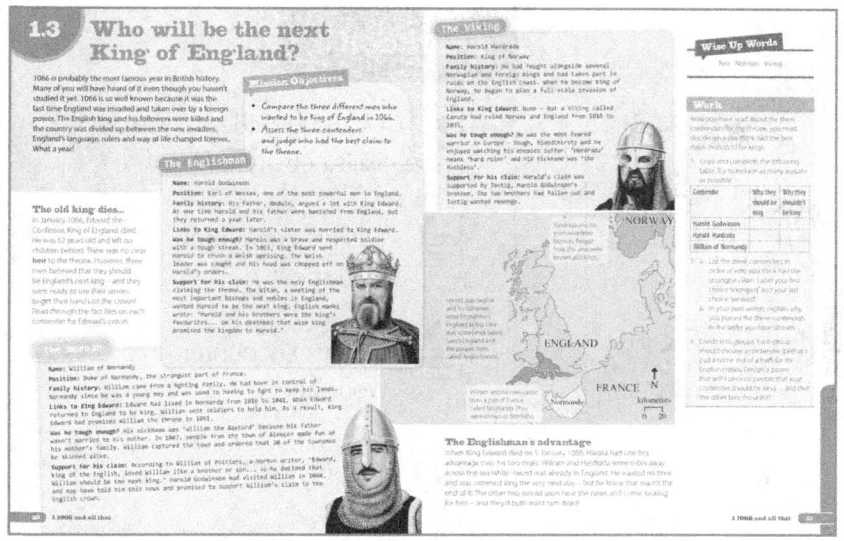

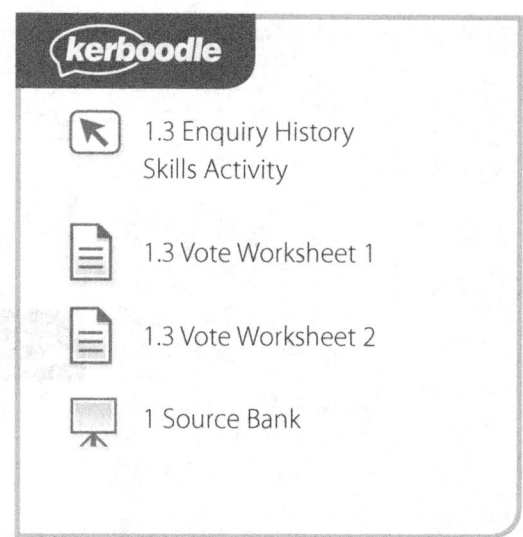

Invasion, Plague and Murder pages 20–21

## Lesson summary

Students will complete a research task to find out about the three men who wished to be King of England in 1066.

### What are the lesson outcomes?

**All** students will know the identities of the three contenders who wished to become the new King of England.

**Most** students will know reasons why each contender believed they should be king.

**Some** students will be able to explain who had the best claim to the throne.

## Starter suggestion

- Think, pair, share: Students should be given 30 seconds to consider what characteristics the new King of England should have. They should then be given one minute to discuss their ideas with a neighbour. This should feed into a class discussion where each pair shares their ideas with the class in order to create a list of characteristics the new King of England should have.

## Main learning suggestions and assessment

### What activities will take place?

**Task 1:** Students should read pages 20–21 and complete 1.3 Vote Worksheet 1 or 1.3 Vote Worksheet 2, researching reasons why each contender should or should not be king. Students should be able to identify, for each contender: Who am I? What's my job? Where am I from? Why should I be king? Why shouldn't I be king?

### How will students demonstrate their understanding?

**Task 2:** Students can assess their own knowledge by completing 1.3 Enquiry History Skills Activity, identifying contenders by various facts.

## Plenary suggestions

- Students should complete the voting slip on their worksheet giving a reason why they have placed each contender in each position. The results could be compiled into a class vote to see who the class have decided should become the new king.

## Differentiation suggestions

### Support

- Lower ability students can use 1.3 Vote Worksheet 2, which includes sentences starters to support their writing.

### Extension: Hungry for more?

- Hot seating activity: To develop and assess understanding, students could take part in a hot seating activity. Each student is given the role of one of the contenders, and they should plan their responses to the following questions: Why should you be king? Why would you make a good king? Who is the strongest contender to the throne? What is your biggest weakness?
  - This can be run as a class discussion with students being invited to the front to give their answers to the questions. The class can then respond by offering individual thoughts or questions, or by working in small groups to discuss each response in turn.

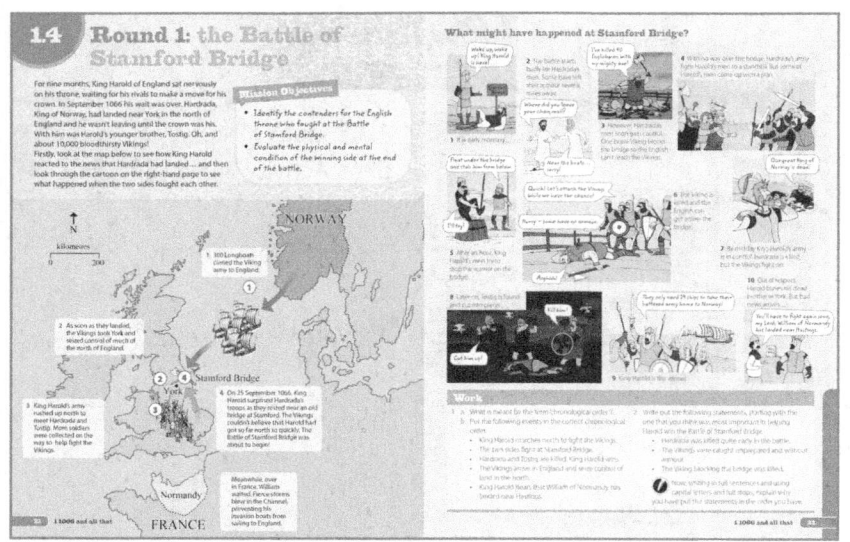

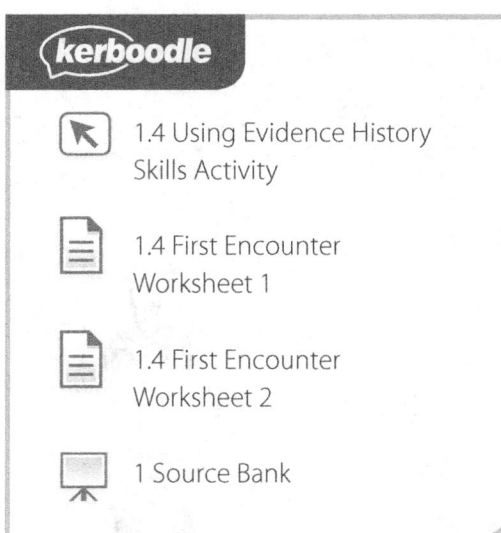

Invasion, Plague and Murder pages 22–23

## Lesson summary

Students will understand the chronology of the Battle of Stamford Bridge and form ideas about who is likely to become king after the battle.

### What are the lesson outcomes?

**All** students will know the events of the Battle of Stamford Bridge.

**Most** students will know the events of the Battle of Stamford Bridge and be able to identify reasons why Harold won.

**Some** students will know the events of the Battle of Stamford Bridge and be able to explain which was the most important reason for Harold's victory.

## Starter suggestion

- Working individually or in pairs, students can write on sticky notes one thing that they already know and one thing that they would like to know about the Battle of Stamford Bridge. For example, 'I know who the three contenders were'; 'I know William came from Normandy'; 'I want to know who becomes king'; 'I want to know who had the best army'.

- These notes would be best displayed such that you can return to them during the lesson or plenary as students find out the things they want to know.

## Main learning suggestions and assessment

### What activities will take place?

**Task 1:** Students should read through the information on pages 22–23. Using this information, and 1.4 First Encounter Worksheet 1, they should create a storyboard showing the events of the Battle of Stamford Bridge, filling in the eight boxes. Each box should contain three keywords and symbols that help to tell the story.

**Task 2:** Students can gain greater insight into the battle through the primary source analysis task in 1.4 Using Evidence History Skills Activity.

### How will students demonstrate their understanding?

**Task 3:** Why did Harold become king? Students should use 1.4 First Encounter Worksheet 2 to complete Work activity **2** on page 23. They should organise the three statements in order of importance, with the most important at the top and the least important at the bottom. In each part they should complete the sentence to explain its position.

## Plenary suggestions

- Students could write down something that they have learned on one more sticky note, to show what they have learned. You may wish to ask students to share these ideas with each other or with small groups.

## Differentiation suggestions

### Support

- 1.4 First Encounter Worksheet 2 includes sentence starters to support lower ability students.

### Extension: Hungry for more?

- Higher ability students could organize a debate on who they believe will be the next King of England in 1066.

# 1.5 Match of the day!

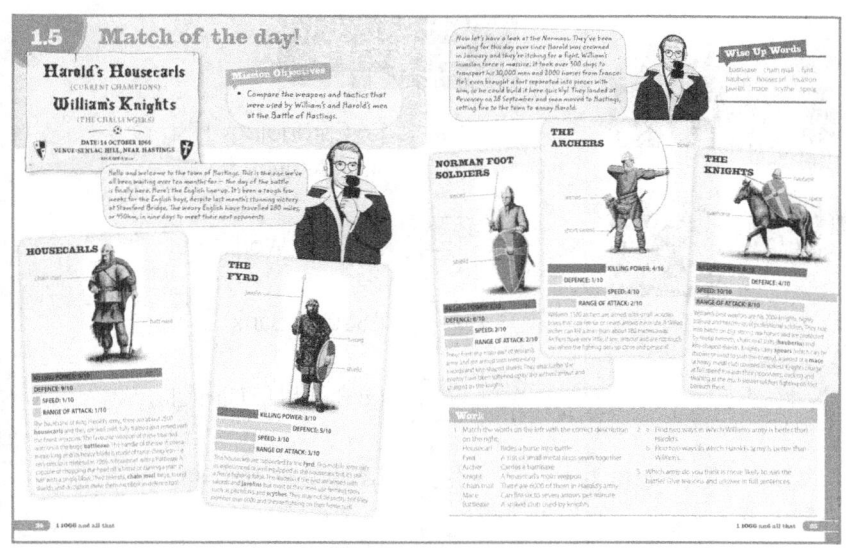

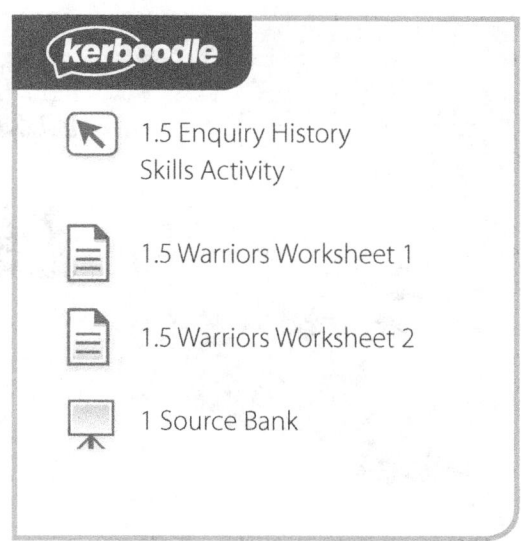

Invasion, Plague and Murder pages 24–25

## Lesson summary
Students will develop their own knowledge about the weapons and tactics used in the Battle of Hastings, and create resources to play a 'Match of the Day' game.

### What are the lesson outcomes?
**All** students will be able to identify the weapons and tactics used by the soldiers at the Battle of Hastings.

**Most** students will be able to describe in detail the weapons and tactics used by the different soldiers at the Battle of Hastings.

**Some** students will be able to explain whether Harold or William had the strongest army.

## Starter suggestion
- You could organize a class vote on who will become king after the Battle of Hastings. Students could think back to the previous lesson on the Battle of Stamford Bridge, remembering why Harold's army was successful there.

## Main learning suggestions and assessment
### What activities will take place?
**Task 1:** Students should read through the information on pages 24–25 and complete Work activities **1–3**. Using 1.5 Warriors Worksheet 1, students can create their own 'Match of the Day' cards, filling in the information required to play the game. For each card students should decide on a symbol which can represent each soldier, colour in their ratings correctly, and write one sentence explaining each soldier's job.

### How will students demonstrate their understanding?
**Task 2:** Students can use the interactive activity 1.5 Enquiry History Skills Activity to sort the strengths and weaknesses of William's and Harold's armies.

## Plenary suggestions
- Students can play the game using the cards they have created. They should also make the numbered die and colour it in as directed on the worksheet. To play the game, the person with the highest dice roll goes first. For each round, roll the dice. The colour shown on the dice will decide which rating to compare. The person with the highest rating is given all the cards from that round, and the poem with the lowest rolls the dice to decide the next round. The first person to get all the cards is the winner.

## Differentiation suggestions
### Support
- Students can complete Work activity **1** to gain an understanding of which soldiers fought on each side, before completing 1.5 Warriors Worksheets 1 and 2.

### Extension: Hungry for more?
- You could ask higher ability students to choose one type of solider to do more research on and produce a mini fact file. They could investigate how many there were, fighting style, and what other battles they fought in, for example.

Invasion, Plague and Murder pages 26–27

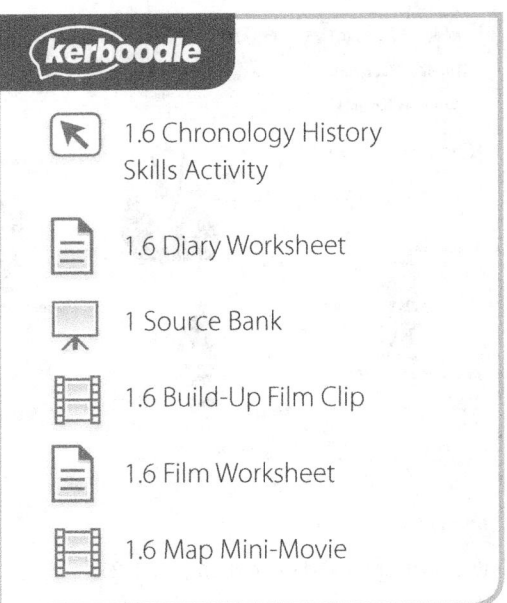

**kerboodle**

- 1.6 Chronology History Skills Activity
- 1.6 Diary Worksheet
- 1 Source Bank
- 1.6 Build-Up Film Clip
- 1.6 Film Worksheet
- 1.6 Map Mini-Movie

## Lesson summary

Students will develop a chronoligical understanding of the morning of the Battle of Hastings.

### What are the lesson outcomes?

**All** students will be able to describe what happened at the Battle of Hastings.

**Most** students will be able to explain Harold's tactics at the Battle of Hastings.

**Some** students will be able to evaluate who is more likely to win the battle.

## Starter suggestion

- Debate stations: Identify two areas of the classroom, one for Harold and one for William. Students should choose who they believe will be the next king, then go to the appropriate area. They should work with their group to decide three reasons for their choice. Their ideas should be shared and discussed with the class.

## Main learning suggestions and assessment

### What activities will take place?

**Task 1:** Students should read pages 26–27 and complete Work activities **1–3**. Students could also watch 1.6 Build-Up Film Clip and/or 1.6 Map Mini-Movie, which both explain the movements of both sides in an audio-visual way. A film worksheet accompanies 1.6 Build-Up Film Clip, and assesses students' understanding of what they have seen and read.

**Task 2:** Once they are confident about the events of the morning of the battle, they could complete 1.6 Chronology History Skills Activity to consolidate their learning.

### How will students demonstrate their understanding?

**Task 3:** Students could complete their own timeline showing the events of the Battle of Hastings.

**Task 4:** Students can use 1.6 Diary worksheet to create a diary entry for one of William's footsoldiers, explaining how successfully they felt the battle went in the morning. This worksheet includes key word prompts.

## Plenary suggestions

- Exit note: Students could write an exit note, to hand in as they leave class, stating one thing they have learned in this lesson.

## Differentiation suggestions

### Support

- 1.6 Diary worksheet includes key word prompts for lower ability students.

### Extension: Hungry for more?

- Students could work in pairs, with one of them taking on the role of Harold Godwinson and the other taking on the role of William of Normandy. Ask each of them to spend one minute making a list of the strengths and weaknesses of their character, then share these with their partners. Who does each pair think will win? Why?

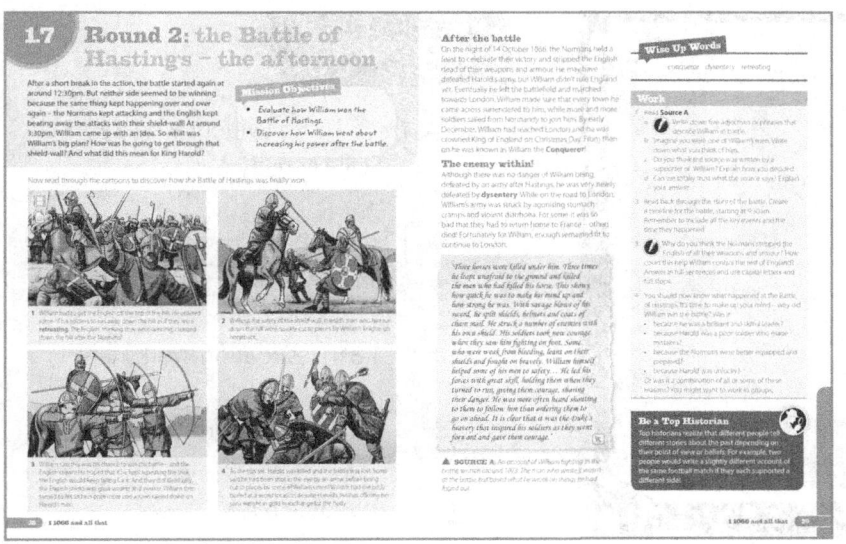

Invasion, Plague and Murder pages 28–29

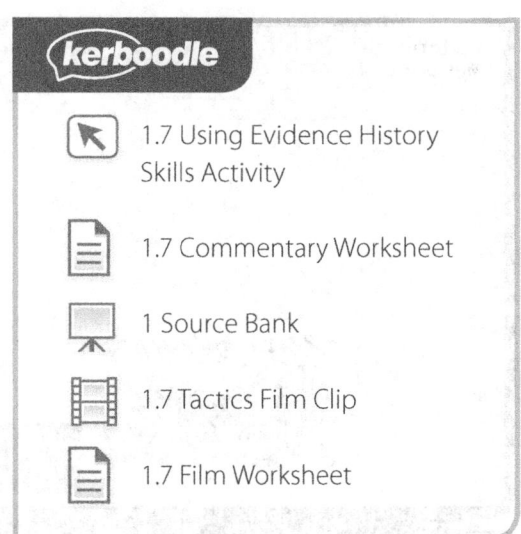

## Lesson summary

Students will learn about the events of the Battle of Hastings and create a script for an audio commentary explaining why they believe William won.

### What are the lesson outcomes?

**All** students will be able to describe what happened at the Battle of Hastings.

**Most** students will be able to describe at least one reason why William won the Battle of Hastings.

**Some** students will be able to explain and link together reasons why William won the Battle of Hastings.

## Starter suggestion

● High five: Students should identify five things that they already know about the Battle of Hastings.

## Main learning suggestions and assessment

### What activities will take place?

**Task 1:** Students should read pages 28–29 and complete 1.7 Using Evidence History Skills Activity to gain further understanding of two written historical sources.

**Task 2:** 1.7 Tactics Film Clip follows on from 1.6 Build-Up Film Clip. Here, William discusses the tactic that won him the battle. Students could also complete the accompanying film worksheet either during or after viewing.

### How will students demonstrate their understanding?

**Task 3:** Students should use the information they have gathered to create an audio commentary on the Battle of Hastings. This can be recorded as a podcast or presented to the class. It should be one minute long and it should include a description of the events of the Battle of Hastings. It should also explain why William won the battle.

Students should use 1.7 Commentary Worksheet to organize their ideas, using the descriptors to help them structure their work.

## Plenary suggestions

● Students can self-assess their own work and peer-assess a partner's work on 1.7 Commentary Worksheet. Encourage them to decide whether they or their partner should be awarded 'good', 'better', or 'best' and explain why.

## Differentiation suggestions

### Support

● Lower ability students should use the sentence starters on 1.7 Commentary Worksheet to help them organize their work.

● On page 29 of the *Student Book*, students are asked to create a timeline. You could show them pages 6–7 and 8–9 to model the conventions of a timeline.

### Extension: Hungry for more?

● You could ask higher ability students to think about what problems they think Harold might face immediately after the battle. What problems do they think he might face in the long term?

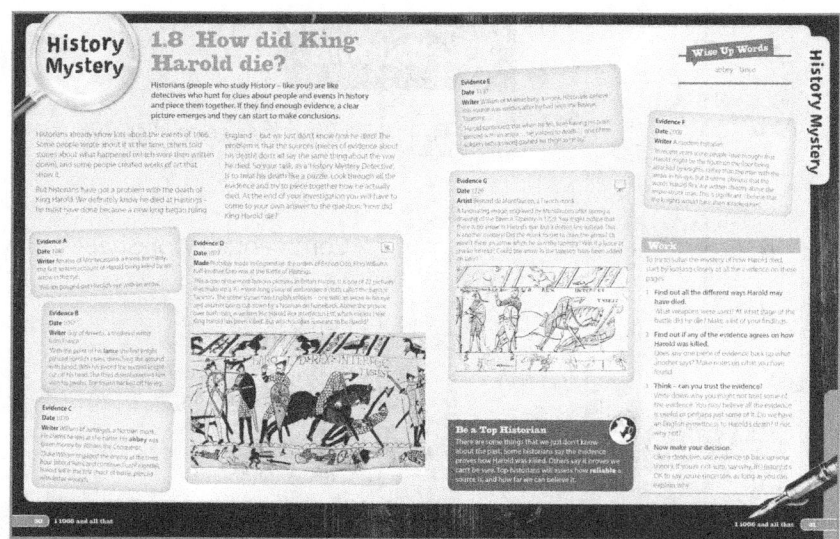

Invasion, Plague and Murder pages 30–31

## kerboodle

↖ 1.8 Using Evidence History Skills Activity 1

↖ 1.8 Using Evidence History Skills Activity 2

▤ 1.8 Investigation Worksheet 1

▤ 1.8 Investigation Worksheet 2

🖥 1 Source Bank

## Lesson summary

Students will investigate how King Harold died, using a variety of sources. They will write a report to explain how they believed Harold died and use evidence to support their ideas.

### What are the lesson outcomes?

**All** students will know the events of Harold Godwinson's death and be able to say how they think he died.

**Most** students will be able to justify their explanation of how King Harold died with support from evidence.

**Some** students will be able to justify their explanation with support from evidence and question the reliability of each source.

## Starter suggestion

- Students (individually or in pairs) can use sticky notes to identify one thing that they already know and one thing that they would like to know about this lesson. For example, 'I know… that King Harold died at Hastings'; 'I know… that some people say he was shot in the eye'; 'I want to know… how Harold died'; 'I want to know… whether we can know for certain how he died'.

## Main learning suggestions and assessment

### What activities will take place?

**Task 1:** Students should read through the information on pages 30–31. Using 1.8 Investigation Worksheet 1 they should analyse the various sources. For each one they should decide how it says Harold died, and they should decide if they can trust it. They should be able to explain why or why not. Students should annotate the sources with their answers.

## How will students demonstrate their understanding?

**Task 2:** Students will write a report entitled 'How did Harold die?'. They should organize their work under four headings: Introduction; Evidence which said Harold died by an arrow to the eye; Evidence which said Harold died by being cut down; Conclusion. Students should write their report using evidence to support each side, making their own decision about how Harold died. 1.8 Investigation Worksheet 2 provides hints for each section of the report.

## Plenary suggestions

- Students should write a sticky note that states one thing they have learned this lesson. They can then stick their notes to a large piece of paper or area of the classroom labelled 'I've Learned'. You may wish to get students to share these ideas with each other or the class.

## Differentiation suggestions

### Support

- 1.8 Investigation Worksheet 2 supports lower ability students by helping them to organize their report.

- 1.8 Using Evidence History Skills Activities 1 and 2 help students understand and interrogate the sources they are working with. You may wish to complete them with students as they come to **Evidence B**, **C**, **D** and **E**.

### Extension: Hungry for more?

- Peer assessment activity: Encourage students to peer assess another student's work, based on the descriptors. They should identify two things the student has done well and set one target to help their peer improve.

# Overview:
# Chapter 2 The Norman Conquest

## Helping you deliver KS3 History National Curriculum

The Norman Conquest is specifically mentioned in the 2014 National Curriculum Key Stage 3 History example list. This chapter explores historical concepts such as continuity and change, cause and consequence, similarity and difference, and significance.

Students are provided with opportunities to select and combine information from sources to answer questions. They are asked to identify links between different events and show how one event led to another. Each lesson identifies particularly important historical terminology (and some difficult concepts) such as feudal, motte, bailey, loyalty conquests, and massacred. Students are encouraged to spell, understand, and deploy these words correctly through a variety of tasks.

The Big Picture

## Why are we teaching 'The Norman Conquest'?

Covering the conquest of England through source analysis allows students to see how William used 'shock and awe' tactics to brutally suppress the people of England. We then look at the three main ways in which William consolidated his position. Many students may look at castles in a new light after discovering that the concept of castles was introduced to Britain by the Normans as a way of keeping control.

We decided to look at the Domesday Book in a degree of detail because of both its importance to William and its value to us. It is a peerless historical source that provides a comprehensive picture of life and development in 11th century England, and reinforces the importance of sources in the study of history.

## Skills and processes covered in this chapter

| | | 2.1A | 2.1B | 2.2 | 2.3 | 2.4 |
|---|---|---|---|---|---|---|
| **History Skills** | Historical enquiry | ✓ | ✓ | ✓ | ✓ | ✓ |
| | Using evidence and source work | ✓ | ✓ | | ✓ | |
| | Chronological understanding | | | | | |
| | Understanding cultural, ethnic and religious diversity | | | | | |
| | Change and continuity | ✓ | | ✓ | ✓ | ✓ |
| | Cause and consequence | | | ✓ | | |
| | Significance | ✓ | ✓ | | ✓ | |
| | Interpretations | | | | | |
| | Making links/connections | | | ✓ | | |
| | Explores similarities and differences | | | | | |
| **Literacy and Numeracy** | Key words identified/deployed | | | | | |
| | Extended writing | | | ✓ | | |
| | Encourages reading for meaning | | | | ✓ | |
| | Focuses on structuring writing | | | | | ✓ |
| | Asks students to use writing to explore and develop ideas | ✓ | ✓ | ✓ | ✓ | |
| | Learn through talk/discussion | | | ✓ | | |
| | Numeracy opportunities | | | | | |
| **Activity types** | Creative task | | | | ✓ | ✓ |
| | Emphasizes role of individual | ✓ | ✓ | | ✓ | ✓ |
| | Group work | | | ✓ | ✓ | |
| | Independent research | | | ✓ | ✓ | |
| | Develops study skills | | | ✓ | ✓ | |

The final element of consolidation was the introduction of the feudal system. It not only teaches students about the nature of power, but introduces them to the concepts of delegation, hierarchy, and loyalty.

## Lesson sequence

| Lesson title | NC references | Objectives | Outcomes |
|---|---|---|---|
| **2.1A The conquest of England pp32–33**<br><br>**2.1B The conquest of England pp34–35** | The Norman Conquest | • Examine William's key problems when he became King of England and analyse how he dealt with them. | **All** students will know at least one problem William faced as king, and how he solved it.<br>**Most** students will be able to explain the problems faced by William as the new King of England, and his solutions.<br>**Some** students will be able to explain how William solved the problems he faced as king, and if they think his solutions were effective. |
| **2.2 William the castle-builder pp36–37** | The Norman Conquest | • Understand what is meant by a 'motte and bailey' castle.<br>• Assess the advantages and disadvantages of these castles. | **All** students will be able to correctly label the parts of a motte and bailey castle.<br>**Most** students will be able to write a diary entry about attacking a motte and bailey castle, using keywords correctly.<br>**Some** students will be able to identify some problems of attacking a motte and bailey castle. |
| **2.3 The Domesday Book pp38–39** | The Norman Conquest | • Explain the purpose of the Domesday Survey and the Domesday Book. | **All** students will know what the Domesday Book was and why it was made.<br>**Most** students will be able to explain what sort of questions were asked in the Domesday Survey.<br>**Some** students will be able to identify how the English people reacted to the survey. |
| **2.4 The feudal system: who's the boss? pp40–41** | The Norman Conquest; Society, economy and culture: for example, feudalism | • Examine the feudal system and be able to illustrate exactly how it worked. | **All** students will know the hierarchy of the feudal system.<br>**Most** students will know the duties and benefits of each member in the hierarchy.<br>**Some** students will be able to explain how the skills or characteristics of each member in the hierarchy made them suited to their role. |

## Ideas for enrichment

A trip to a castle is an obvious enrichment activity here. Many castles, such as Warwick Castle, Conwy Castle, Kenilworth Castle, and the Tower of London, cater fantastically for school students. Stafford Castle, Beeston Castle, and Pleshey Castle are also great places to visit. The geographical extent of Norman castle building will almost certainly mean that there will be a castle within reasonable distance of most schools. A research project about a castle's history is a classic chronology study idea, and one that could equally be applied to Chapter 3: Castles.

An extension task could challenge students to track down the nearest town or village to their local area that has a Domesday Book entry. Point them in the direction of the website www.domesdaymap.co.uk. This is a wonderful opportunity for a local history project that can really help history come to life.

Before you lead the lesson on the feudal system, you could get students thinking about a hierarchy that exists in a situation that they are familiar with. For example, they could consider the hierarchy of staff and students at school, or managers, coaches, and players in a football club. This will set the lesson up nicely!

# 2.1A The conquest of England

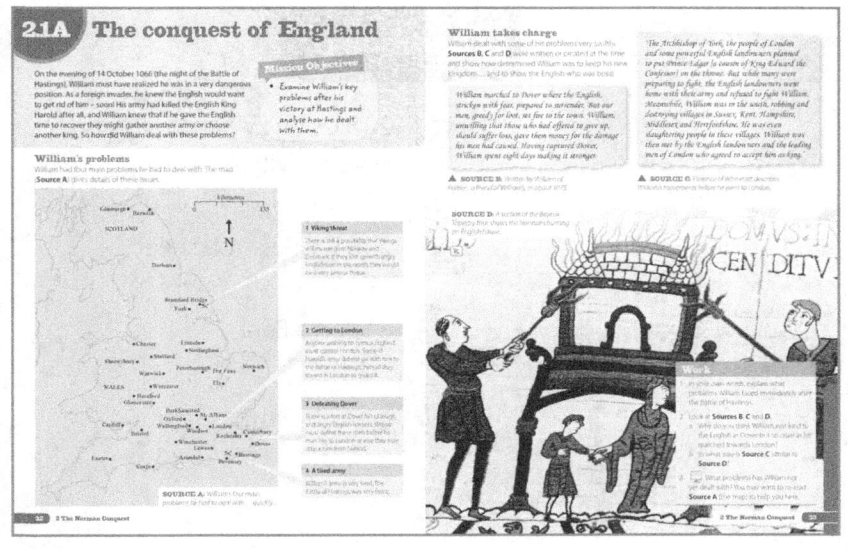

Invasion, Plague and Murder pages 32–33

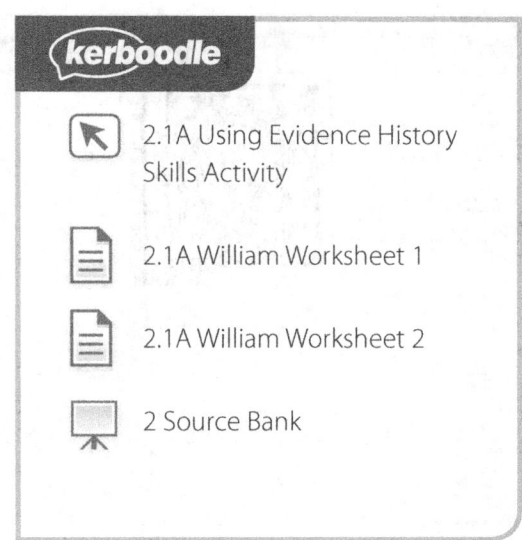

- 2.1A Using Evidence History Skills Activity
- 2.1A William Worksheet 1
- 2.1A William Worksheet 2
- 2 Source Bank

## Lesson summary

Students will understand the problems William faced when he became King of England.

### What are the lesson outcomes?

**All** students will know at least one problem William faced as king, and how he solved it.

**Most** students will be able to explain the problems faced by William as the new King of England, and his solutions.

**Some** students will be able to explain how William solved the problems he faced as king, and if they think his solutions were effective.

## Plenary suggestions

- Be a DJ!: Students could identify the top five things they have learned from this lesson, and read these out in a DJ style.

## Differentiation suggestions

### Support

- Lower ability students can use 2.1 William Worksheet 2 which includes questions to help them develop their answers.

### Extension: Hungry for more?

- Students could create their own version of the Bayeux Tapestry showing William arriving in Dover. It should be historically accurate and students may even choose to write headings in Latin.

## Starter suggestion

- Key questions: Pose three key questions to unlock the lesson:
  - Who was crowned King of England in 1066?
  - Why did William win the Battle of Hastings?
  - Can you think of three problems William might face as the new king?

## Main learning suggestions and assessment

### What activities will take place?

**Task 1:** Students should read the information on pages 32–33. Using 2.1A William Worksheet 1 or 2.1A William Worksheet 2, they should complete Work activity **1** to understand the problems William faced as king. Worksheet 1 is aimed at higher ability while Worksheet 2 is lower ability.

### How will students demonstrate their understanding?

**Task 2:** Students should use 2.1A Using Evidence History Skills Activity to develop a greater understanding of **Source B** and **Source D**. They should then complete Work activities **2** and **3**.

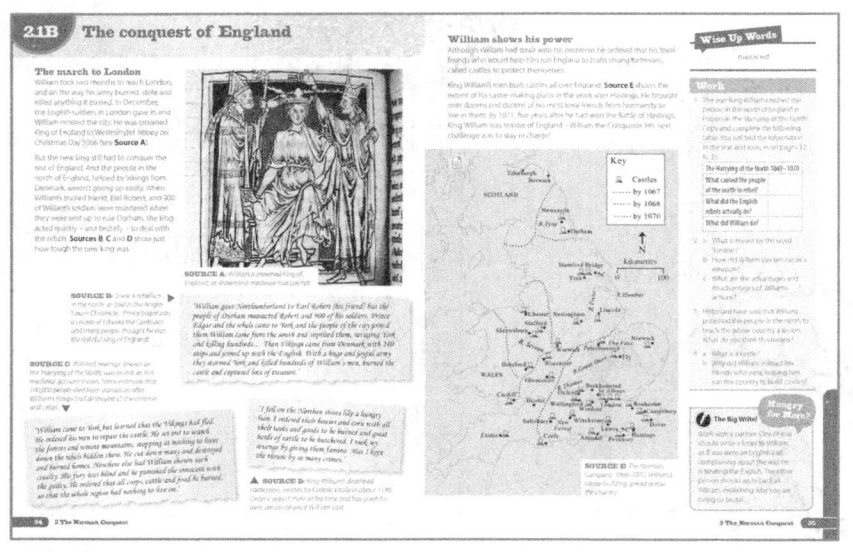

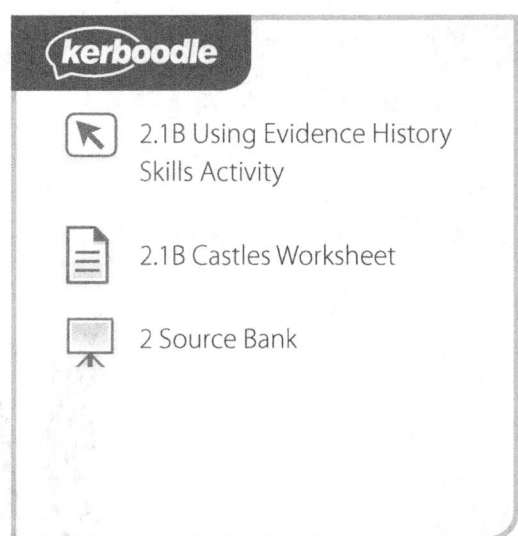

Invasion, Plague and Murder pages 34–35

## Lesson summary

Students will understand the problems William faced when he became King of England.

### What are the lesson outcomes?

**All** students will know at least one problem William faced as king, and how he solved it.

**Most** students will be able to explain the problems faced by William as the new King of England, and his solutions.

**Some** students will be able to explain how William solved the problems he faced as king, and if they think his solutions were effective.

## Starter suggestion

- Post it!: Ask students to write, on sticky notes, one problem they can remember William facing as the new King of England, recapping from last lesson.

## Main learning suggestions and assessment

### What activities will take place?

**Task 1:** Students should read the information on pages 34–35 and complete 2.1B Castles Worksheet to understand why William built so many castles.

### How will students demonstrate their understanding?

**Task 2:** Students should complete Work activities **1** and **2** and use 2.1B Using Evidence History Skills Activity to analyse the 'Harrying of the North'.

**Task 3:** Class debate: Ask students to consider the statement 'Historians have said that William punished the people in the North to teach the whole country a lesson.' Encourage students to explain, in their own words, what this statement means. This might be run as a hands-up activity or as a 'think,

pair, share' session. Encourage students to use any evidence they can think of to support the statement.

## Plenary suggestions

- Ask students the question 'Do you agree with the way William treated people in the North?' They should then vote 'yes' or 'no', according to whether they believe William's actions were the right way to treat the people of England. If possible, provide students with red and green voting cards, or ask them to write 'yes' or 'no' on mini whiteboards. Ask them to justify their decisions.

## Differentiation suggestions

### Support

- To help lower ability students in **Task 3**, you may wish to look at each source individually, and encourage students to write five adjectives to describe William's actions in each source. This should help students to consider how English people viewed their new king.

- In the *Student Book*, the Big Write activity invites students to write one of two letters. Students may need help with letter conventions. You could remind them to include their address, the recipient's address, the date, to write in paragraphs and to end appropriately with a signature.

### Extension: Hungry for more?

- Students could research a castle local to them that was built by the Normans. They could try to find out when was it built, what its history is, if any famous events happened there, and what it is used for now.

# 2.2 William the castle-builder

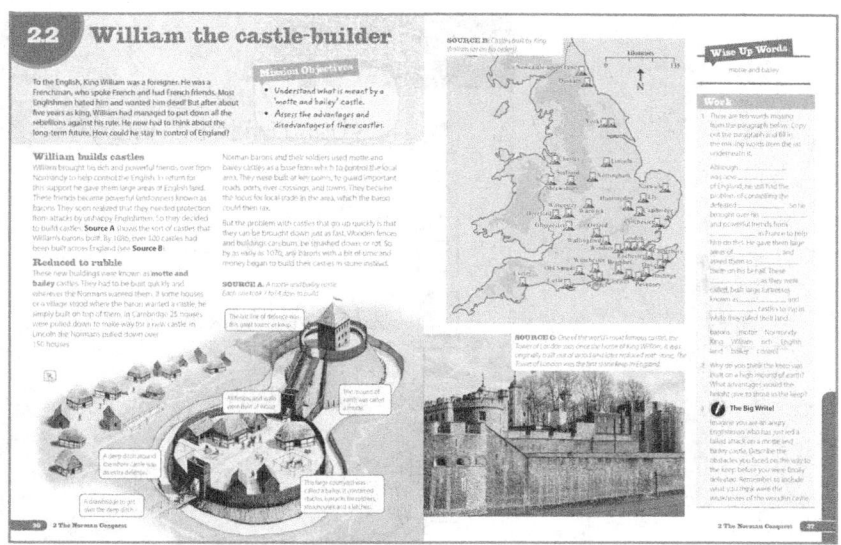

Invasion, Plague and Murder pages 36–37

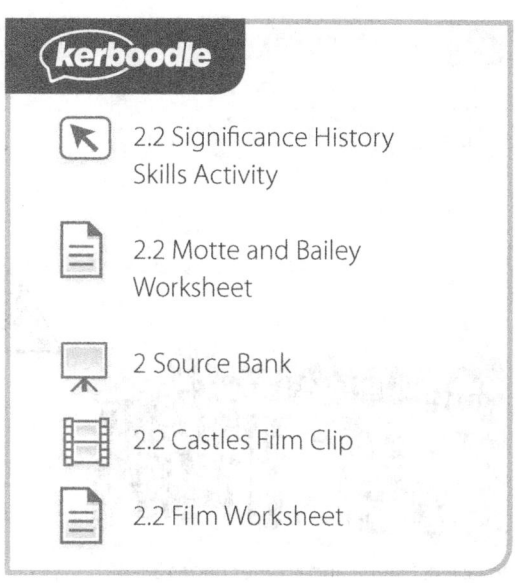

kerboodle

- 2.2 Significance History Skills Activity
- 2.2 Motte and Bailey Worksheet
- 2 Source Bank
- 2.2 Castles Film Clip
- 2.2 Film Worksheet

## Lesson summary

Students will understand the reasons why William built castles after the Norman invasion.

### What are the lesson outcomes?

**All** students will be able to correctly label the parts of a motte and bailey castle.

**Most** students will be able to write a diary entry about attacking a motte and bailey castle, using keywords correctly.

**Some** students will be able to identify some problems of attacking a motte and bailey castle.

## Starter suggestion

- 3, 5, 7: Ask each student to identify three things they know about William of Normandy, then work with a partner to share and come up with five things they know about him. Each pair should then team up with another one or two pairs to list their top seven facts about William of Normandy.

## Main learning suggestions and assessment

### What activities will take place?

**Task 1:** Students should read the information on pages 36–37 and complete 2.2 Significance History Skills Activity to label a motte and bailey castle. Students should also complete 2.2 Motte and Bailey Worksheet. Students can watch 2.2 Castles Film Clip on William the castle-builder.

**Task 2:** Students can complete Work activity **1**. They could work as a class to fill in the gaps using the writing tools to annotate the *Invasion, Plague and Murder Kerboodle Book* version on your interactive whiteboard.

### How will students demonstrate their understanding?

**Task 3:** In this lesson's Big Write activity each student should imagine they are an angry English person who has just led an attack on a motte and bailey castle. They should describe the obstacles they faced on the way to the keep before they were finally defeated. They should remember to include what they think were the weaknesses of the wooden castle. They should try to include key words. This writing could take the form of an account, a diary entry or a letter to a friend.

## Plenary suggestions

- Attacking a castle!: Display **Source A** from either the source bank or the *Kerboodle Book*. Explain to students that they have five minutes to come up with a plan to attack this castle. Encourage them to identify the weaknesses of the motte and bailey castle and to use the correct keywords.

## Differentiation suggestions

### Support

- For Work activity **3**, you may wish to direct students' attention to the cartoon and labels on page 36 in order to give them a starting point for the castle defences they might like to write about. You may also wish to provide an opening sentence for lower ability students.

### Extension: Hungry for more?

- Students could imagine being an English warrior who is angry with William the Conqueror. They should imagine that they are about to attack a motte and bailey castle. What are the weaknesses of this type of castle? How would they attack it? Students should make a plan by themselves, or with a partner.

# 2.3 The Domesday Book

Invasion, Plague and Murder pages 38–39

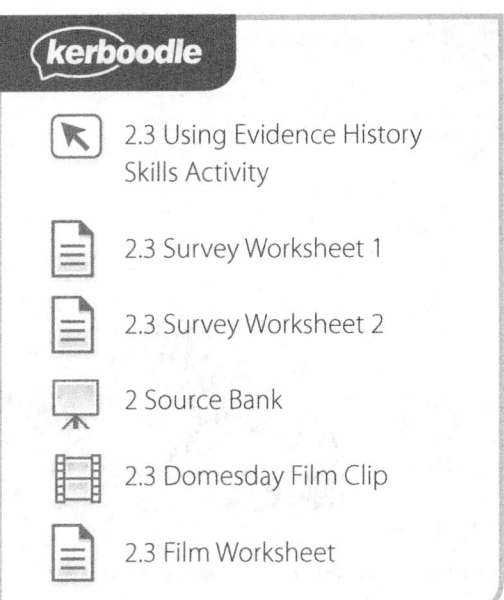

- 2.3 Using Evidence History Skills Activity
- 2.3 Survey Worksheet 1
- 2.3 Survey Worksheet 2
- 2 Source Bank
- 2.3 Domesday Film Clip
- 2.3 Film Worksheet

## Lesson summary

Students will investigate how William the Conqueror intended to use the Domesday Book to learn more about his new kingdom.

### What are the lesson outcomes?

**All** students will know what the Domesday Book was and why it was made.

**Most** students will be able to explain what sort of questions were asked in the Domesday Survey.

**Some** students will be able to identify how the English people reacted to the survey.

## Starter suggestion

- School survey!: Tell students that they are going to help you complete a survey of the classroom. Tell them it is important that they are as specific as possible. For example, ask them to count items like student books, desks, and crayons. After three minutes, ask them what they have found out. Try to encourage them to think about why this information would be useful. Prompt them to think about the changes that would have to be made if the survey were to be carried out across the whole school, or in every school in your area.

## Main learning suggestions and assessment

### What activities will take place?

**Task 1:** Students should read the information on pages 38–39. To further develop their understanding of the topic, they should complete 2.3 Using Evidence History Skills Activity to compare **Source A** with **Source C**. Students should complete Work activities **2** and **3**.

### How will students demonstrate their understanding?

**Task 2:** Students should complete 2.3 Survey Worksheet 1. This worksheet will develop their understanding of what the Domesday Book was and why William wanted the survey carried out. Students can watch 2.3 Domesday Film Clip to learn more about the Domesday Book and complete 2.3 Film Worksheet to assess their understanding.

**Task 3:** Role-play activity: Students should work in pairs. Within each pair students should allocate themselves the role of either the steward or the official in **Source A**. They should develop three questions that the official might have asked, and three answers the steward might have given for that village. Encourage students to think about how they might react to the questions and to the Domesday Book. These can be presented to the rest of the class.

## Plenary suggestions

- One more thing: Students could identify one thing they have learned this lesson, to complete the sentence 'One thing I have learned is…'.

## Differentiation suggestions

### Support

- When reading the sources on pages 38 and 39, encourage lower ability students to first read the captions in order to understand the context of the sources and the language being used.

### Extension: Hungry for more?

- Students could complete 2.3 Survey Worksheet 2. This worksheet uses three sources to allow students to develop their understanding of the reaction of people to the Domesday Book.

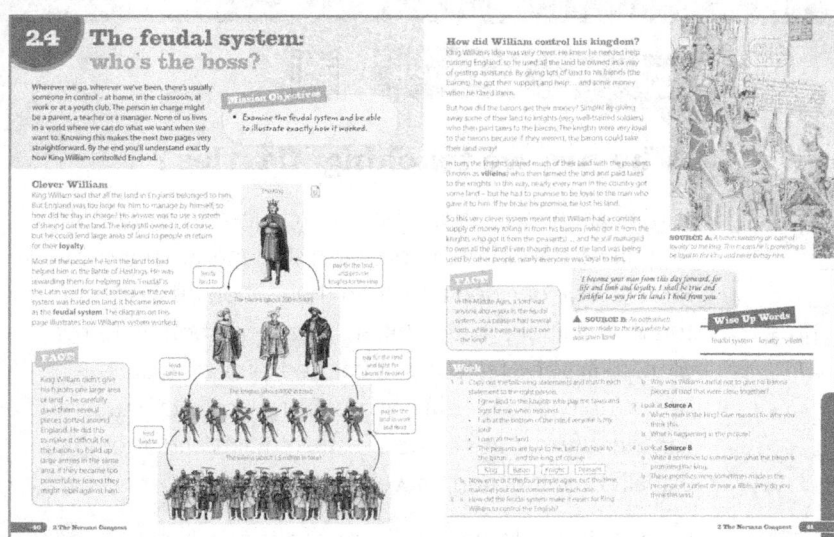

Invasion, Plague and Murder pages 40–41

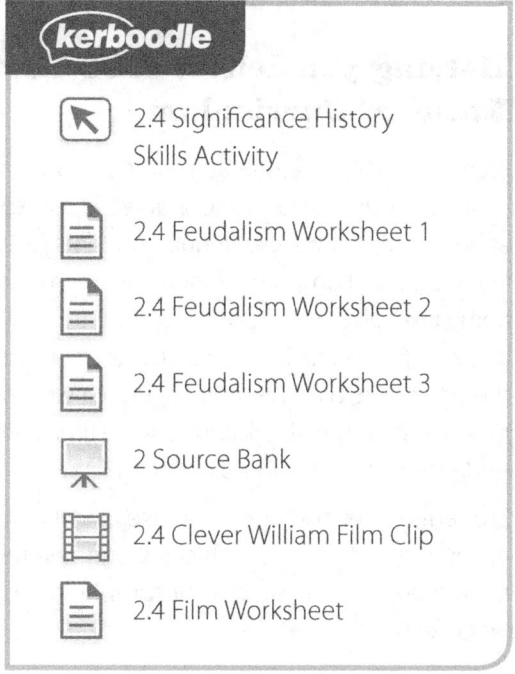

kerboodle

▶ 2.4 Significance History Skills Activity

▤ 2.4 Feudalism Worksheet 1

▤ 2.4 Feudalism Worksheet 2

▤ 2.4 Feudalism Worksheet 3

🗔 2 Source Bank

🎞 2.4 Clever William Film Clip

▤ 2.4 Film Worksheet

## Lesson summary

Students will understand how the feudal system affected people in living in the Middle Ages.

### What are the lesson outcomes?

**All** students will know the hierarchy of the feudal system.

**Most** students will know the duties and benefits of each member in the hierarchy.

**Some** students will be able to explain how the skills or characteristics of each member in the hierarchy made them suited to their role.

## Starter suggestion

● You could ask students to create a hierarchy of the school. Allocate the following roles: one head teacher; two deputy head teachers; five or more teachers; ten or more students. Once students have been allocated their roles they should organize themselves into a triangle hierarchy. Hopefully they will realize that the head teacher should be at the top of the hierarchy, and the students should be at the bottom! You could prompt the students with some questions, for example: Who has the most power? Who has the least power? What is each person's job? What does each person expect in return for their hard work?

## Main learning suggestions and assessment

### What activities will take place?

**Task 1:** Students should read the information on pages 40–41 and complete 2.4 Feudalism Worksheet 1 to understand how the feudal system worked. Encourage them to consider the same prompt questions as in the starter: Who has the most power? Who has the least power? What is each person's job? What does each person expect in return for their hard work? Their understanding can be assessed through 2.4 Significance History Skills Activity on the problems William faced.

### How will students demonstrate their understanding?

**Task 2:** Students should complete Work activity **3**. Students can watch 2.4 Clever William Film Clip on the feudal system.

 **Task 3:** Students should create their own job application for one role in the feudal system.

## Plenary suggestions

● Hot seat: Give students four minutes to plan their responses to the following questions: What is your job? What are your responsibilities? What are the rewards? Do you like your role? Invite four students to the front to be 'interviewed' by the rest of the class. Encourage them to get into character! The 'audience' should ask the questions and respond to the answers. You may wish to swap students' roles throughout to allow more students to participate.

## Differentiation suggestions

### Support

● Students can use 2.4 Feudalism Worksheet 2 to help them create their own job application for a role in the feudal system.

### Extension: Hungry for more?

● Ask students to consider how society is structured today. How is the different from and similar to the feudal system?

## Helping you deliver KS3 History National Curriculum

A chapter all about castles is a natural follow-on from the chapter about the Norman Conquest. The lessons looking at how castles developed require students to recognize and describe change and continuity over a long timescale. Some tasks give students the opportunity to identify causes and explain the relationships between them. Others ask them to select, organize, and deploy relevant information to produce structured work and to show their knowledge and understanding of local and national history.

Students are encouraged to make use of correct historical terminology throughout this unit and several keywords are required for the successful completion of some of the work sections.

## The Big Picture

### Why are we teaching 'Castles'?

In our experience, having been introduced to castles when examining the Norman Conquest, students are hungry for more! So we decided to extend the section on castles in this new edition. The evolution of castles – both in terms of materials and features – is charted, providing an ideal opportunity to undertake a local history project. Students can identify features of local castle remains and attempt to explain their function, as well as date them.

We also decided to look at the methods people developed to attack castles. The siege of Rochester Castle in 1215 provides an excellent case study. Students never fail to be amazed that it was burning pigs that ended the siege! We also attempt to convey some of the flavour of everyday life in a castle.

## Skills and processes covered in this chapter

| | | 3.1A | 3.1B | 3.2A | 3.2B | 3.3A | 3.3B | 3.4 |
|---|---|---|---|---|---|---|---|---|
| **History Skills** | Historical enquiry | ✓ | ✓ | ✓ | ✓ | ✓ | ✓ | ✓ |
| | Using evidence and source work | ✓ | ✓ | ✓ | | | | |
| | Chronological understanding | ✓ | ✓ | | | | | |
| | Understanding cultural, ethnic and religious diversity | | | | | | | |
| | Change and continuity | ✓ | ✓ | | | | ✓ | ✓ |
| | Cause and consequence | | | ✓ | ✓ | | | |
| | Significance | | | | | | | |
| | Interpretations | | | | | | | |
| | Making links/connections | | ✓ | | ✓ | ✓ | ✓ | ✓ |
| | Explores similarities and differences | | | | | | ✓ | ✓ |
| **Literacy and Numeracy** | Key words identified/deployed | ✓ | | ✓ | | ✓ | ✓ | |
| | Extended writing | | | | ✓ | | | |
| | Encourages reading for meaning | ✓ | | ✓ | | ✓ | ✓ | ✓ |
| | Focuses on structuring writing | | ✓ | | | ✓ | ✓ | |
| | Asks students to use writing to explore and develop ideas | ✓ | | | | | | |
| | Learn through talk/discussion | ✓ | | ✓ | ✓ | | | |
| | Numeracy opportunities | | | | | | | |
| **Activity types** | Creative task | | | | | ✓ | ✓ | ✓ |
| | Emphasizes role of individual | ✓ | | | | | | |
| | Group work | | | ✓ | ✓ | ✓ | | |
| | Independent research | ✓ | | ✓ | | | ✓ | |
| | Develops study skills | | ✓ | | | | | |

The final section explains why castle building came to an end, as this is not often readily apparent to students. Looking at the various roles that castles play today is a good opportunity to explain how they are maintained.

## Lesson sequence

| Lesson title | NC references | Objectives | Outcomes |
|---|---|---|---|
| **3.1A How did castles develop? pp42–43**<br><br>**3.1B How did castles develop? pp44–45** | Society, economy and culture: 1066–1509 | • Investigate how and why castles changed after 1066. | **All** students will be able to identify the components of a motte and bailey castle and a concentric castle.<br>**Most** students will be able to describe at least three ways in which castles changed during the Middle Ages.<br>**Some** students will be able to explain at least two reasons why castles changed during the Middle Ages. |
| **3.2A The siege of Rochester Castle pp46–47**<br><br>**3.2B The siege of Rochester Castle pp48–49** | Society, economy and culture: 1066–1509 | • Recall the names of at least five weapons, methods, or tactics used to get into a castle.<br>• Summarize how each of these weapons, methods, or tactics was designed to work.<br>• Explain in detail how King John eventually got into Rochester Castle. | **All** students will be able to describe five weapons, methods, or tactics used to get into a castle under siege, using the correct historical terms.<br>**Most** students will be able to explain five weapons, methods, or tactics used to get into a castle under siege, using the correct historical terms.<br>**Some** students will be able to explain in detail more than five weapons, methods, or tactics used to get into a castle under siege, using the correct terms and providing historical examples. |
| **3.3A Who's who in a castle? pp50–51**<br><br>**3.3B Who's who in a castle? pp52–53** | Society, economy and culture: 1066–1509 | • Examine what day-to-day life in a castle was like and know the names and jobs of the people who lived there. | **All** students will be able to know at least five different roles of workers in a medieval castle.<br>**Most** students will be able to describe what role different workers had in a medieval castle.<br>**Some** students will be able to identify what characteristics made people successful for each role in a medieval castle. |
| **3.4 Where have all our castles gone? pp54–55** | Society, economy and culture: 1066–1509 | • Discover how the use and look of castles has changed since the Middle Ages.<br>• Examine why the golden age of castle-building ended and what we do to protect castles today. | **All** students will be able to explain why castles were built in medieval times and describe how they have changed up to the present day.<br>**Most** students will be able to explain why castles have been changed, developed, and extended over the years.<br>**Some** students will carry out research into how castles are protected today by modern organizations. |
| **Assessing Your Learning 1 pp56-57** | The Norman Conquest | • Create the content summaries for a new castle website using knowledge learned in Chapter 2 The Norman Conquest and Chapter 3 Castles. | **Good:** Students will describe what castles were, what they looked like, how they were built and how they changed.<br>**Better:** Students will do all of the above and explain both how AND why castles changed.<br>**Best:** Students will do all of the above, using the correct historical terms and dates, as well as justifying their choice of topic for section 6. |

## Ideas for enrichment

As in the previous chapter, as visit to a local castle would provide an excellent opportunity for enrichment.

You could consider asking students to take on and rehearse the role of a character from a castle, using the information on who's who in a castle. This could become a type of quiz where other students have to guess what the roles are.

In collaboration with the Geography department, you could ask students to plot castles on a map, colour coding them to show their ages. This activity could cover your county. Students would need to research all the castles in the county and group them into decades or centuries according to when they were built. The map would be a useful tool for showing how castle-building spread across the county.

Strongly recommended TV programmes include the Discovery Channel's *Bloody Britain: The Siege of Rochester*, presented by Rory McGrath and PBS's *Secrets of Lost Empires: Medieval Siege*.

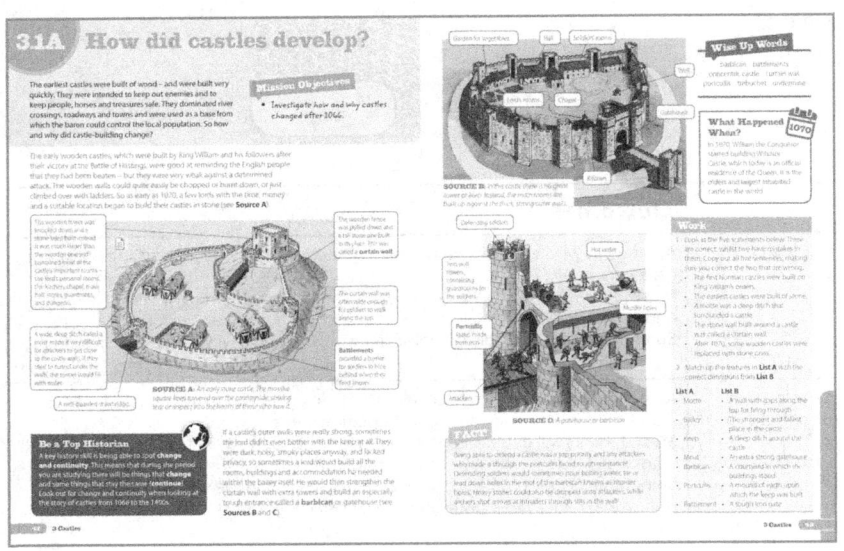
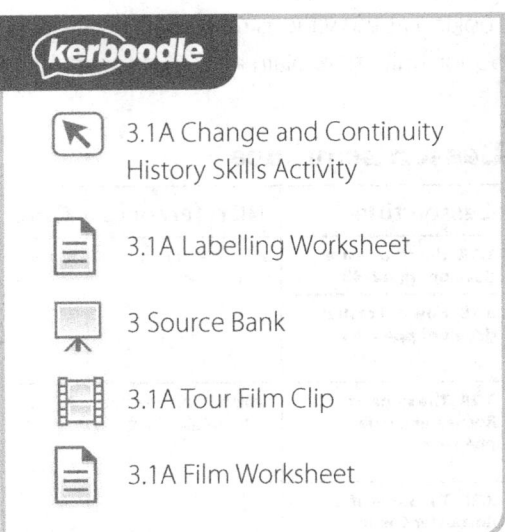

Invasion, Plague and Murder pages 42–43

## Lesson summary

Students will develop their understanding of the components of motte and bailey castles and concentric castles, alongside understanding reasons why castles developed.

### What are the lesson outcomes?

**All** students will be able to identify the components of a motte and bailey castle and a concentric castle.

**Most** students will be able to describe at least three ways in which castles changed during the Middle Ages.

**Some** students will be able to explain at least two reasons why castles changed during the Middle Ages.

## Starter suggestion

- Ask students to team up with a partner and take turns to tell each other what they already know about why William might have built castles in England.

## Main learning suggestions and assessment

### What activities will take place?

**Task 1:** Students should read the information on pages 42–43 and complete 3.1A Labelling Worksheet to label a stone castle. Students can also complete 3.1A Change and Continuity History Skills Activity.

### How will students demonstrate their understanding?

**Task 2:** Students should be able to recognize the key features of Goodrich Castle when viewing 3.1A Tour Film Clip and successfully complete 3.1A Film Worksheet. When questioned, students should be able to recognize more detailed features such as the barbican, portcullis etc.

## Plenary suggestions

- Hangman: Students could play hangman with the following keywords: portcullis; murder hole; moat; battalion.

## Differentiation suggestions

### Support

- As there are many new Wise Up Words in this lesson, it might be a good idea to ask the students to do a quick test on them. Once the words have been introduced in the lesson, ask them to spell and/or give a brief definition of some or all of the new words. Ask them to then self- or peer-mark their work.

### Extension: Hungry for more?

- Ask students to research a real castle and find a picture of it that shows as many of the castle features that have been covered in this lesson as possible. For each feature, they should write a short description of how it functioned and why it was important to that castle. This would make a good homework task.

# 3.1B How did castles develop?

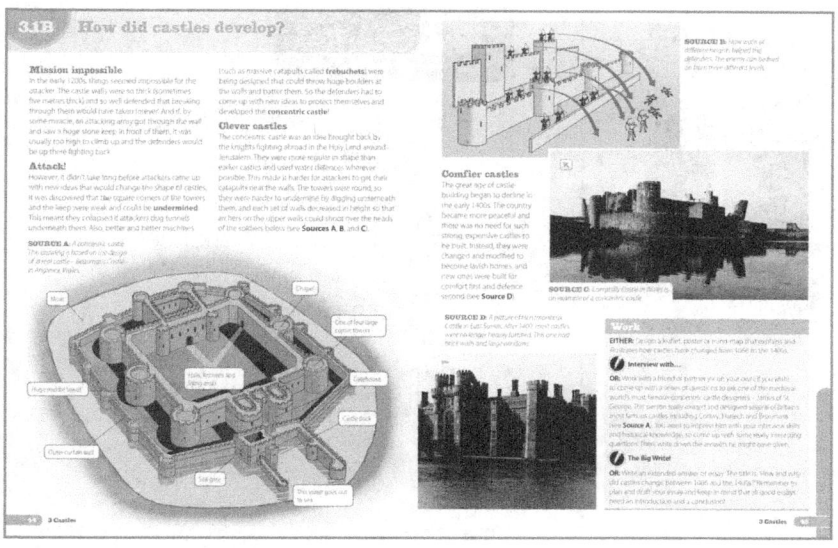

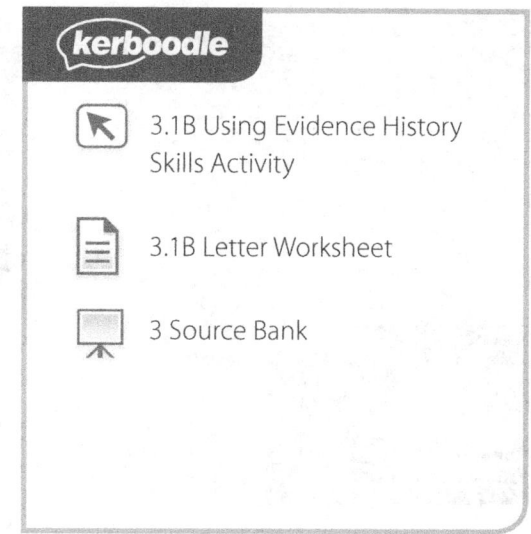

Invasion, Plague and Murder pages 44–45

## Lesson summary

Students will develop their understanding of the components of motte and bailey castles and concentric castles, alongside understanding reasons why castles developed.

### What are the lesson outcomes?

**All** students will be able to identify the components of a motte and bailey castle and a concentric castle.

**Most** students will be able to describe at least three ways in which castles changed during the Middle Ages.

**Some** students will be able to explain at least two reasons why castles changed during the Middle Ages.

## Starter suggestion

- 3, 5, 7: Ask students to identify three things that they already know about castles. Then, working in pairs, they should share their ideas and come up with five things that they know about castles. Finally students should share their ideas in a group and come up with the top seven things that they know about castles.

## Main learning suggestions and assessment

### What activities will take place?

**Task 1:** Students should read the information on pages 44–45. To develop their understanding of the topic further, they should complete 3.1B Using Evidence History Skills Activity.

### How will students demonstrate their understanding?

**Task 2:** Students should use 3.1B Letter Worksheet to write a letter, posing as medieval barons. They should explain how and why they have developed their castles.

**Task 3:** Students should choose one of three activities:

- Design a leaflet, poster, or mind-map that explains and illustrates how castles changed between 1066 and the 1400s.
- Work with a partner to come up with a series of questions to pose to the castle designer James of St George.
- Complete the essay 'How and why did castles change between 1066 and the 1400s?'.

You may wish to model the conventions of a good essay for your students. They may need to consider how to structure, open and conclude an essay with an example. This is a skill to develop throughout Key Stage 3 in readiness for GCSE exams where extended writing is likely to dominate.

## Plenary suggestions

- Top five: Ask students to create a list of the top five facts they have learned about medieval castles.

## Differentiation suggestions

### Support

- Lower ability students can use 3.1B Letter Worksheet to help them organize their work. The worksheet includes sentence starters and key words.

### Extension: Hungry for more?

- Ask students to peer-assess other students' letters from 3.1B Letter Worksheet. Ask them to consider:
  - Have they explained at least three ways they have developed their castles?
  - Have they explained one reason why they have updated their castles?
  - Is their work organized into full sentences?
  - Is their work well presented and interesting to read?
- Higher ability students could attempt the essay question, first making a draft of their work. They should include both an introduction and a conclusion.

# 3.2A The siege of Rochester Castle

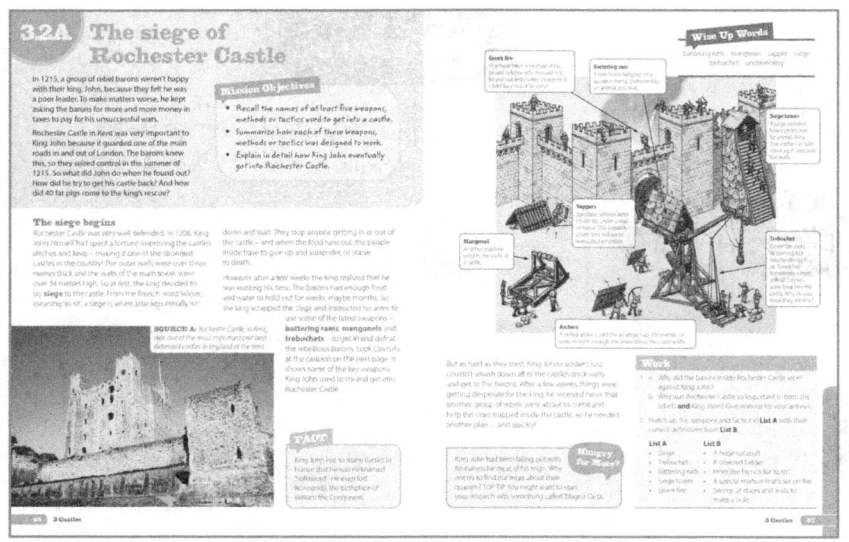

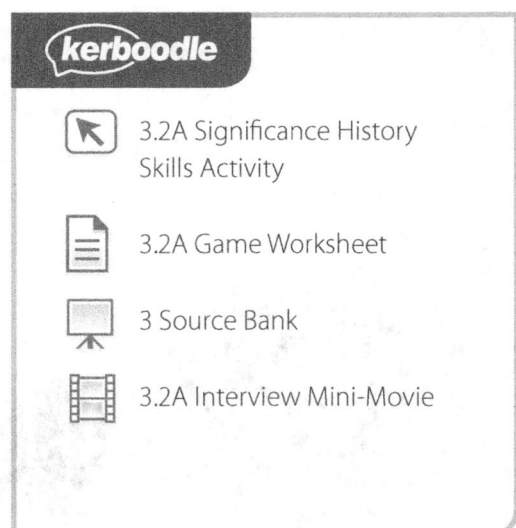

Invasion, Plague and Murder pages 46–47

## Lesson summary

Students will learn how soldiers laid siege to a castle, learning about the different weapons, methods, and tactics used.

### What are the lesson outcomes?

**All** students will be able to describe five weapons, methods, or tactics used to get into a castle under siege, using the correct historical terms.

**Most** students will be able to explain five weapons, methods, or tactics used to get into a castle under siege, using the correct historical terms.

**Some** students will be able to explain in detail more than five weapons, methods, or tactics used to get into a castle under siege, using the correct terms and providing historical examples.

## Starter suggestion

- Ask students to consider **Source A**. Give them one minute to come up with as many ways of attacking a castle as they can think of.

## Main learning suggestions and assessment

### What activities will take place?

**Task 1:** Students should read the information on pages 46–47 and complete 3.2A Significance History Skills Activity, completing a paragraph on the importance of Rochester Castle.

**Task 2:** Students could watch 3.2A Interview Mini-Movie, which provides a visual summary of the siege. Here, a medieval journalist reports on the events at Rochester Castle.

### How will students demonstrate their understanding?

**Task 3:** Students should complete Work activities **1** and **2**.

## Plenary suggestions

- Students could split into pairs and play 'Say what you Siege!', using 3.2A Game Worksheet. Ask students to sit back to back: student one with the worksheet, student two with paper and a pencil. Student one has three minutes to say what they see, describing the images they have in front of them. However they cannot use the key words at the bottom of the worksheet to describe the features of the diagram. Their partner has to draw what is being described. Once their time is up allow all the students to look at the diagram on the worksheet and compare it with their own drawings.

## Differentiation suggestions

### Support

- Lower ability students should use the glossary at the back of the *Student Book* to become familiar with the Wise Up Words on page 47.

### Extension: Hungry for more?

- Ask students to research another historic siege and write a short script for a radio report. They could even interview soldiers from both sides!

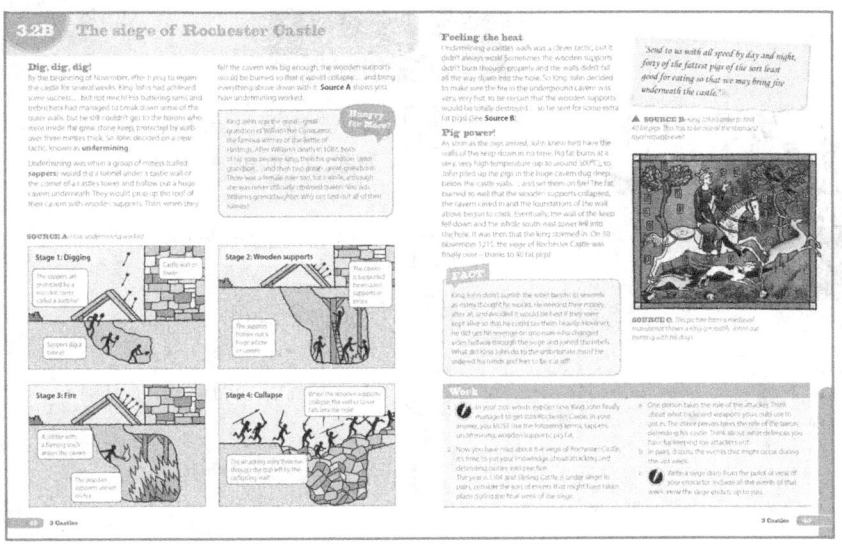

Invasion, Plague and Murder pages 48–49

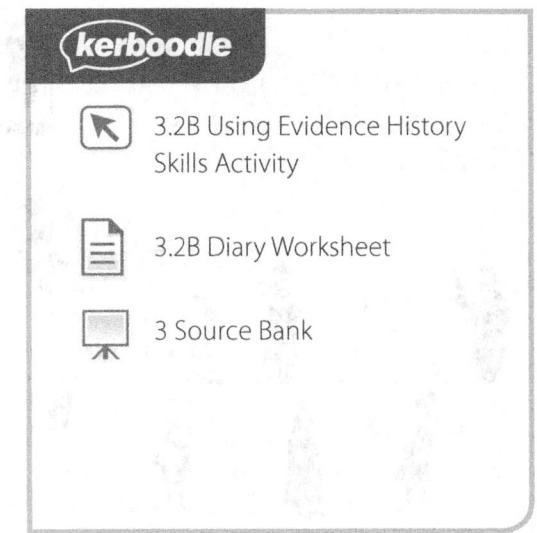

**kerboodle**

3.2B Using Evidence History Skills Activity

3.2B Diary Worksheet

3 Source Bank

## Lesson summary

Students will learn how soldiers laid siege to a castle, learning about the different weapons, methods, and tactics used.

### What are the lesson outcomes?

**All** students will be able to describe five weapons, methods, or tactics used to get into a castle under siege, using the correct historical terms.

**Most** students will be able to explain five weapons, methods, or tactics used to get into a castle under siege, using the correct historical terms.

**Some** students will be able to explain in detail more than five weapons, methods, or tactics used to get into a castle under siege, using the correct terms and providing historical examples.

## Starter suggestion

- Student as teacher: Students should choose one of the Wise Up Words from either page 48 or pages 46–47 (the previous lesson). Ask them to do some quick research (using a dictionary or the glossary in the back of the *Student Book*) to teach a partner what their chosen word means.

## Main learning suggestions and assessment

### What activities will take place?

**Task 1:** Students should complete 3.2B Using Evidence History Skills Activity to learn more about different methods used to attack a castle.

### How will students demonstrate their understanding?

**Task 2:** Students should imagine that the year is 1304 and Stirling Castle is under siege! What events do they think would take place in the final week of the siege? One student should take on the role of attacker. They should make a list of tactics and weapons they could use to get in. The other person is to take on the role of the baron defending his castle. They should make a list of the defences the castle has that will keep the attackers out.

**Task 3:** Explain that their final task is to create a siege diary from the point of view of their character. They should use the success criteria on 3.2B Diary Worksheet to support their writing. They should include all the events that they decided happened during the week of the siege (including how it ends!), and use the correct historical key words.

## Plenary suggestions

- Ask students to note down three things that they have learned and two questions they would like to ask. This can lead into a whole-class discussion on progress, areas of weakness, and how students can continue to develop in the following lessons.

## Differentiation suggestions

### Support

- Offer lower ability students the opportunity to work in groups of four when completing **Task 2**. This activity works well if students have access to mini whiteboards, as these allow them to add to, adapt, and display their ideas.

### Extension: Hungry for more?

- Ask students to peer-assess a partner's siege diary. They should think about whether their partner has:

  o included all the correct siege terms
  o described at least four methods of attacking a castle
  o explained who won the siege and why.

# 3.3A  Who's who in a castle?

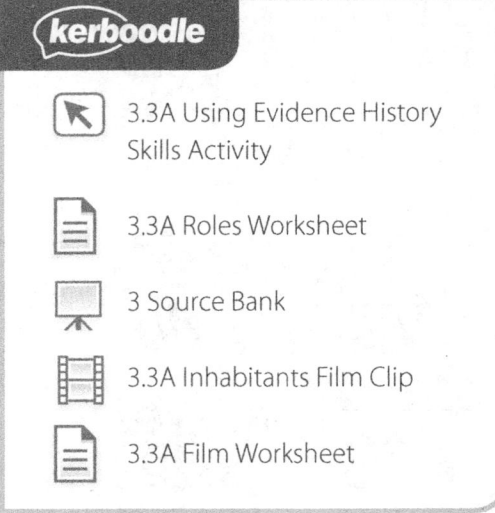

Invasion, Plague and Murder pages 50–51

## Lesson summary

Students will complete two activities to develop their understanding of who worked in a medieval castle and whether or not they would have liked to have worked there.

### What are the lesson outcomes?

**All** students will be able to know at least five different roles of workers in a medieval castle.

**Most** students will be able to describe what role different workers had in a medieval castle.

**Some** students will be able to identify what characteristics made people successful for each role in a medieval castle.

## Starter suggestion

- Hands up!: Ask students to come up with five jobs they think would be necessary in running a medieval castle.

## Main learning suggestions and assessment

### What activities will take place?

**Task 1:** Students should read the information on pages 50–51. Using 3.3A Roles Worksheet they should record, for each person who worked in a castle: job title; daily activities; job rating. The job rating goes from one to ten, depending on how keen the student would be to do it!

**Task 2:** Watch 3.3A Inhabitants Film Clip with the class, where the baroness talks about people who live in the castle. You could ask students to complete the accompanying film worksheet after watching. This film clip also leads into 5.6 Dancing Film Clip.

## How will students demonstrate their understanding?

**Task 3:** To test their understanding, students can complete 3.3A Using Evidence History Skills Activity, focussing on the role of the castle jester.

**Task 4:** Using the writing tools in the *Invasion, Plague and Murder Kerboodle Book*, students can complete the crossword in Work activity **1** on the interactive whiteboard. This can be completed as a whole-class activity.

## Plenary suggestions

- Hands up!: Ask students to think back to the starter. Were the ideas they came up with correct? Can they now describe five jobs they think would be necessary in running a medieval castle?

## Differentiation suggestions

### Support

- Work activity **1** is particularly well suited to lower ability students.

### Extension: Hungry for more?

- You may wish to extend Work activity **2** for higher ability students by asking them to plan a recruitment drive for one or more roles in the castle. They could film a television advert, for example.

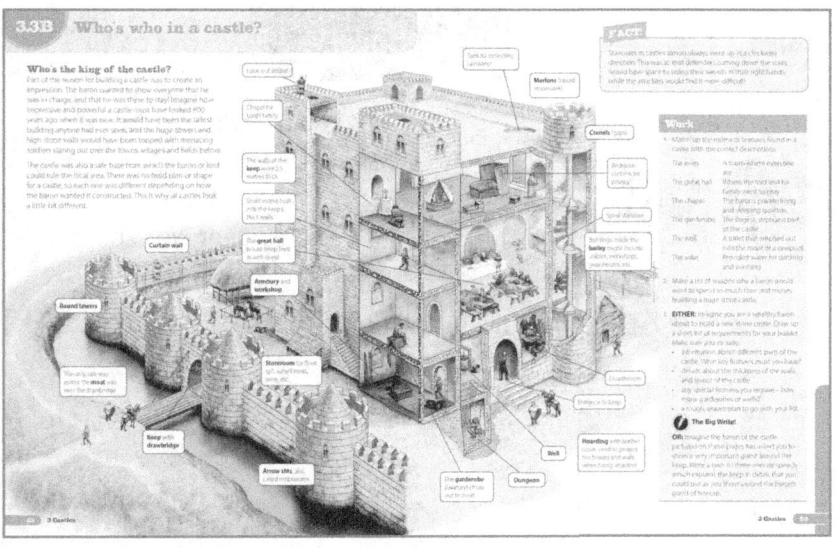

Invasion, Plague and Murder pages 52–53

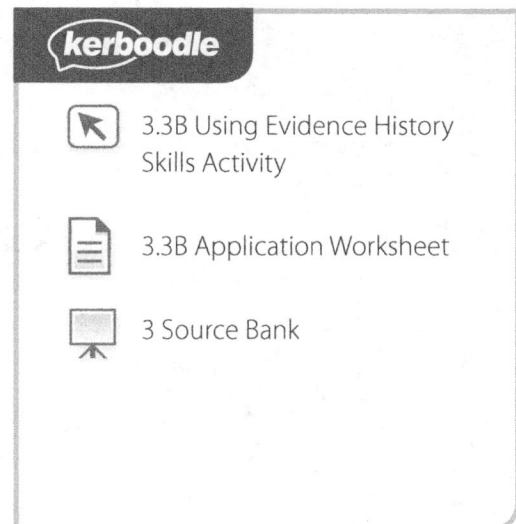

3.3B Using Evidence History Skills Activity

3.3B Application Worksheet

3 Source Bank

## Lesson summary

Students will complete two activities to develop their understanding of who worked in a medieval castle and whether or not they would have liked to have worked there.

### What are the lesson outcomes?

**All** students will be able to know at least five different roles of workers in a medieval castle.

**Most** students will be able to describe what role different workers had in a medieval castle.

**Some** students will be able to identify what characteristics made people successful for each role in a medieval castle.

## Starter suggestion

- Ask students to think about what they have already learned about castles and come up with the top five most important jobs that they think were needed to run a medieval castle.

## Main learning suggestions and assessment

### What activities will take place?

**Task 1**: Students should study the diagram on pages 52 and 53, and complete 3.3B Using Evidence History Skills Activity. This includes a new source depicting castle life for students to analyse.

**Task 2:** Students should write a letter applying for a job of their choice in the castle. They should explain to the steward which job they are applying for, and they should outline the tasks they expect to do. They should say why they believe they should be employed. Ask students to look at the success criteria on 3.3B Application Worksheet to help them develop their answers.

### How will students demonstrate their understanding?

**Task 3:** Students should complete Work activities **1** and **2**.

**Task 4:** Students should complete one activity from Work activity **3**. Here there is a Big Write opportunity as students are asked to write a speech. You may wish to offer them a model of a good speech. 3.1A Tour Film Clip could be used as a model.

## Plenary suggestions

- Exit note: Students should complete the sentences: 'Before this lesson I could already…' and 'Now I can also…' on sticky notes, and hand these in as they leave the class.

## Differentiation suggestions

### Support

- Students can use 3.3B Application Worksheet to create their job application, using the subheadings available.

### Extension: Hungry for more?

- Students could research a stone castle which was built near them. Can they find out the history of the castle? When was it built? How has it changed over time?

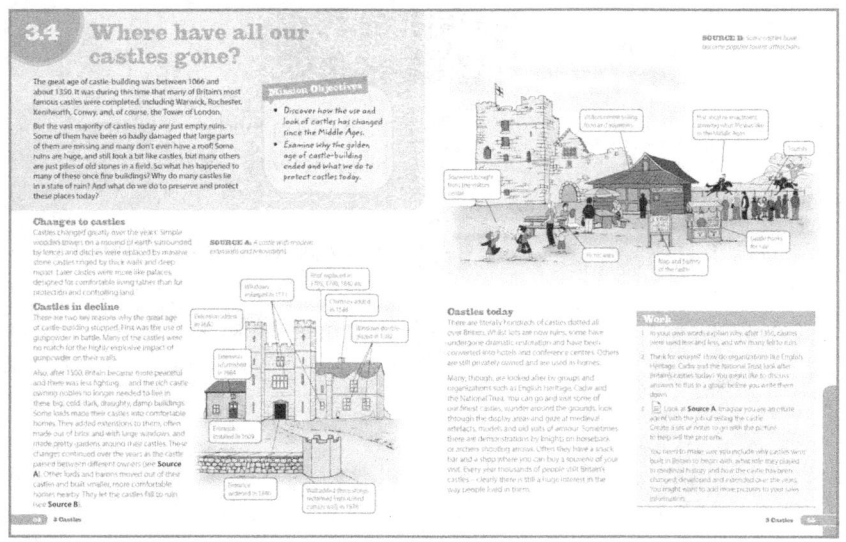
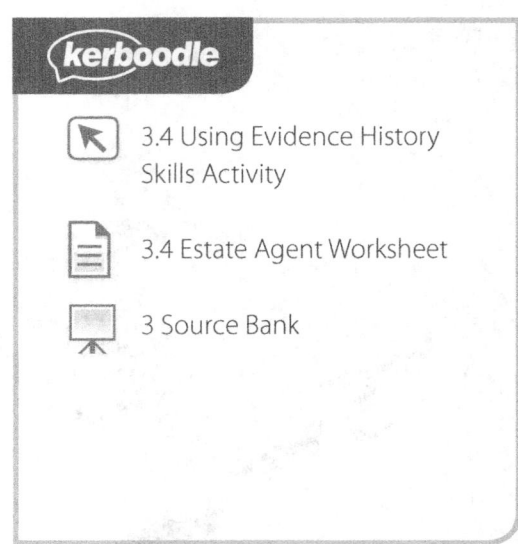

Invasion, Plague and Murder pages 54–55

### Lesson summary
Students will develop their understanding of how and why castles have changed over the years, forming a decision about the role they believe castles have in modern times.

### What are the lesson outcomes?
**All** students will be able to explain why castles were built in medieval times and describe how they have changed up to the present day.

**Most** students will be able to explain why castles have been changed, developed, and extended over the years.

**Some** students will carry out research into how castles are protected today by modern organisations.

### Starter suggestion
- What is the question?: Ask students to offer ideas for questions that would have the following answers: concentric castle; King William; motte and bailey castle; oubliette; garderobe.

### Main learning suggestions and assessment
#### What activities will take place?
**Task 1:** Students should read the information on pages 54–55 and complete Work question **1**. They should explain why castles were used less and less after 1350, and why many turned into ruins. To develop a further understanding of the topic they should complete 3.4 Using Evidence History Skills Activity, to consider how and why we should look after the buildings.

#### How will students demonstrate their understanding?
**Task 2:** Students should write a speech that could be used to show a guest around the castle on pages 54–55.

**Task 3:** Students should use 3.4 Estate Agent Worksheet to complete Work activity **3**. Students should imagine that they are estate agents with the job of selling the castle in **Source A**. They should complete their adverts, labelling the image of the castle and creating a description to help sell the property. Students should use the success criteria to help organize their work, explaining why castles were built, what role they played in medieval history, and how the castle has been changed, extended, and developed.

### Plenary suggestions
- Students could complete a 'think, pair, share' activity. Give them two minutes to think of their own responses to the questions 'Why did people stop building and living in castles? What might you expect to see if you visited a castle today?'. They should then work in pairs for two minutes to discuss their ideas with their partners. Finally, they should share their ideas in a whole class discussion.

### Differentiation suggestions
#### Support
- For Work activity **3**, you might like to show students some examples of real estate agent listings to give them an idea of the tone and what kind of features are usually highlighted.

#### Extension: Hungry for more?
- Students could consider how castles are looked after today. Ask students to research how organizations like English Heritage, Cadw, and the National Trust preserve and protect Britain's castles. You could set this up as a research task or group discussion.

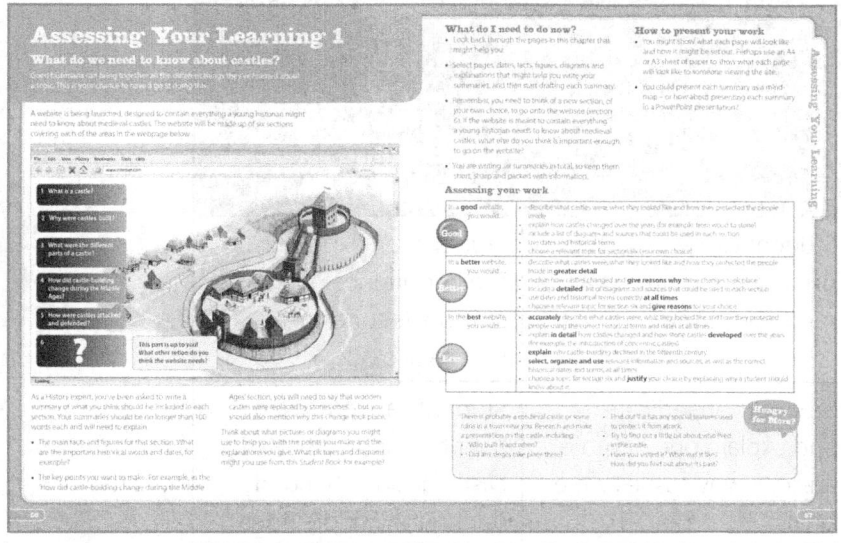

Invasion, Plague and Murder, Student Book pages 56–57

## Assessment in the *Student Book*

In this assessment task, students are asked to put together a plan for a website that will provide a user with all the information they could need about castles. Since castles were such an iconic aspect of the Norman Conquest, which is specifically mentioned in the 2014 National Curriculum, this assessment encourages students to consolidate and demonstrate their knowledge of this topic.

In the *Student Book* (and on the supporting worksheets), you'll find guidance on success criteria that you can use to help your students understand what their work should include. You could ask them to use these criteria for self- or peer-assessment once they've completed the task.

## Chapter 3  Castles assessment task

A website is being launched, aimed to containing everything a young historian might need to know about medieval castles. The website will be made up of six sections:

1. What is a castle?
2. Why were castles built?
3. What were the different parts of a castle?
4. How did castle building change during the Middle Ages?
5. How were castles attacked and defended
6. Your own choice of topic

As a History expert, you've been asked to write a summary of what you think should be included in each section.

### Student Book

- Assessment task
- Student 'Assessing your work' grid

### kerboodle

 Assessment Task Presentation 1

 Assessment Worksheet 1

Success Criteria Teacher Grid 1

### Teacher Handbook

- Success Criteria Teacher Grid 1

---

**Hungry for More?**

There is probably a medieval castle or some ruins in a town near you. Research and make a presentation on the castle.

## Assessing your work

| In a **good** website, you would… | • describe what castles were, what they looked like and how they protected the people inside<br>• explain how castles changed over the years (for example, from wood to stone)<br>• include a list of diagrams and sources that could be used in each section<br>• use dates and historical terms<br>• choose a relevant topic for section six (your own choice). |
|---|---|
| In a **better** website, you would… | • describe what castles were, what they looked like and how they protected the people inside in **greater detail**<br>• explain how castles changed and **give reasons why** these changes took place<br>• include a **detailed** list of diagrams and sources that could be used in each section<br>• use dates and historical terms correctly **at all times**<br>• choose a relevant topic for section six and **give reasons** for your choice. |
| In the **best** website, you would… | • **accurately** describe what castles were, what they looked like and how they protected people using the correct historical terms and dates at all times<br>• explain **in detail** how castles changed and **how stone castles developed** over the years (for example, the introduction of concentric castles)<br>• **explain** why castle-building declined in the fifteenth century<br>• **select, organize and use** relevant information and sources, as well as the correct historical dates and terms, at all times<br>• choose a topic for section six and **justify** your choice by explaining why a student should know about it. |

**Success criteria teacher grid**

| Assessment criteria | Beginning/ Developing | Securing | Extending |
|---|---|---|---|
| | Current NC Level 3/4 | Current NC Level 5/6 | Current NC Level 7/8 |
| | GCSE Grade Indicator E/D | GCSE Grade Indicator C/B | GCSE Grade Indicator A/A* |
| **Remembering** | Student can identify and describe features of a castle, for example, portcullis | Student can explain the use of the features of a medieval castle | Student can explain the importance of one or more features of a medieval castle |
| **Understanding** | Student appreciates why castles were built in the Middle Ages | Student can indicate and explain one or more reasons why castles were built | Student can formulate their own ideas as to why castle design changed during the Middle Ages |
| **Applying** | Student can summarize information under the key headings | Student includes correct historical terminology and has selected relevant information for each section | Student independently selects and writes a final summary; they can justify their choice of topic |
| **Analyzing** | Student can identify features which may have changed over time | Student can explain how some features of a castle may have changed over time | Student can explain reasons why features of a castle may have changed over time |
| **Evaluating** | Student can describe why motte and bailey castles were built | Student can explain why medieval castles were built and assess how the use of castles has changed over time | Student can assess how and why the use of castles has changed over time |
| **Creating** | Each summary contains relevant subject knowledge | Summaries are no longer than 100 words and contain relevant subject knowledge | Student independently selects and writes a final summary; work meets all of website brief requirements |

## Helping you deliver KS3 History National Curriculum

This chapter explores religion, one of the most significant aspects of British life in the Middle Ages. Christendom, the importance of religion, the Crusades, and religion in daily life are defined as possible areas of study in the 2014 Key Stage 3 History National Curriculum.

Students will be required to assess the significance of events, individuals, and ideas, and identify similarities and differences between sources. They need to describe what is useful and/or reliable about sources. They also need to analyse the causes and consequences of a variety of events, and examine why different people tell different stories about the past. Formative assessment opportunities will allow you to assess students' abilities to put key events in chronological order, understand difficult concepts, assess significance, and identify turning points.

The Big Picture

## Why are we teaching 'How religious were people in the Middle Ages?'?

Medieval religion provides a stark contrast with today's multifaith and increasingly secular society. The chapter starts off by looking at the role of religion in everyday medieval life. In creating their own doom paintings, students can grasp the paintings' intended purposes.

We decided to examine the lives of monks and nuns to reinforce the importance of religion and the duties performed in its name during the medieval period. Students can empathize with past lives by directly comparing their average day with that of a medieval monk. They also consider possible reasons for becoming monks.

The chapter then looks at the Crusades – the motives, events, and consequences. Students become aware of the level of

## Skills and processes covered in this chapter

| | | 4.1 | 4.2 | 4.3 | 4.4 | 4.5 | 4.6 | 4.7 |
|---|---|---|---|---|---|---|---|---|
| **History Skills** | Historical enquiry | ✓ | ✓ | ✓ | ✓ | ✓ | ✓ | ✓ |
| | Using evidence and source work | ✓ | | ✓ | | | | |
| | Chronological understanding | | | | | | ✓ | |
| | Understanding cultural, ethnic and religious diversity | ✓ | ✓ | ✓ | ✓ | ✓ | ✓ | ✓ |
| | Change and continuity | | | | | | | ✓ |
| | Cause and consequence | | | | | ✓ | | |
| | Significance | | | ✓ | | ✓ | | |
| | Interpretations | | | | | | ✓ | |
| | Making links/connections | | | | | | ✓ | |
| | Explores similarities and differences | ✓ | | | | | | ✓ |
| **Literacy and Numeracy** | Key words identified/deployed | | | | ✓ | ✓ | | ✓ |
| | Extended writing | | | | | ✓ | | |
| | Encourages reading for meaning | | | | | | | ✓ |
| | Focuses on structuring writing | | | ✓ | ✓ | | | |
| | Asks students to use writing to explore and develop ideas | ✓ | | ✓ | | | ✓ | |
| | Learn through talk/discussion | | | | | ✓ | | ✓ |
| | Numeracy opportunities | ✓ | | | | ✓ | ✓ | |
| **Activity types** | Creative task | | ✓ | | ✓ | | | ✓ |
| | Emphasizes role of individual | | | | | | | ✓ |
| | Group work | | | | | | | |
| | Independent research | | | | | | ✓ | |
| | Develops study skills | | | | | ✓ | ✓ | |

religious misunderstanding and intolerance at the time. The final section focuses on the knowledge exchanged during this clash of civilizations. Not only does this inform the students of how and when everyday objects and ideas came to Europe, it also leads them to the self-evident conclusion that more is to be gained from talking than from fighting.

## Lesson sequence

| Lesson title | NC references | Objectives | Outcomes |
|---|---|---|---|
| **4.1 Religious beliefs pp58–59** | Christendom, the importance of religion, and the Crusades<br><br>Society, economy and culture: for example, religion in daily life (parishes, monasteries, abbeys) | • Investigate the importance of religion in medieval times.<br>• Evaluate the role of religion in everyday life. | **All** students will be able to describe how the medieval Church was organized.<br>**Most** students will be able to explain how the medieval Church affected everyday life.<br>**Some** students will be able to use sources to support their findings on the medieval Church. |
| **4.2 A day in the life of a monk pp60–61** | Society, economy and culture: for example, religion in daily life (parishes, monasteries, abbeys) | • Explain why some men became monks and what their daily life involved.<br>• Understand how monks contributed to medieval society. | **All** students will be able to identify reasons why some men became monks.<br>**Most** students will be able to describe and explain the daily activities of monks in a monastery.<br>**Some** students will be able to identify and explain, using their own opinions, the most and least important jobs that monks carried out. |
| **4.3 Was it fun to be a nun? pp62–63** | Society, economy and culture: for example, religion in daily life (parishes, monasteries, abbeys) | • Examine why some women became nuns and what their lives involved.<br>• Explain how they helped the rest of society. | **All** students will be able to identify reasons why some women became nuns.<br>**Most** students will be able to describe and explain the daily activities of nuns in a nunnery.<br>**Some** students will be able to identify at least two reasons why nuns were important in medieval life. |
| **4.4 What were the Wars of the Cross? pp64–65** | Christendom, the importance of religion, and the Crusades | • Summarize why some people of medieval Europe wished to visit the Holy Land.<br>• Discover why Jerusalem was an important city for Christians, Muslims, and Jews.<br>• Examine why the Pope ordered the Crusades. | **All** students will know at least two reasons why Christians went on the Crusades.<br>**Most** students will be able to explain why Jerusalem was an important city for Christians, Muslims, and Jews.<br>**Some** students will be able to use historical examples to explain why the Pope encouraged people to go on the Crusades. |
| **4.5 Cuthbert the Crusader pp66–67** | Christendom, the importance of religion, and the Crusades | • Categorize reasons why people went on Crusades.<br>• Evaluate a number of different routes to the Holy Land. | **All** students will know at least two reasons why Christians went on the Crusades.<br>**Most** students will be able to categorize reasons why Christians went on the Crusades.<br>**Some** students will be able to use historical examples to explain why the Pope encouraged people to go on the Crusades. |
| **4.6 Chronicles of the Crusades pp68–69** | Christendom, the importance of religion, and the Crusades | • Define the period in history known as 'The Crusades'.<br>• Construct a timeline of key events.<br>• Interpret views on Saladin. | **All** students will be able to describe the chronology of the Crusades.<br>**Most** students will be able to explain the key features and results of the main Crusades.<br>**Some** students will be able to identify examples of tolerance and intolerance in the struggle for the Holy Land. |
| **4.7 What did the Crusades do for us? pp70–71** | Christendom, the importance of religion, and the Crusades | • Understand how life in Europe changed and improved after contact with the Muslim World.<br>• Decide which change was the most important and why. | **All** students will be able to explain two or three changes that took place in Europe after contact with the Muslim world.<br>**Most** students will be able to explain which change was the most important and why.<br>**Some** students will be able to justify why people supported the Crusades. |

## Ideas for enrichment

A trip to one of the big medieval monasteries or abbeys such as Glastonbury Abbey, Rievaulx Abbey, Fountains Abbey, or Tintern Abbey would be ideal. If this is impractical, you could ask students to carry out a research project on a local medieval church. Ask them some questions to start them off: When was it built? Who was king at this time? How has the church changed over time?

Alternatively, you could use Ordnance Survey maps or Google Earth to establish the number of churches in your local area. Assign groups to research each church to find out which is the oldest, which denomination they are, and whether they are still in use as churches.

A medieval pilgrimage site in the local area would provide an excellent local history project, especially if a visit to the site could be arranged.

There are many versions of Pope Urban II's speech of 1095, the speech that inspired the First Crusade. Ask students to find several versions and to compare and contrast them. They need to consider the reliability of sources here and the problems associated with the use of evidence.

# 4.1 Religious beliefs

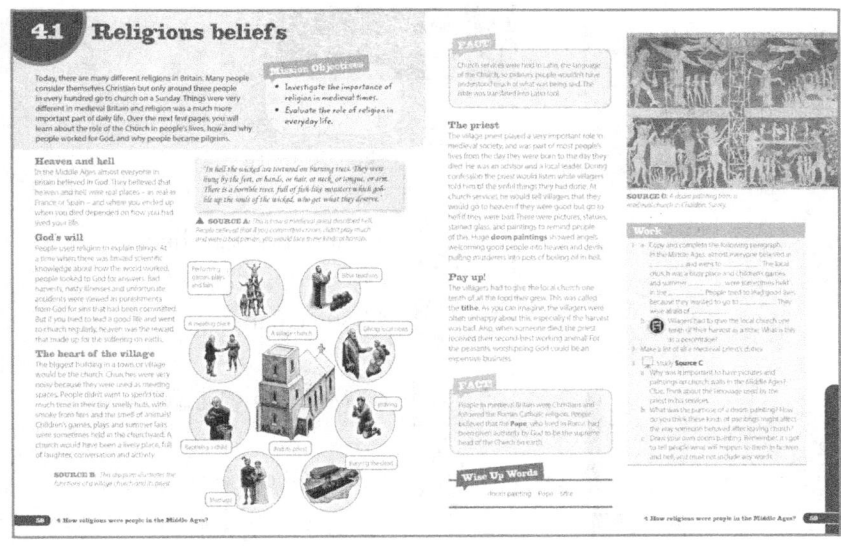

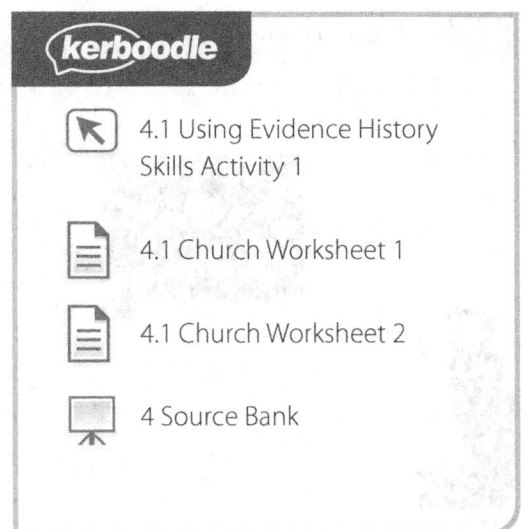

Invasion, Plague and Murder pages 58–59

## Lesson summary

Students should develop their understanding of how and why religion affected everyday life in medieval England.

### What are the lesson outcomes?

**All** students will be able to describe how the medieval Church was organized.

**Most** students will be able to explain how the medieval Church affected everyday life.

**Some** students will be able to use sources to support their findings on the medieval Church.

## Starter suggestion

● High five!: Students could identify five things that they already know about the medieval Church.

## Main learning suggestions and assessment

### What activities will take place?

**Task 1:** Students should read the information on pages 58–59 to gain an understanding of how power was distributed within the Church. They should become familiar with medieval religious beliefs and the role that the Church played in everyday life. They should then complete 4.1 Using Evidence History Skills Activity to learn about another doom painting.

### How will students demonstrate their understanding?

**Task 2:** Students should complete Work activities **1** and **2**.

**Task 3:** Students should complete the table on 4.1 Church Worksheet 1 using **Source B** on page 58. This will show if they understand where people would have gone in the Middle Ages for advice and for education.

**Task 4:** Students should complete 4.1 Church Worksheet 2 to carry out a comparison of the views in **Sources A** and **C**.

## Plenary suggestions

● What is the answer?: Students could use whiteboards to display answers to the following questions.
  ○ What religion did everyone follow in medieval England?
  ○ What did people think would happen to them if they didn't do what the Church said?
  ○ Can you give one reason why people used the Church that had nothing to do with God or religion?

## Differentiation suggestions

### Support

● Lower ability students might benefit from completing 4.1 Using Evidence History Skills Activity before attempting Work activity **3**.

### Extension: Hungry for more?

● You could arrange a visit your local church. Ask students if they can find any images in the church. Can they describe these images? Can they think why these images would have been so important in the Middle Ages?

# 4.2 A day in the life of a monk

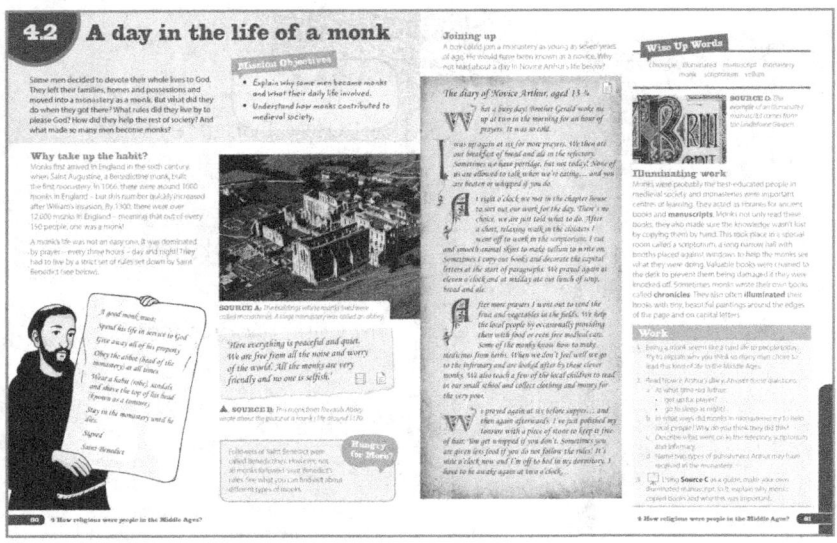

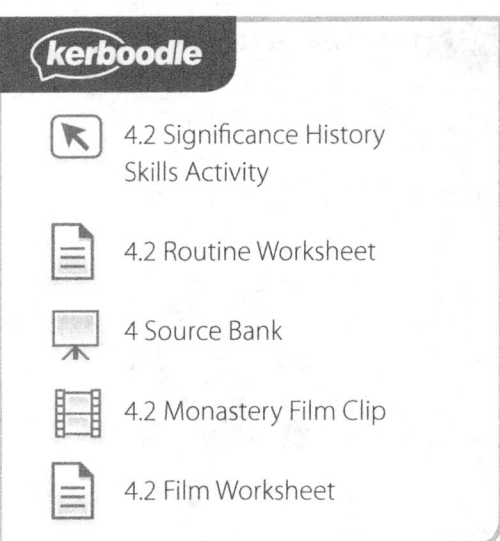

Invasion, Plague and Murder pages 60–61

## Lesson summary

Students should develop their understanding of the roles of monks and monasteries in the Middle Ages.

### What are the lesson outcomes?

**All** students will be able to identify reasons why some men became monks.

**Most** students will be able to describe and explain the daily activities of monks in a monastery.

**Some** students will be able to identify and explain, using their own opinions, the most and least important jobs that monks carried out.

## Starter suggestion

- You could give students access to **Source B** on page 60. This would be best displayed on a whiteboard, using the *Invasion, Plague and Murder Kerboodle Book*. Students could complete a 'think, pair, share' activity. Give them one minute to think of as many reasons as they can to explain why some men became monks. They should then pair up and be given one minute to discuss the reasons they have thought about. Finally they should share their ideas within a class discussion.

## Main learning suggestions and assessment

### What activities will take place?

**Task 1:** Students should read the information on pages 60–61 and watch 4.2 Monastery Film Clip. This clip shows a monk discussing his routine in a monastery and students can assess their understanding of it by completing 4.2 Film Worksheet.

**Task 2:** Students could complete 4.2 Routine Worksheet. They should correctly label the timeline to show the daily life of a monk.

## How will students demonstrate their understanding?

**Task 3:** Students should complete Work activities **1** to **3**. They should also complete 4.2 Significance History Skills Activity to understand the significance of monks and how they helped preserve knowledge in medieval England.

**Task 4:** Students should create a job advert for a monk. They should include details about people's reasons for becoming a monk, how monks should behave, what monks should wear, where and how monks live, and their daily activities.

## Plenary suggestions

- Students could identify three things they have learned in this lesson, and two questions they would like to ask another student or research further.

## Differentiation suggestions

### Support

- There are several new Wise Up Words in this lesson. You could ask students to create a mini glossary, and direct them to the glossary in the *Student Book*, if necessary.

### Extension: Hungry for more?

- Students could use **Source C** and the information on page 61 to create their own illuminated manuscript. On the manuscript, students should explain why monks copied out books by hand and why this was important.

- Explain to students that not all monks stayed in monasteries. Ask them to research St Francis of Assisi. They should find out: where he was from; what the important events that happened in his life were; which religious orders he founded.

# 4.3 Was it fun to be a nun?

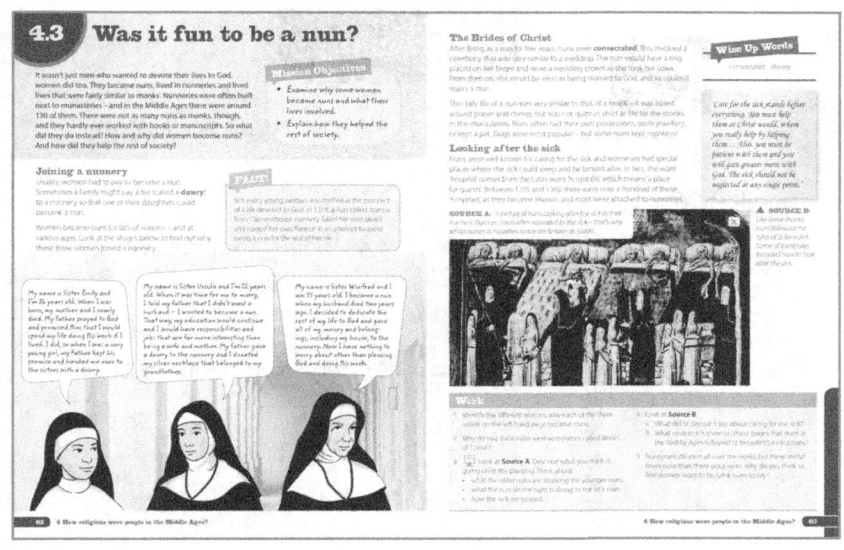
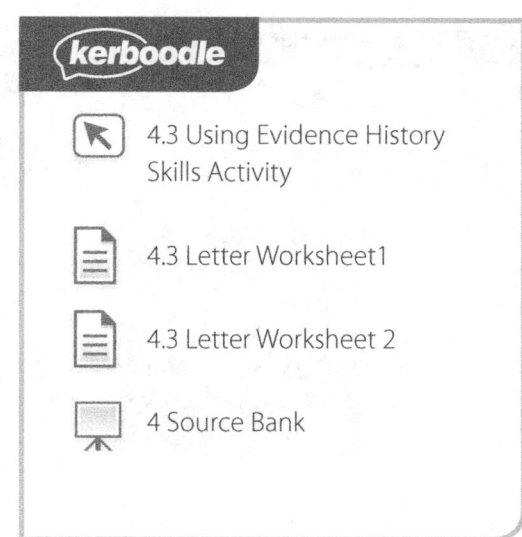

Invasion, Plague and Murder pages 62–63

## Lesson summary

Students should develop their understanding of the jobs that medieval nuns did and how important nuns were to medieval society.

### What are the lesson outcomes?

**All** students will be able to identify reasons why some women became nuns.

**Most** students will be able to describe and explain the daily activities of nuns in a nunnery.

**Some** students will be able to identify at least two reasons why nuns were important in medieval life.

## Starter suggestion

- You could pose the question to students: What do we already know about the medieval Church? Ask students, individually or in pairs, to use post-it notes to identify one thing that they already know and one thing that they would like to know about this topic. Stick these in two groups on the wall.

## Main learning suggestions and assessment

### What activities will take place?

**Task 1:** Students should read the information on pages 62–63 and complete Work activities **1** to **4**. Students should also complete 4.3 Using Evidence History Skills Activity to gain a greater understanding of **Source A**.

### How will students demonstrate their understanding?

**Task 2:** Students should complete 4.3 Letter Worksheet 1 or 4.3 Letter Worksheet 2. Worksheet 1 is aimed at higher ability students, while Worksheet 2 is aimed at lower ability. They should use the success criteria on the worksheet to write a letter, posing as a nun, explaining how they are serving God and helping people.

## Plenary suggestions

- Students could add one sticky note to the group of notes saying what they know about the medieval Church. You may wish to get students to share these ideas with each other or the whole class.

## Differentiation suggestions

### Support

- 4.3 Letter Worksheet 2 is for lower ability students and provides sentences starters.

### Extension: Hungry for more?

- 4.3 Letter Worksheet 1 is for higher ability students and encourages them to use sources to support their writing.

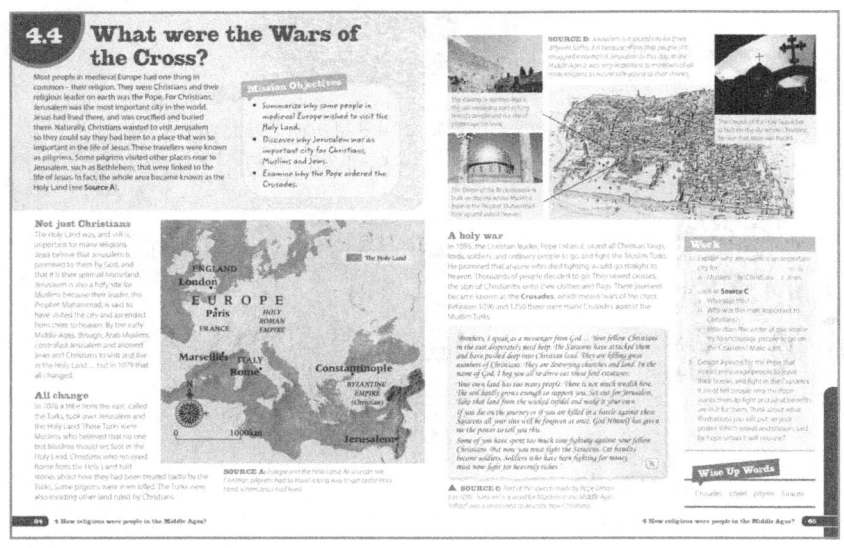

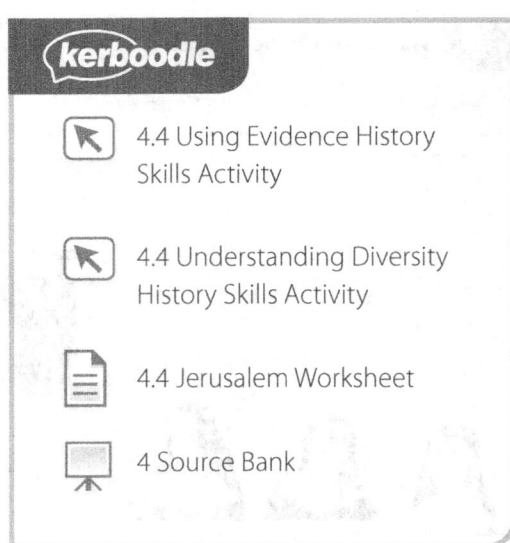

Invasion, Plague and Murder pages 64–65

## Lesson summary
Students will understand the claims that different religions had over Jerusalem and be able to explain reasons why the Pope ordered the Crusades.

### What are the lesson outcomes?
**All** students will know at least two reasons why Christians went on the Crusades.

**Most** students will be able to explain why Jerusalem was an important city for Christians, Muslims, and Jews.

**Some** students will be able to use historical examples to explain why the Pope encouraged people to go on the Crusades.

## Starter suggestion
- Ask students what they think the word 'multicultural' means? Do they think they live in a multicultural society? Do they think medieval society was multicultural?

## Main learning suggestions and assessment
### What activities will take place?
**Task 1:** Students should read the information on pages 64–65 and complete 4.4 Jerusalem Worksheet. They should be able to label a map of Jerusalem explaining why three religions had claims to it, and explain why some Christians went on Crusades.

**Task 2:** Students should complete 4.4 Understanding Diversity History Skills Activity to understand why the city of Jerusalem is important to three religions.

### How will students demonstrate their understanding?
**Task 3:** Students should complete Work activities **1** and **2**, as well as 4.4 Using Evidence History Skills Activity, which closely examines Pope Urban's rallying speech to Christians.

**Task 4:** Students should design a poster for the Pope that would encourage people to leave their homes and fight on the Crusades. They should use the success criteria to organise their poster, ensuring that they tell people why the Pope wants them to fight and how fighting will benefit them.

## Plenary suggestions
- Post it: Students could complete a sticky note to complete the sentence 'Today I have learned …'.

## Differentiation suggestions
### Support
- The idea of Jerusalem as a 'Holy Land' is often a difficult concept to grasp. You may wish to use the source bank for this chapter to display the map shown in **Source A** at the start of the lesson, to make sure students have a firm understanding of the location of Jerusalem in relation to Britain, Europe and historically Christian areas.

### Extension: Hungry for more?
- Students could write a short essay entitled 'Why people went on Crusades'. They should try to give as many reasons as possible, aiming for five, and split their essay into a paragraph for each one. In each paragraph they should state the reason and try to explain how each reason motivated people to go.

# 4.5 Cuthbert the Crusader

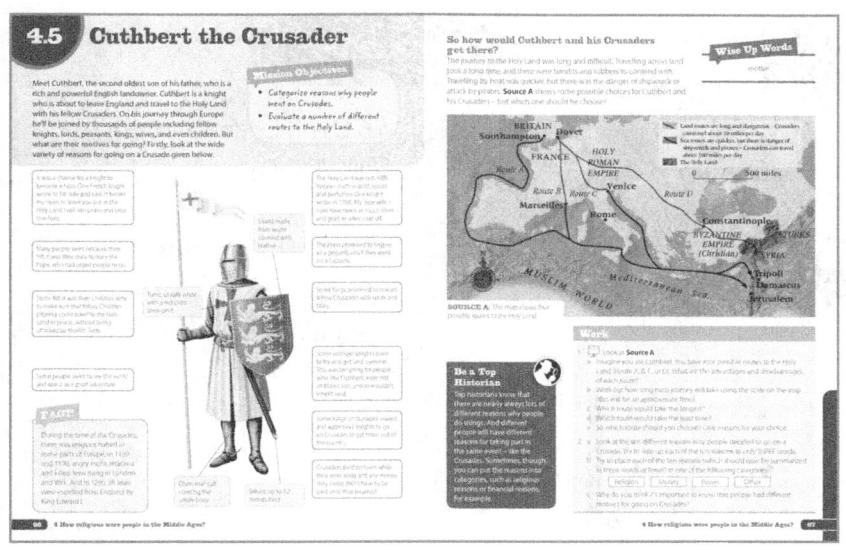

Invasion, Plague and Murder pages 66–67

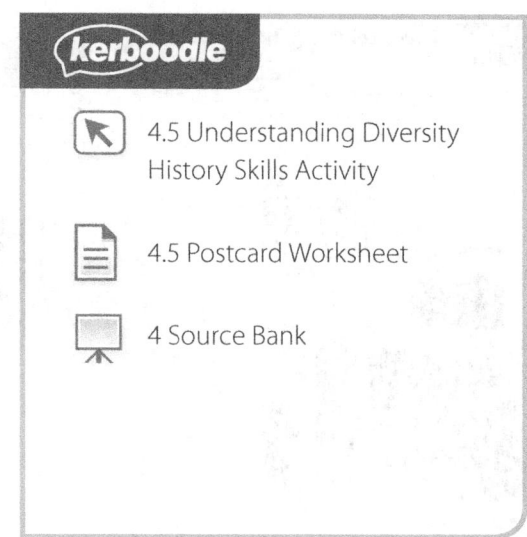

4.5 Understanding Diversity History Skills Activity

4.5 Postcard Worksheet

4 Source Bank

## Lesson summary

Students will be able to explain reasons why people went on the Crusades and evaluate the different routes they could take.

### What are the lesson outcomes?

**All** students will know at least two reasons why Christians went on the Crusades.

**Most** students will be able to categorize reasons why Christians went on the Crusades.

**Some** students will be able to use historical examples to explain why the Pope encouraged people to go on the Crusades.

## Starter suggestion

- Think, pair, share: Ask students the question 'Why did people go on Crusades?' Give them 30 seconds to think of reasons, and then one minute to discuss their ideas with a partner. This should feed into a class discussion where each pair shares their ideas with the class in order to create a list of reasons.

## Main learning suggestions and assessment

### What activities will take place?

**Task 1:** Students should read the information on pages 66–67 and complete Work activity **1**.

### How will students demonstrate their understanding?

**Task 2:** Students should complete 4.5 Understanding Diversity History Skills Activity, sorting the information to understand more about reasons for participating in the Crusades.

**Task 3:** Students should write a postcard, as a crusading knight, explaining why they have chosen to go on a Crusade. 4.5 Postcard Worksheet provides a framework for the postcard.

## Plenary suggestions

- Exit note: Students could complete the following sentence 'Before this lesson I could already … Now I can also …'.

## Differentiation suggestions

### Support

- For Work activity **1**, when calculating the journey time for possible routes, it might be a good idea to pair lower ability students with students who have high numeracy skills.

### Extension: Hungry for more?

- Students could pick one route from this lesson and write three entries from a crusader's diary, explaining where they are and the problems they have faced along their journey.

- Higher ability students may wish to include religious and historical examples from the speeches of the Pope, or from other Crusades, to support their writing.

# 4.6 Chronicles of the Crusades

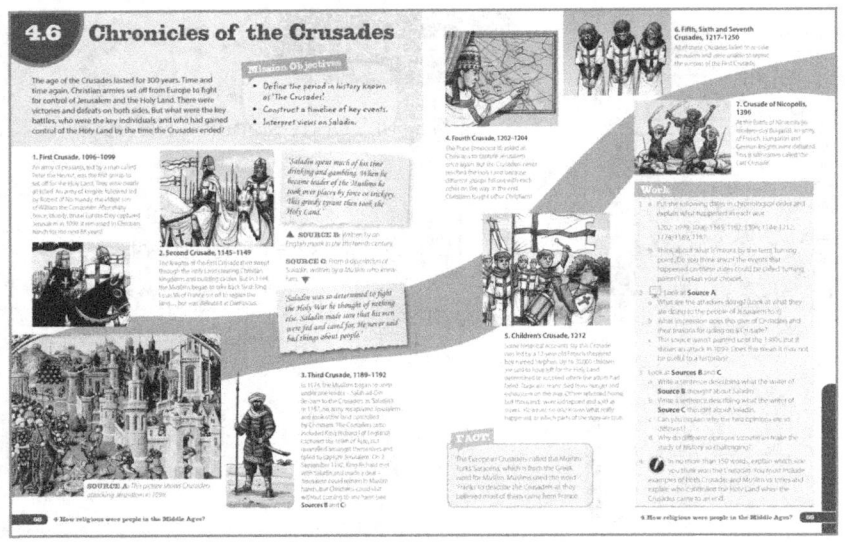

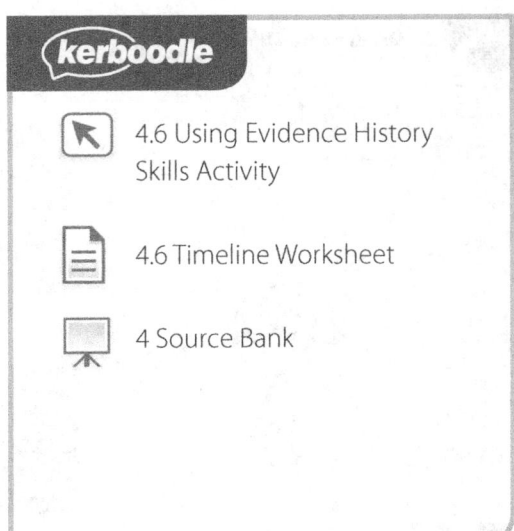

Invasion, Plague and Murder pages 68–69

## Lesson summary

Students will develop a chronological understanding of the Crusades, creating a timeline. They will also attempt to identify examples of tolerance and intolerance during the Crusades.

### What are the lesson outcomes?

**All** students will be able to describe the chronology of the Crusades.

**Most** students will be able to explain the key features and results of the main Crusades.

**Some** students will be able to identify examples of tolerance and intolerance in the struggle for the Holy Land.

## Starter suggestion

- High five!: Students could try to identify five reasons why people went on Crusades.

## Main learning suggestions and assessment

### What activities will take place?

**Task 1:** Students should read the information on pages 68–69 and create a timeline of the main events of the Crusades. For each Crusade they should find out the dates, the leaders, who took part, what happened, and the result. Students should work through their timeline and highlight, in one colour, examples of Christian armies being intolerant. In another colour they should highlight examples of Muslim armies being intolerant.

### How will students demonstrate their understanding?

**Task 2:** Students should complete 4.7 Using Evidence History Skills Activity.

**Task 3:** Students should complete Work activities **2** to **4**.

## Plenary suggestions

- Do you know the answer?: Give each student one piece of paper. They should write down a question, and an answer, about something they have learned about the Crusades so far. Students should then move around the classroom. When a student meets a partner they should read out their question and allow the other student to answer. If the student answers incorrectly, the first student should tell them the answer. Then the other student should read out their question. When each exchange is finished, the students should swap their bits of paper and move on to a new partner, completing the process four more times if possible. At the end, ask students what they have remembered about the Crusades, from this activity.

## Differentiation suggestions

### Support

- 4.6 Timeline Worksheet provides a framework for lower ability students to create their timelines.

### Extension: Hungry for more?

- You could set students the challenge of creating an obituary for the Muslim leader Saladin. They should explain who Saladin was, what sort of leader he was, how and when he fought the Christians, and if he was successful. Ask them to consider if they think he was a cruel or tolerant leader, and to use this to set the tone of their obituary.

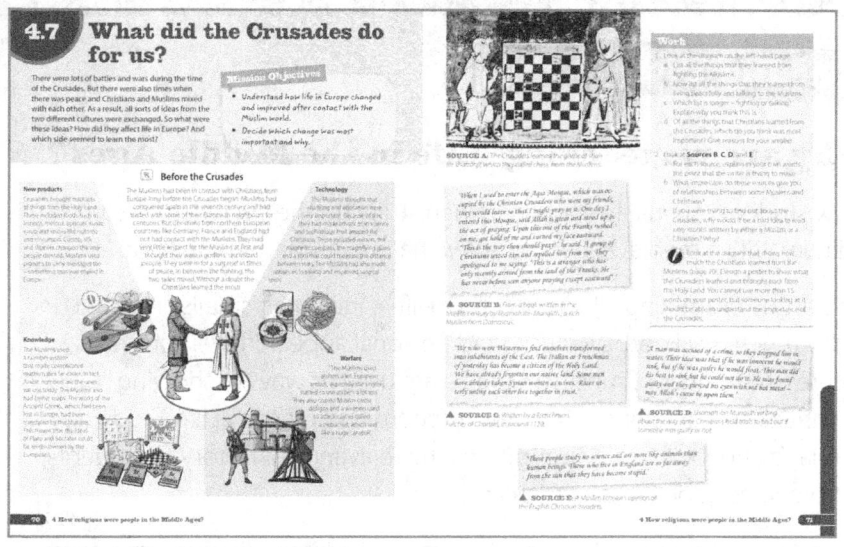

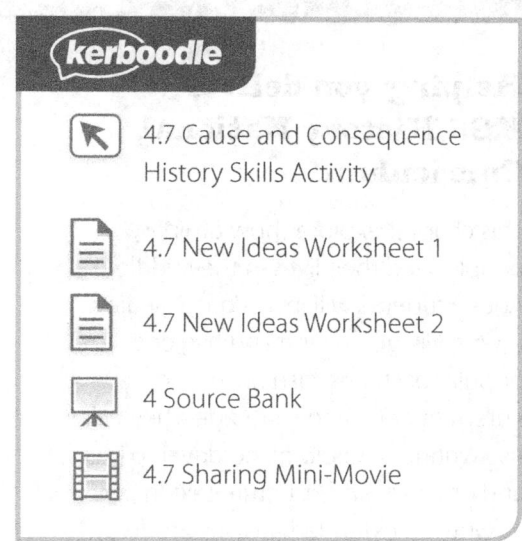

Invasion, Plague and Murder pages 70–71

## Lesson summary

Students will develop an understanding of why people supported the Crusades and whether they were right to do so.

### What are the lesson outcomes?

**All** students will be able to explain two or three changes that took place in Europe after contact with the Muslim world.

**Most** students will be able to explain which change was the most important and why.

**Some** students will be able to justify why people supported the Crusades.

## Starter suggestion

- Ask students to act out using the following things that were brought back from the Crusades: spices; a compass; a mirror; a bow and arrow; a game of chess. One student should act out each thing, without saying anything. The other members of the class should try to guess what each thing is.

## Main learning suggestions and assessment

### What activities will take place?

**Task 1:** Students should read the information on pages 70–71 and complete 4.7 New Ideas Worksheet 1. This will help them to complete Work activity **1**.

**Task 2:** Students should watch 4.7 Sharing Mini-Movie, where a Christian and Muslim discuss what they have learned from one another.

### How will students demonstrate their understanding?

**Task 3:** Students should complete a 'hot seat' activity to encourage them to decide how the Crusades changed life in Europe and the Holy Land. Students should work in pairs and be assigned a role as either a crusading knight or a Muslim fighter. Give students ten minutes to prepare answers to five questions:

- Why do you think the Crusades are happening?
- How are people encouraged to go on a Crusade?
- What has your country gained or lost through the Crusades?
- Do you think going on the Crusades was the right thing to do?
- Why did people support the Crusades?

## Plenary suggestions

- Traffic lights: Students could be given coloured sticky notes to write on. The green note should contain a concept that they could teach to a partner. The amber note should contain a concept that they are happy with and understand. The red note should contain a question that they would like to ask to help their understanding.

## Differentiation suggestions

### Support

- 4.7 New Ideas Worksheet 1 helps lower ability students to create their answers for the hot seat activity in **Task 2**.

- Work activity **3** asks students to create a poster. You may wish to model a more visual poster to help them understand the conventions required.

### Extension: Hungry for more?

- Students could research other things resulting from the Crusades that have not been discussed in the lesson. They could design an advert to sell these goods back in England.

## Helping you deliver KS3 History National Curriculum

This chapter explores how ordinary people lived their lives in the Middle Ages. Students will investigate medieval towns, villages, health and hygiene, popular pastimes, fashion, music, entertainment, and language. They will use writing to explore and develop ideas, and organize and structure text in order to write an extended answer. Students will also select and combine information from sources to answer questions, put events in chronological order, and define difficult concepts, such as heraldry.

## The Big Picture

### Why are we teaching 'Life in the Middle Ages'?

Many students are really engaged when studying the everyday lives of ordinary British medieval people, so we have extended this section.

We start by examining village and town life – including smells and basic bodily functions! Football, music, and personal appearance – common features in the lives of most students – are used as ways of showing similarities and differences between modern and medieval life. Studying language and food again strengthens the relevance of history to students, and provides good cross-curricular links.

We examine chivalry and knights. We also consider medieval tournaments, and the original purpose of heraldry.

We end this chapter by examining the lives of women. The contrast with modern attitudes to gender equality can seem amusing in the classroom,

## Skills and processes covered in this chapter

|  |  | 5.1A | 5.1B | 5.2A | 5.2B | 5.3 | 5.4 | 5.5 | 5.6 | 5.7 | 5.8 | 5.9 | 5.10 | 5.11 | 5.12 | 5.13 | 5.14 |
|---|---|---|---|---|---|---|---|---|---|---|---|---|---|---|---|---|---|
| **History Skills** | Historical enquiry | ✓ | ✓ | ✓ | ✓ | ✓ | ✓ | ✓ | ✓ | ✓ | ✓ | ✓ | ✓ | ✓ | ✓ | ✓ | ✓ |
|  | Using evidence and source work |  | ✓ |  | ✓ | ✓ | ✓ | ✓ | ✓ | ✓ |  | ✓ |  | ✓ | ✓ | ✓ | ✓ |
|  | Chronological understanding |  |  |  |  |  | ✓ |  |  |  |  |  |  |  |  |  |  |
|  | Understanding cultural, ethnic and religious diversity |  |  |  |  |  | ✓ |  | ✓ |  |  |  |  |  |  | ✓ |  |
|  | Change and continuity |  |  |  |  | ✓ | ✓ | ✓ | ✓ | ✓ | ✓ | ✓ |  |  |  | ✓ |  |
|  | Cause and consequence |  |  | ✓ |  | ✓ |  |  |  |  | ✓ |  |  |  |  |  |  |
|  | Significance |  |  |  |  |  |  |  |  |  |  |  |  | ✓ | ✓ |  | ✓ |
|  | Interpretations |  |  |  |  |  |  |  |  |  |  |  |  |  |  |  | ✓ |
|  | Making links/connections |  | ✓ |  |  |  |  |  |  |  |  |  |  |  |  | ✓ |  |
|  | Explores similarities and differences | ✓ | ✓ |  |  | ✓ | ✓ |  |  |  |  |  | ✓ |  |  | ✓ | ✓ |
| **Literacy and Numeracy** | Key words identified/deployed | ✓ |  | ✓ |  |  |  |  |  | ✓ | ✓ | ✓ |  | ✓ | ✓ | ✓ |  |
|  | Extended writing |  |  |  |  |  |  |  |  |  |  |  |  |  |  |  | ✓ |
|  | Encourages reading for meaning | ✓ |  |  |  |  |  | ✓ | ✓ |  | ✓ |  |  |  |  |  | ✓ |
|  | Focuses on structuring writing |  |  |  |  | ✓ |  |  |  |  |  |  |  |  |  |  | ✓ |
|  | Asks students to use writing to explore and develop ideas |  | ✓ | ✓ | ✓ |  | ✓ |  | ✓ | ✓ |  | ✓ | ✓ | ✓ | ✓ | ✓ | ✓ |
|  | Learn through talk/discussion |  |  |  |  |  | ✓ |  |  |  |  |  |  | ✓ | ✓ |  |  |
|  | Numeracy opportunities |  |  |  |  |  |  |  |  |  |  |  |  |  |  |  |  |
| **Activity types** | Creative task | ✓ |  | ✓ | ✓ | ✓ |  |  |  |  |  |  | ✓ | ✓ |  | ✓ |  |
|  | Emphasizes role of individual |  |  |  |  |  |  |  |  |  |  |  |  |  |  |  | ✓ |
|  | Group work |  |  | ✓ |  |  | ✓ |  |  |  |  |  |  | ✓ | ✓ |  |  |
|  | Independent research | ✓ |  |  |  |  | ✓ |  | ✓ |  |  |  | ✓ |  | ✓ | ✓ | ✓ |
|  | Develops study skills |  |  |  | ✓ |  |  |  |  |  |  |  |  |  |  | ✓ | ✓ |

but the irrationality of sexism and prejudice is quickly grasped when students examine the power struggle between Stephen and Matilda.

## Lesson sequence

| Lesson title | NC references | Objectives | Outcomes |
|---|---|---|---|
| **5.1A  What was life like in a medieval village?** pp72–73 <br><br> **5.1B  What was life like in a medieval village?** pp74–75 | Society, economy and culture: for example, farming, trade and towns | • Investigate village life during the Middle Ages. <br> • Recall how a medieval villager spent his day. | **All** students will be able to describe what life was like in a medieval village. <br> **Most** students will be able to navigate and label correctly the various parts of a medieval village. <br> **Some** students will be able to use historical sources to support their findings. |
| **5.2A  What was life like in a medieval town?** pp76–77 <br><br> **5.2B  What was life like in a medieval town?** pp78–79 | Society, economy and culture: for example, farming, trade and towns | • Explain what life was like in a medieval town and what a town might look like. <br> • Discover why towns grew. <br> • Assess how buying and selling was organized. | **All** students will be able to describe what life was like in a medieval town. <br> **Most** students will be able to use sources to find out information about life in a medieval town. <br> **Some** students will be able to support their writing with evidence from sources. |
| **5.3  How smelly were the Middle Ages?** pp80–81 | Society, economy and culture 1066–1509 | • Explore how and why standards of cleanliness and personal hygiene were different from today. | **All** students will be able to identify how people in England kept clean in the Middle Ages. <br> **Most** students will be able to explain two reasons why standards of cleanliness and personal hygiene were very different from today. <br> **Some** students will be able to support their writing using evidence from sources. |
| **5.4  Could you have fun in the Middle Ages?** pp82–83 | Society, economy and culture 1066–1509 | • Investigate how both rich and poor spent their spare time in the Middle Ages. <br> • Categorize some of the major differences between sport today and sport in the Middle Ages. | **All** students will be able to describe three things people did for fun in the Middle Ages. <br> **Most** students will be able to explain which activities we still do today, and how they have changed. <br> **Some** students will be able to explain reasons why these activities may have changed. |
| **5.5  Has football changed much since the Middle Ages?** pp84–85 | Society, economy and culture 1066–1509 | • Discover the origins of football in Britain. <br> • Evaluate how football in the Middle Ages differs from football today. | **All** students will be able to identify reasons for and against banning mob football. <br> **Most** students will be able to explain reasons for and against banning mob football. <br> **Some** students will be able to make a judgement about whether mob football should have been banned or not. |
| **5.6  Let me entertain you** pp86–87 | Society, economy and culture 1066–1509 | • Investigate the important role music played within medieval life. | **All** students will be able to identify five medieval musical instruments. <br> **Most** students will be able to explain one reason why music was so important in the Middle Ages. <br> **Some** students will be able to complete a source analysis activity on a miracle play. |
| **5.7  Keeping in fashion** pp88–89 | Society, economy and culture 1066–1509 | • Understand the role fashion played in the lives of the rich and how fashion changed during the Middle Ages. | **All** students will be able to identify how the rich dressed during the Middle Ages. <br> **Most** students will be able to explain how fashion changed for the rich during the Middle Ages. <br> **Some** students will be able to explain the role fashion played in the lives of the rich. |
| **5.8  The story of the English language** pp90–91 | Society, economy and culture 1066–1509 | • Investigate the origins of the main language spoken in Britain today. | **All** students will be able to identify which languages make up the English language we speak today. <br> **Most** students will be able to explain why different languages were used in the Middle Ages. <br> **Some** students will be able to use sources to support their writing. |
| **5.9  Come dine with me!** pp92–93 | Society, economy and culture 1066–1509 | • Compare food in medieval times with the foods we eat today. <br> • Judge which diet is healthiest. | **All** students will be able to describe the types of food that the rich and poor ate in the Middle Ages. <br> **Most** students will be able to explain why food eaten in the Middle Ages was different from the food we have today. <br> **Some** students will be able to explain how healthy medieval people were. |
| **5.10  Knight life** pp94–95 | Society, economy and culture: for example, feudalism 1066–1509 | • Consider the role of the knight in medieval society and how aspects of medieval history still have relevance today. | **All** students will be able to describe the steps to becoming a knight. <br> **Most** students will be able to explain the role of knights in medieval society. <br> **Some** students will be able to explain the importance of knights in medieval society and whether they still have an impact on modern life. |
| **5.11  Welcome to the tournament** pp96–97 | Society, economy and culture 1066–1509 | • Explain why tournaments took place. <br> • Investigate what different activities took place in a medieval tournament. | **All** students will be able to identify the activities that took place in a medieval tournament. <br> **Most** students will be able to imagine what it would be like at a tournament. <br> **Some** students will be able to explain why tournaments were important for a knight's training. |
| **5.12 What was heraldry?** pp98–99 | Society, economy and culture 1066–1509 | • Analyse the rules of heraldry. <br> • Explain why heraldry was important in medieval society. | **All** students will be able to describe what a heraldry shield is. <br> **Most** students will be able to create a heraldry shield that uses correctly the rules of heraldry. <br> **Some** students will be able to explain the relevance of heraldry for knights and the importance of heraldry in tournaments. |
| **5.13 Enough of history: what about *herstory?*** pp100–101 | Society, economy and culture 1066–1509 | • Compare the rights of women today with those of women in the Middle Ages. <br> • Explain why there was little written about the lives of women. | **All** students will be able to identify some of the jobs that medieval women did in European society. <br> **Most** students will be able to describe similarities and differences between the lives of women today and those living in the Middle Ages. <br> **Some** students will be able to explain whether they believed medieval English society was tolerant towards women. |
| **5.14 Matilda: the forgotten queen** pp102–103 | Society, economy and culture 1066–1509 | • Investigate why Matilda thought she should have been crowned queen in 1135. <br> • Explain the reasons why she wasn't. <br> • Judge who won the struggle between Stephen and Matilda. | **All** students will understand why Matilda thought she should have been crowned queen in 1135. <br> **Most** students will understand the reasons why she was not crowned queen. <br> **Some** students will decide who won in the struggle between Stephen and Matilda. |

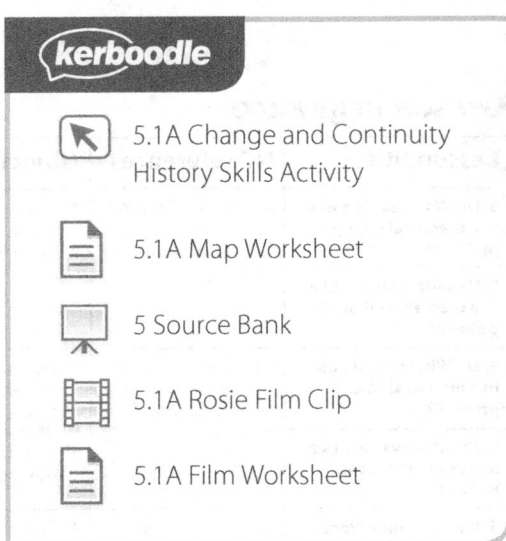

Invasion, Plague and Murder pages 72–73

## Lesson summary

Students will develop an understanding of life in a medieval village.

### What are the lesson outcomes?

**All** students will be able to describe what life was like in a medieval village.

**Most** students will be able to navigate and label correctly the various parts of a medieval village.

**Some** students will be able to use historical sources to support their findings.

## Starter suggestion

- List-o-rama!: Tell students they have 30 seconds to list as many features of their local town or city as they can. Ask them to put a star next to any features on their lists that they think would be present in a medieval town or city.

## Main learning suggestions and assessment

### What activities will take place?

**Task 1:** Students should read the information on pages 72–73 and complete Work activity **1**. They should complete 5.1A Change and Continuity History Skills Activity to consider how much villages have changed, or stayed the same, since medieval times.

**Task 2:** Students should watch 5.1A Rosie Film Clip, in which village girl Rosie talks about what her village is like. Students could complete 5.1A Film Worksheet during or after viewing the clip.

### How will students demonstrate their understanding?

**Task 3:** Students should complete the activity on 5.1A Map Worksheet, labelling a medieval village. Students should read the instructions on 5.1A Map Worksheet to work out the locations of nine places within a medieval village, labelling them correctly using the key, and providing a description of what activities happened there.

## Plenary suggestions

- Freeze frame: Split the class into around nine groups of three or four students. Allocate each group one location within a medieval village. Explain that they have three minutes to create their own freeze frame of an activity they would expect to see in their location. Remind students of the importance of teamwork, body language, and facial expressions. Ask them to keep their location secret and encourage other groups to guess what the location is.

## Differentiation suggestions

### Support

- Lower ability students may wish to create their own glossary of key words for a medieval village to help them understand how the different buildings and areas were used.

### Extension: Hungry for more?

- Students could use the map they have created to plan a treasure hunt. They should plot the route and get a partner to find the treasure.

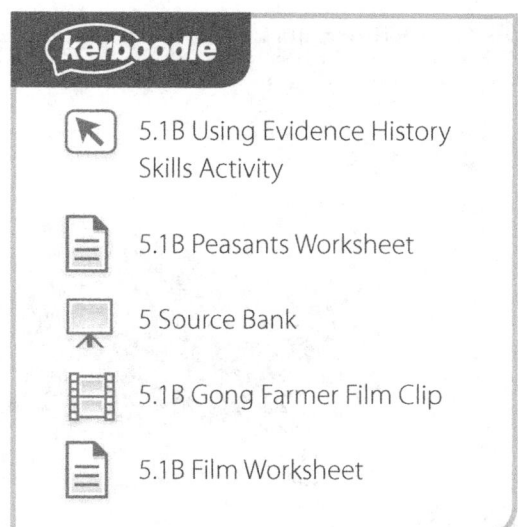

Invasion, Plague and Murder pages 74–75

## Lesson summary

Students will develop an understanding of life in a medieval village.

### What are the lesson outcomes?

**All** students will be able to describe what life was like in a medieval village.

**Most** students will be able to navigate and label correctly the various parts of a medieval village.

**Some** students will be able to use historical sources to support their findings.

## Starter suggestion

- Hangman!: Students can play a game of hangman to revise the correct names of places in a medieval village.

## Main learning suggestions and assessment

### What activities will take place?

**Task 1:** Students should read the information on pages 74–75 and complete Work activities **1** to **3**. They should complete 5.1B Using Evidence History Skills Activity to gain a greater understanding of life in a medieval village.

**Task 2:** Students should watch 5.1B Gong Farmer Film Clip. Here, the local gong farmer discusses his role in the village. Students should complete 5.1B Film Clip to help them consider what they have seen.

### How will students demonstrate their understanding?

**Task 3:** Students should complete 5.1B Peasants Worksheet to understand what villagers' homes and daily lives were like by completing the tasks.

## Plenary suggestions

- One more thing!: Students should complete the sentence to state what they have learned in this lesson: One thing I have learned is …

## Differentiation suggestions

### Support

- Encourage lower ability students to revise and make sure they understand the Wise Up Words from this lesson and the previous one.

### Extension: Hungry for more?

- Students should study **Source C** and write a 100-word essay answering the following question: How useful is **Source C** in helping us to learn about peoples' lives in the Middle Ages? You should encourage higher ability students to use evidence from sources to support their writing.

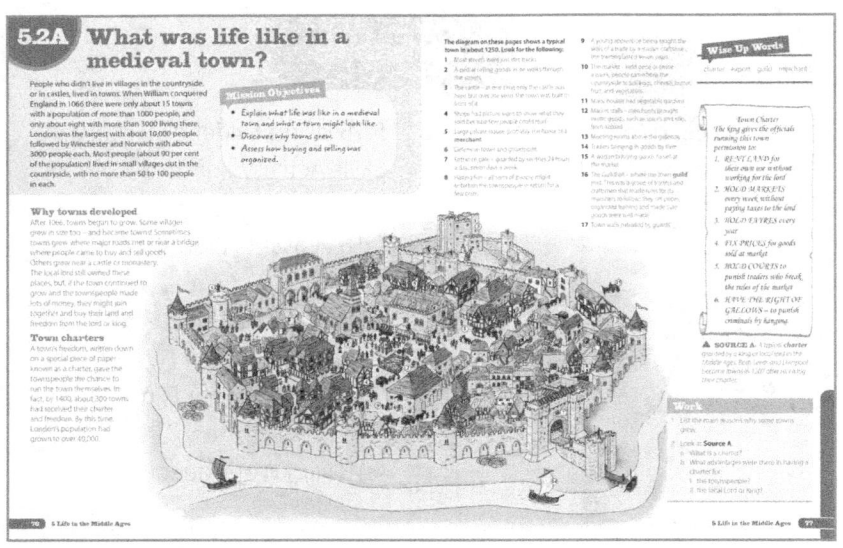

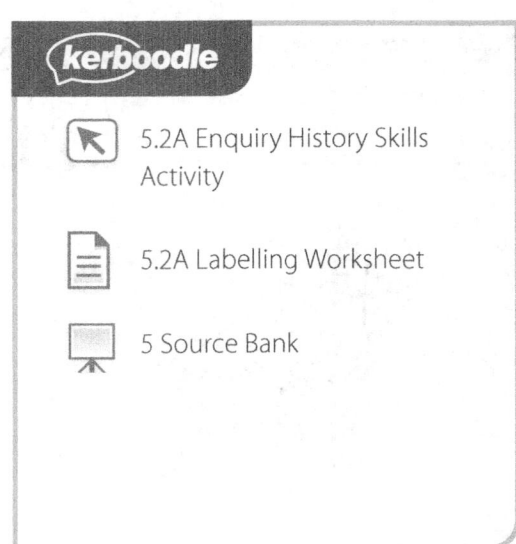

Invasion, Plague and Murder pages 76–77

## Lesson summary

Students will develop their ability to use sources to support and extend their understanding of life in a medieval town.

### What are the lesson outcomes?

**All** students will be able to describe what life was like in a medieval town.

**Most** students will be able to use sources to find out information about life in a medieval town.

**Some** students will be able to support their writing with evidence from sources.

## Starter suggestion

● 3, 5, 7: Explain to students that they should already know about life in a medieval village. Ask them to work individually for 30 seconds to think of three buildings they might expect to discover in a medieval town. Ask them to share their ideas with a partner and between them come up with five buildings they might expect to discover. Finally students should work in small groups to come up with a final list of seven buildings they might expect to discover. Ask students to feed back on their findings.

## Main learning suggestions and assessment

### What activities will take place?

**Task 1:** Students should read the information on pages 76–77 and complete Work activities **1** and **2**. They should complete 5.2A Enquiry History Skills Activity to explore why towns grew around certain landmarks.

### How will students demonstrate their understanding?

**Task 2:** Students should complete 5.2A Labelling Worksheet, labelling the image of a medieval town.

## Plenary suggestions

● Charades!: Students could play a game of charades to guess the following keywords: saddler; baker; weaver; carpenter.

## Differentiation suggestions

### Support

● *Ask students to research the definitions of the Wise Up Words in this lesson. They could use the glossary at the back of the Student Book if they need extra support. Then, ask students to volunteer their definitions. Agree on the best as a class and ask everyone to copy these definitions down in their book in a mini glossary.*

### Extension: Hungry for more?

● Higher ability students should attempt Work activity **2** to develop their source skills. Ask students to look at the town charter in **Source A**. Could they come up with a charter for their own school? What rules would they include?

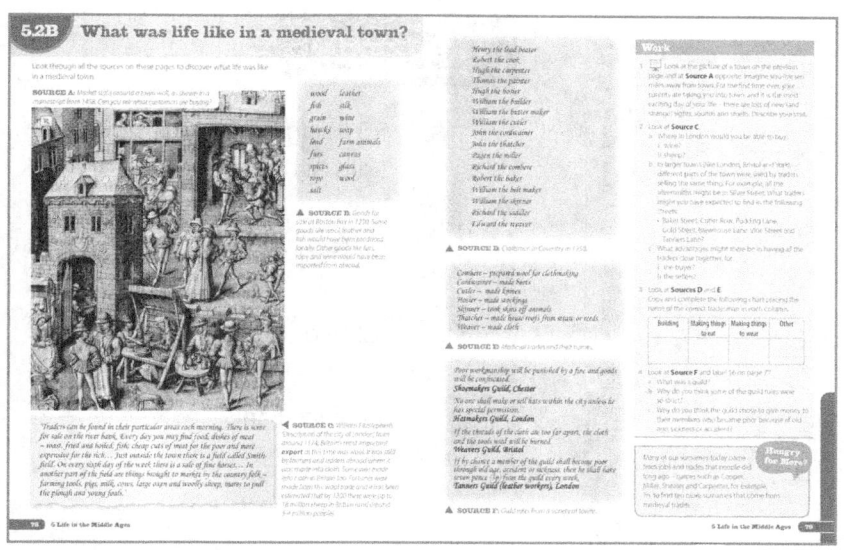

Invasion, Plague and Murder pages 78–79

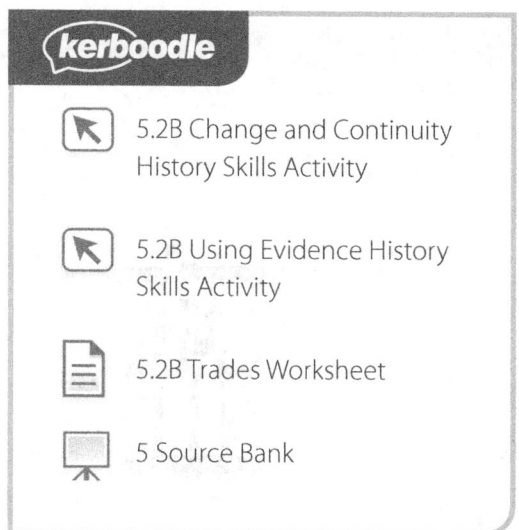

## Lesson summary

Students will develop their ability to use sources to support and extend their understanding of life in a medieval town.

### What are the lesson outcomes?

**All** students will be able to describe what life was like in a medieval town.

**Most** students will be able to use sources to find out information about life in a medieval town.

**Some** students will be able to support their writing with evidence from sources.

## Starter suggestion

- Ask students to read **Source C**. They should make a list of the different things they could buy at a medieval market.

## Main learning suggestions and assessment

### What activities will take place?

**Task 1:** Students should read the information on pages 78–79 and complete 5.2B Using Evidence History Skills Activity to investigate **Source A** and so gain a greater understanding of life in a medieval town.

### How will students demonstrate their understanding?

**Task 2:** Students should complete Work questions **1** to **4**. They could also complete 5.2B Change and Continuity History Skills Activity and 5.2B Trades Worksheet to gain a greater understanding of the jobs and businesses in a medieval town.

**Task 3:** During medieval times, signs on shops did not contain any words as most people at this time could not read or write. Ask students to work in pairs to create a sign for one of the shops in a medieval town. Remind them of the success criteria: there must be no words; there should be two or three symbols; they should think about the activities or goods involved in the business; they should use colour to make the sign attractive.

## Plenary suggestions

- Mission achieved?: Students could try to answer the following questions: What were five jobs that you could do in the Middle Ages? Can you list three ways in which life in a medieval town was different from life today? What was a town charter?

## Differentiation suggestions

### Support

- Students should look at **Source A** and **Source C** and complete the following question: Does **Source C** support what you can see happening in **Source A**?

### Extension: Hungry for more?

- Many of our surnames today come from jobs and trades that people did long ago, for example names such as Miller, Shearer, and Carpenter. Ask students to find ten more surnames that come from medieval trades.

# 5.3 How smelly were the Middle Ages?

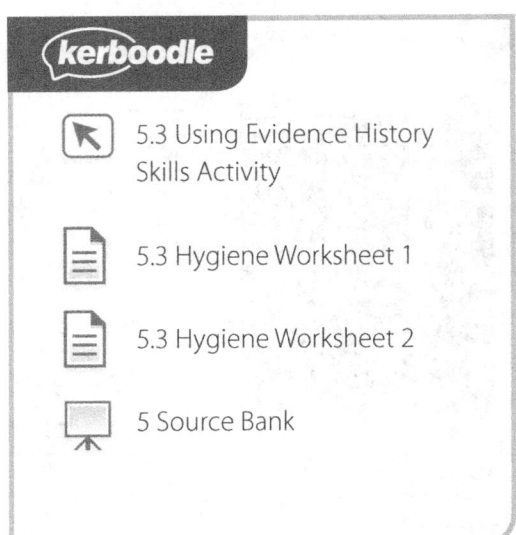

Invasion, Plague and Murder pages 80–81

## Lesson summary

Students will create a leaflet for foreigners visiting England, explaining what to expect 'when nature calls'! They will organize their own work and use sources to support their writing.

### What are the lesson outcomes?

**All** students will be able to identify how people in England kept clean in the Middle Ages.

**Most** students will be able to explain two reasons why standards of cleanliness and personal hygiene were very different from today.

**Some** students will be able to support their writing using evidence from sources.

## Starter suggestion

- Students could write out a list of things that they have done over the last few days in order to keep themselves clean, tidy, and as germ-free as possible. Ask volunteers to feed back to the rest of the class.

## Main learning suggestions and assessment

### What activities will take place?

**Task 1:** Students should read the information on pages 80–81 and use 5.3 Hygiene Worksheet 1 to record a list of things that medieval people did to keep themselves clean, tidy, and as germ-free as possible. They should also write down a list of reasons why people in the Middle Ages were not as clean as we are today. Ask students to feed their ideas back to the rest of the class.

### How will students demonstrate their understanding?

**Task 2:** Students should complete 5.3 Using Evidence History Skills Activity to investigate **Source D**. This will give

them a greater understanding of how public health changed in the Middle Ages.

**Task 3:** Students should complete Work activities **1** and **2**.

**Task 4:** Students should either complete Work question **3** or 5.3 Hygiene Worksheet 2 to create a leaflet about medieval toilets. They should imagine that they have been asked to help inform a group of foreign visitors coming to medieval England. What should the visitors expect to find 'when nature calls'? Students are required to use history skills such as using evidence and exploring similarities and differences whilst reading for meaning to structure their writing to suit a particular audience.

## Plenary suggestions

- Student as the teacher!: Students could tell the class three ways in which standards of cleanliness were different in the Middle Ages, and explain the reason for one of these.

## Differentiation suggestions

### Support

- For Work activity **3** you might like to show students a few examples of information leaflets, so they can familiarize themselves with the format and layout before they start drafting their own.

### Extension: Hungry for more?

- Higher ability students should start to include historical sources as examples to support their writing.

- Students could read **Source D**, then create a poster based on it. They must imagine that the poster will be displayed on Town Hall notice boards to tell people the key points about the new Public Health Act.

# 5.4 Could you have fun in the Middle Ages?

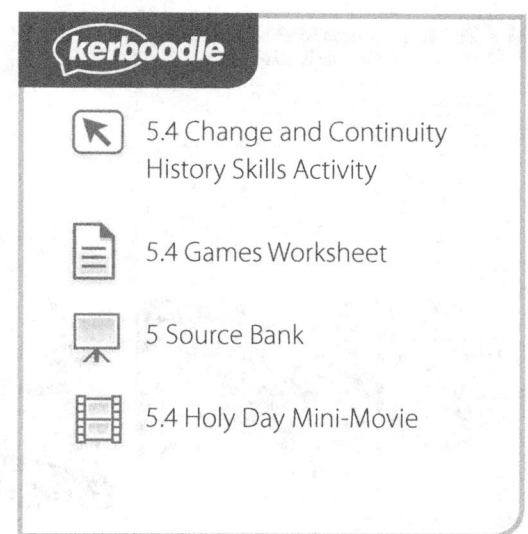

Invasion, Plague and Murder pages 82–83

## Lesson summary

Students will understand how people had fun in the Middle Ages, organizing and creating a poster to advertise a medieval holy day. Students should learn the importance of holy days in medieval society.

### What are the lesson outcomes?

**All** students will be able to describe three things people did for fun in the Middle Ages.

**Most** students will be able to explain which activities we still do today, and how they have changed.

**Some** students will be able to explain reasons why these activities may have changed.

## Starter suggestion

- Allow students 20 seconds, working in pairs, to come up with three games that they think might have been played during medieval times. Students should then watch 5.4 Holy Day Mini-Movie. In pairs, ask students to pick two examples: one game we do not play today and one game we do play. Can they explain to another pair why they think this is? What has changed?

## Main learning suggestions and assessment

### What activities will take place?

**Task 1:** Students should read the information on pages 82–83 and complete 5.4 Games Worksheet. Students should write on the worksheet the name and a description of each sport.

### How will students demonstrate their understanding?

**Task 2:** Students should complete Work questions **1** and **2**. They should then complete 5.4 Change and Continuity History Skills Activity to categorize medieval and modern day sports.

**Task 3:** Students should use the information across the spread to complete Work activity **3**, which asks them to create a poster to advertise a medieval holy day in their town. They should follow the conventions of a poster and use pictures.

## Plenary suggestions

- Do you know: Ask all students to stand up behind their chairs. Begin this activity by asking one student a 'do you know…' question. For example, 'do you know which game involved the player being blindfolded?'. If the student can say the correct answer, they can ask another student a 'do you know' question, and sit down. Students can answer with 'I don't know', but they cannot sit down until they get an answer correct!

## Differentiation suggestions

### Support

- For Work activity **3** you might like to show students a few examples of posters designed to advertise events, so they can familiarize themselves with the format and layout before they start drafting their own.

### Extension: Hungry for more?

- Students could think about whether they have played or enjoyed any of the games or sports mentioned in this lesson. Have any of the sports changed? If so, how or why?

69

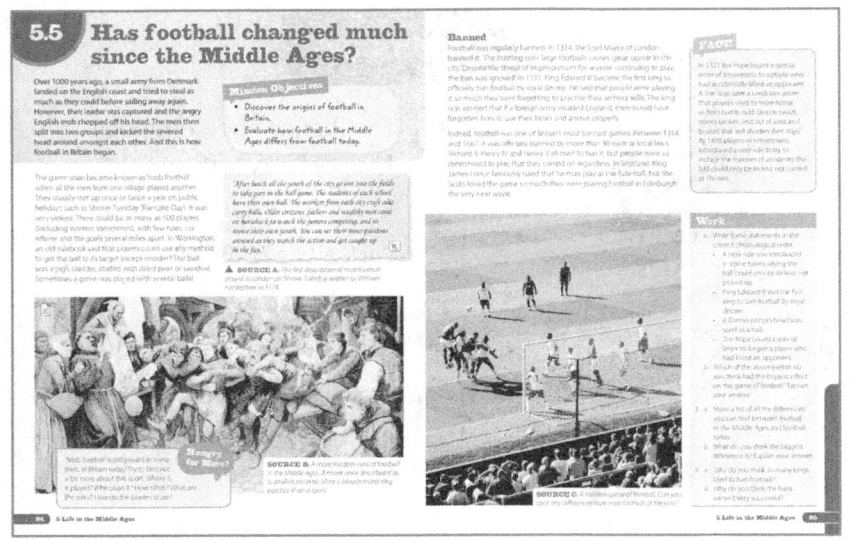

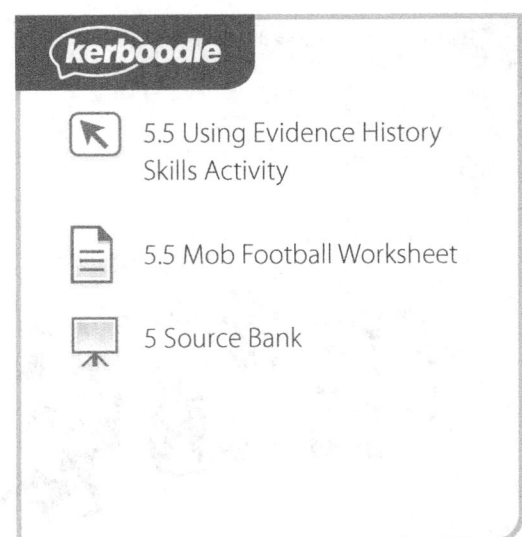

Invasion, Plague and Murder pages 84–85

## Lesson summary
Students should explain the origins of football, and the reasons for and against the banning of mob football.

### What are the lesson outcomes?
**All** students will be able to identify reasons for and against banning mob football.

**Most** students will be able to explain reasons for and against banning mob football.

**Some** students will be able to make a judgement about whether mob football should have been banned or not.

## Starter suggestion
- 3, 5, 7: Allow students 20 seconds of thinking time to come up with three games that might have been played during medieval times. Allow them 30 seconds to share their findings with a partner, explaining to them that they need to come up with five games between them. Finally students should work in small groups to come up with seven games between them. Each group should feed back to the class on their findings.

## Main learning suggestions and assessment
### What activities will take place?
**Task 1:** Students should read the information on pages 84–85 and complete Work questions **1** to **4**.

### How will students demonstrate their understanding?
**Task 2:** Students should complete 5.5 Using Evidence History Skills Activity to compare **Source A** and **Source B**, and gain a greater understanding of them. Students could alternatively complete a source investigation using 5.5 Mob Football Worksheet.

## Plenary suggestions
- Be a DJ!: Ask students if they can identify five differences between medieval and modern football.

## Differentiation suggestions
### Support
- 5.5 Mob Football Worksheet includes step by step questions to help students analyse the sources.

### Extension: Hungry for more?
- Higher ability students should be encouraged to consider the usefulness of **Source A** and **Source B**.

- Mob football is still played in some parts of Britain today. Ask students to find out a bit more about this sport. Where is it played? Who plays it? How often? What are the rules? How do the players score?

# 5.6 Let me entertain you

Invasion, Plague and Murder pages 86–87

## Lesson summary

Students should investigate the role that music played in medieval life.

### What are the lesson outcomes?

**All** students will be able to identify five medieval musical instruments.

**Most** students will be able to explain one reason why music was so important in the Middle Ages.

**Some** students will be able to complete a source analysis activity on a miracle play.

## Starter suggestion

- Student as the teacher!: Students must choose one of the Wise Up Words on page 87. They should explain to a partner what they think the word means, and why they think this.

## Main learning suggestions and assessment

### What activities will take place?

**Task 1**: Students should read the information on pages 86–87 and complete Work activities **1** to **4**.

**Task 2**: Watch 5.6 Dancing Film Clip with the class, where the baroness shows the teacher how people danced in the Middle Ages. You could ask students to complete the accompanying film worksheet after watching. This film clip also follows on from 3.3A Inhabitants Film Clip.

### How will students demonstrate their understanding?

**Task 3**: Students should complete 5.6 Significance History Skills Interactive to gain a greater understanding of miracle plays.

**Task 4**: Students should complete 5.6 Miracle Play Worksheet.

## Plenary suggestions

- One more thing: Students should complete the following sentence to state what they have learned in this lesson: 'One thing I have learned is…'. You can either pick students to tell the class one thing they have learned, or they can write on sticky notes that they hand in at the end of the lesson.

## Differentiation suggestions

### Support

- Visual and audio resources are very helpful for this lesson. As well as watching 5.6 Dancing Film Clip, other films on medieval instruments and performance are available online and would be a good way in to the lesson.

### Extension: Hungry for more?

- Encourage higher ability students to use evidence from sources to support their analysis of 5.6 Miracle Play Worksheet.

- Ask students to read **Source B**. Encourage them to come up with their own song that would tell other students what they have learned about life in the Middle Ages. They should include verses and a chorus, and they could make the song rhyme and even come up with a tune to sing it to!

# 5.7 Keeping in fashion

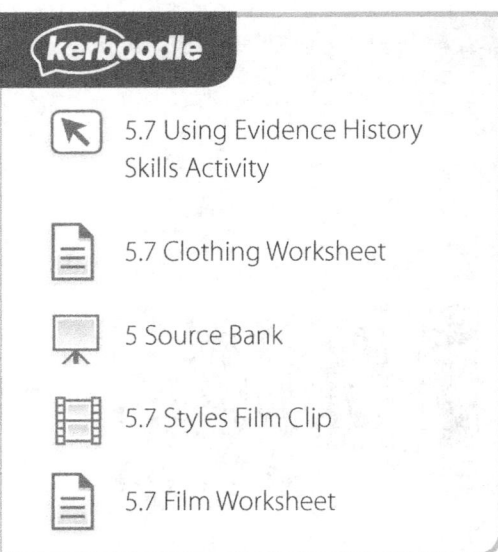

Invasion, Plague and Murder pages 88–89

## Lesson summary

Students should understand the role that fashion played in the lives of rich medieval people and how fashion changed during the Middle Ages.

### What are the lesson outcomes?

**All** students will be able to identify how the rich dressed during the Middle Ages.

**Most** students will be able to explain how fashion changed for the rich during the Middle Ages.

**Some** students will be able to explain the role fashion played in the lives of the rich.

## Starter suggestion

- Goal setting: Students could set themselves two targets for this lesson. One should be based on knowledge; another should be based on a skill.

## Main learning suggestions and assessment

### What activities will take place?

**Task 1:** Students should read the information on pages 88–89 and complete Work activity **1,** allowing them to develop an understanding of fashion in medieval times. Their understanding can be further developed by watching 5.7 Styles Film Clip, and completing the accompanying film worksheet.

### How will students demonstrate their understanding?

**Task 2:** Students should complete 5.7 Using Evidence History Skills Activity and 5.7 Clothing Worksheet to investigate medieval fashion.

**Task 3:** Students should complete Work activity **2.** This is a Big Write opportunity that allows students creative freedom to write a magazine extract. You could share some age-appropriate modern magazines to model the genre before they start work. Students are asked to explore and develop ideas (perhaps as part of a group) and carry out independent research in order to create an appropriate double-page spread that uses the correct historical terms accurately.

## Plenary suggestions

- Hangman!: Students could play the game using keywords from this lesson: poulaines; tunic; steeple hat; linen.

## Differentiation suggestions

### Support

- In order to help students grasp the idea of fashion as an indication of social status and wealth, you could show pictures of celebrities wearing extravagant clothes and ask them why they are dressed like that. Make the point that often, people are trying to show off their wealth and status, and this is just what rich people did in the Middle Ages too.

### Extension: Hungry for more?

- Higher ability students should be encouraged to consider the usefulness of the source on 5.7 Clothing Worksheet.

- Encourage students to use the Internet or textbooks to find two different images of medieval fashion. One image should show what rich people would have worn, and the other should show what peasants would have worn. Ask them to write 100 words to summarize how and why each image is different.

# 5.8 The story of the English language

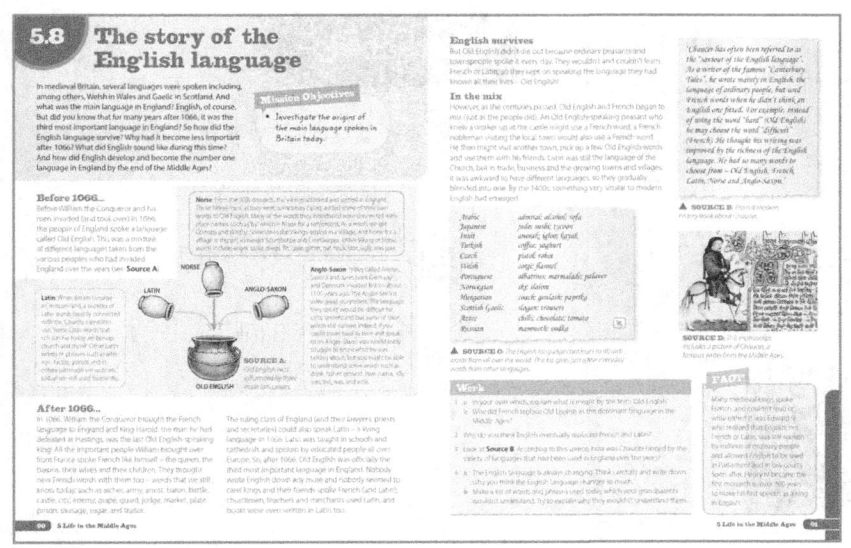

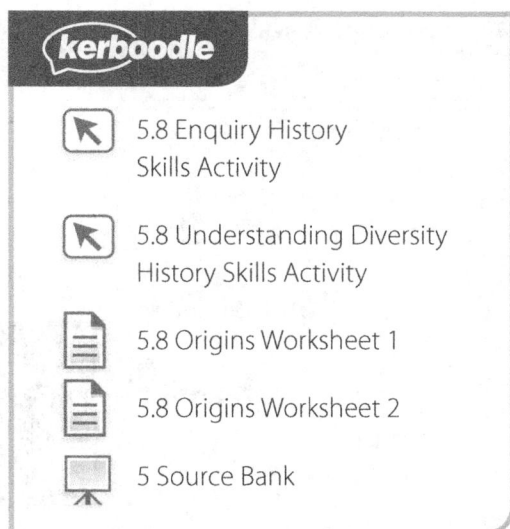

Invasion, Plague and Murder pages 90–91

## Lesson summary

Students will develop their understanding of how the English language developed. They will develop their writing by using either the text or sources to find answers and support their ideas.

### What are the lesson outcomes?

**All** students will be able to identify which languages make up the English language we speak today.

**Most** students will be able to explain why different languages were used in the Middle Ages.

**Some** students will be able to use sources to support their writing.

## Starter suggestion

- What is the language?: Give students a range of words, and ask them to guess whether the word is Anglo-Saxon, Latin, French, or Norse. This activity works well with miniature whiteboards. Use **Source A** and the text on page 90 to get some ideas.

## Main learning suggestions and assessment

### What activities will take place?

**Task 1:** Students should read the information on pages 90–91 and complete Work activities **1** and **2**.

### How will students demonstrate their understanding?

**Task 2:** Students should complete 5.8 Enquiry History Skills Activity and 5.8 Understanding Diversity History Skills Activity to understand more about the origins of some English words.

**Task 3:** Students should complete Work activities **3** and **4**.

**Task 4:** Students should complete either 5.8 Origins Worksheet 1 or 5.8 Origins Worksheet 2 on the story of the English language, to increase their understanding of how the English language developed. Worksheet 1 is intended for higher ability students, while Worksheet 2 can be used with lower ability students.

## Plenary suggestions

- Communication game!: Students could work in pairs. Explain to students that they have to communicate with their partner one thing they have learned today. However, they cannot use speech to communicate! Encourage them to think of the different methods of communication that they could use. After this activity you could discuss the importance of language within our society. Why is language so important?

## Differentiation suggestions

### Support

- 5.8 Origins Worksheet 2 is intended for lower ability students, and encourages them to identify information from the *Student Book* text.

### Extension: Hungry for more?

- 5.8 Origins Worksheet 1 is for higher ability students – it encourages more independent thinking and analysis.

- Students could create their own crossword or wordsearch using Old English words.

73

# 5.9 Come dine with me!

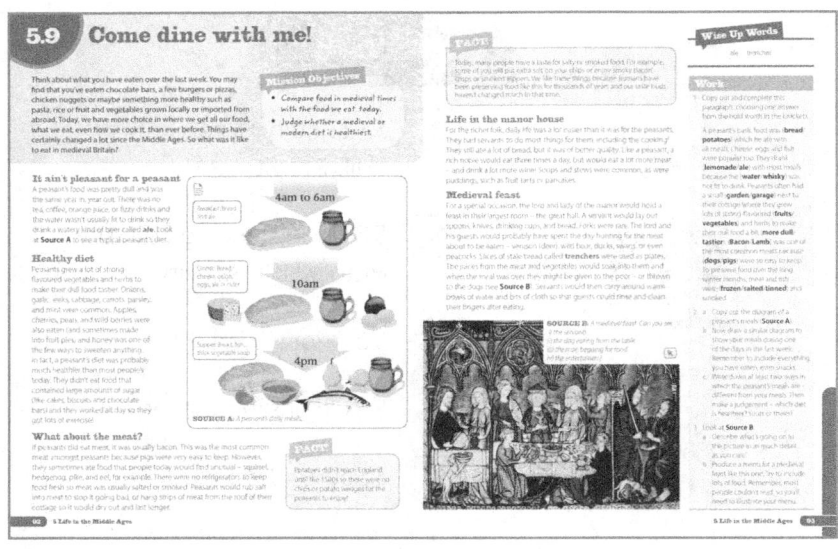

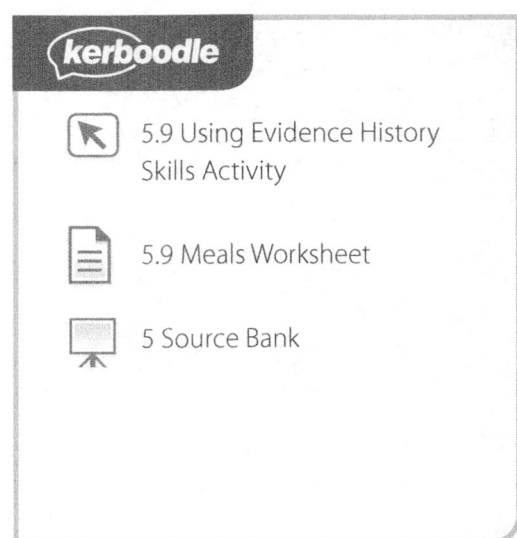

Invasion, Plague and Murder pages 92–93

## Lesson summary

Students will understand how the food and drink we have today differs from the food and drink people had in the Middle Ages.

### What are the lesson outcomes?

**All** students will be able to describe the types of food that the rich and poor ate in the Middle Ages.

**Most** students will be able to explain why food eaten in the Middle Ages was different from the food we have today.

**Some** students will be able to explain how healthy medieval people were.

## Starter suggestion

- Ask students to write down three items of food they ate yesterday on three separate post-it notes. Designate two areas in the classroom: one for post-it notes of food that they think would have been available in medieval times, and one for post-it notes of food that they think would not have been available.

## Main learning suggestions and assessment

### What activities will take place?

**Task 1:** Students should read the information on pages 92–93 and complete Work activity **1**.

**Task 2:** Students should complete 5.9 Using Evidence History Skills Activity to gain a greater understanding of **Source B**.

### How will students demonstrate their understanding?

**Task 3:** Students should complete Work activity **2**. They should use 5.9 Meals Worksheet and **Source A** to create a

diagram of a rich noble's daily meals, and a second diagram to show their own eating habits for a day.

**Task 4:** Students should complete Work activity **3**.

## Plenary suggestions

- Tell your neighbour: Students could summarize two facts that they have learned this lesson and tell these to a partner.

## Differentiation suggestions

### Support

- Through careful and appropriate questioning, you could work through the answer choices available to complete Work activity **1** in the *Student Book*. For work activity **2**, students could begin by writing down what they have eaten today/yesterday or this week in order to prepare for the comparison exercise

### Extension: Hungry for more?

- There are many foods that we eat every day that were not available in the Middle Ages. Ask students to find out roughly when the following foods arrived in Britain: chocolate; coffee; potatoes; pineapples; tea; saffron.

- Higher ability students can practise their source skills by completing Work activity **3**.

# 5.10 Knight life

Invasion, Plague and Murder pages 94–95

## Lesson summary

Students will understand the role of knights, the importance of knights in medieval society, and how aspects of medieval history still have relevance today.

### What are the lesson outcomes?

**All** students will be able to describe the steps to becoming a knight.

**Most** students will be able to explain the role of knights in medieval society.

**Some** students will be able to explain the importance of knights in medieval society and whether they still have an impact on modern life.

## Starter suggestion

- Students, either individually or in pairs, could use post-it notes to identify one thing that they already know and one thing that they would like to know about this lesson. For example, 'I know that knights were part of the feudal system'; 'I know that knights were medieval warriors'; 'I want to know about the weapons that knights fought with'; 'I want to know why William needed knights'. Ask them to stick these in two separate areas in the classroom.

## Main learning suggestions and assessment

### What activities will take place?

**Task 1:** Students should read the information on pages 94–95 and complete Work activities **1** and **2**.

**Task 2:** Students should watch 5.10 Knighthood Film Clip, where a village girl describes the life of a knight to the teacher, and then complete 5.10 Film Worksheet.

## How will students demonstrate their understanding?

**Task 3:** Students should complete 5.10 Significance History Skills Activity to gain a better understanding of the vocabulary used in this lesson.

**Task 4:** Students should use 5.10 Ceremony Worksheet to create a storyboard about becoming a knight. Students should show the steps of the ceremony that a medieval man went through to become a knight.

**Task 5:** Students should complete Work activities **3** and **4**.

## Plenary suggestions

- Students could add one sticky note to the group of notes stating what they now know. You may wish to get students to share these ideas with each other or with the class.

## Differentiation suggestions

### Support

- Students could be organized into mixed ability groups to complete Work activity **4**. Encourage higher ability students to support lower ability members of their group by becoming a mentor or group leader.

### Extension: Hungry for more?

- Ask students to carry out research on the knighting ceremony in modern Britain. How has it changed? Why are people knighted in today's world? What knights do they know? What about 'female knights' in modern Britain?

- Students could research the life of a famous medieval knight, including battles he fought in, where he lived, and any fascinating facts. Examples are Sir Henry Percy, John Hawkwood and William Marshal, Earl of Pembroke.

# 5.11 Welcome to the tournament

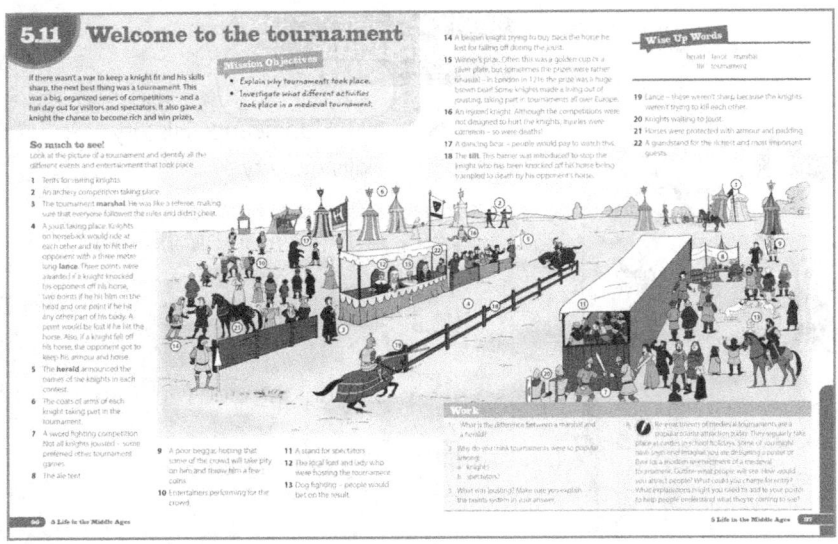
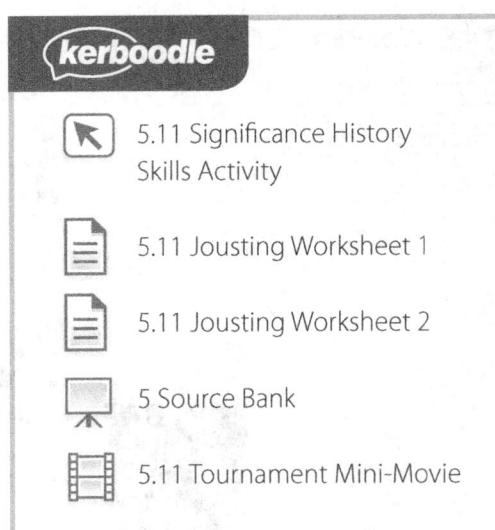

Invasion, Plague and Murder pages 96–97

## Lesson summary

Students will understand which activities took place in a medieval tournament and why they were important for a knight's training.

### What are the lesson outcomes?

**All** students will be able to identify the activities that took place in a medieval tournament.

**Most** students will be able to imagine what it would be like at a tournament.

**Some** students will be able to explain why tournaments were important for a knight's training.

## Starter suggestion

- Students should have access to 5.11 Jousting Worksheet 1. Try to prevent them having access to the labelled diagram in the *Student Book*. Students could pick one character on the worksheet, and be given three minutes to try to answer the following questions: What is your job? What are you doing? Are you enjoying the day? Why? They could then watch 5.11 Tournament Mini-Movie to see if their answers are correct.

## Main learning suggestions and assessment

### What activities will take place?

**Task 1:** Students should read the information on pages 96–97 and complete 5.11 Significance History Skills Activity to gain a better understanding of tournaments.

**Task 2:** Students should complete 5.11 Jousting Worksheet 1. They should label the ten activities happening on the worksheet.

### How will students demonstrate their understanding?

**Task 3:** Students should complete Work activities **1** to **4**.

**Task 4:** Students should complete 5.11 Jousting Worksheet 2, which asks them to write a letter home describing what being at a tournament was like.

## Plenary suggestions

- Freeze-frame: In small groups, students could create a freeze-frame of a specific activity that may have taken place at a medieval tournament. Remind students of the importance of teamwork, body language, and facial expressions. Ask students to keep the subject of their freeze-frame a secret and encourage other groups to guess what is happening.

## Differentiation suggestions

### Support

- Encourage lower ability students to use the Wise Up Words when completing Work activities **1** to **4**, to help them develop their writing.

### Extension: Hungry for more?

- Students could research the Chronicles of Jean Froissart. What can they learn about tournaments from his writing?

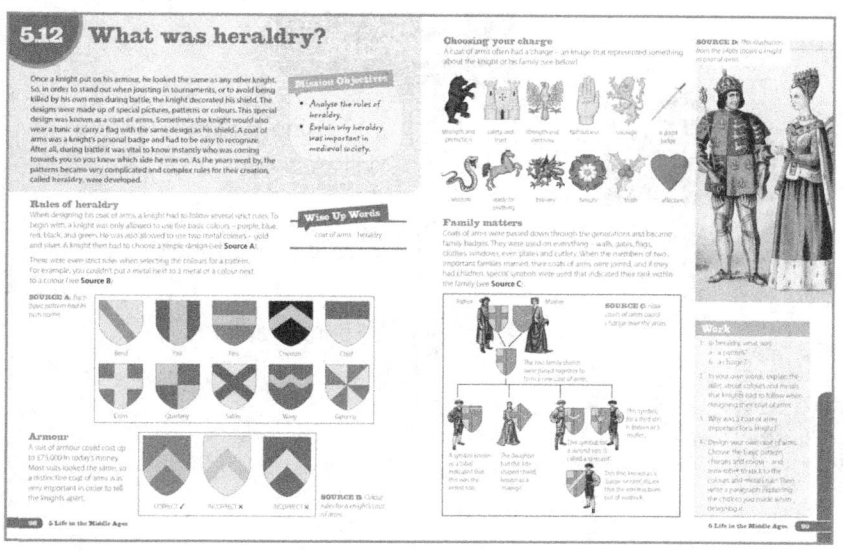

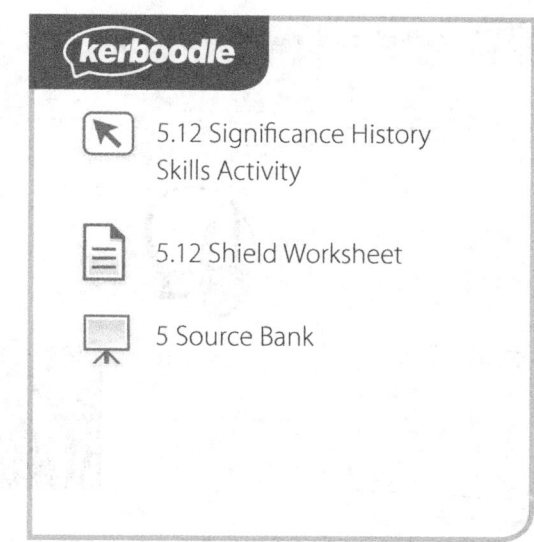

Invasion, Plague and Murder pages 98–99

## Lesson summary

Students will create their own heraldry shield, and develop their understanding of the rules of heraldry and why they were important in medieval society.

### What are the lesson outcomes?

**All** students will be able to describe what a heraldry shield is.

**Most** students will be able to create a heraldry shield that uses correctly the rules of heraldry.

**Some** students will be able to explain the relevance of heraldry for knights and the importance of heraldry in tournaments.

## Starter suggestion

- Ask students to think of any symbols they know of, and what these symbols mean. Try to encourage them to think of symbols that they might see around school, at home, or in shops. Why are symbols so important in daily life? Ask students to think of symbols that could represent themselves.

## Main learning suggestions and assessment

### What activities will take place?

**Task 1:** Students should read the information on pages 98–99 and complete 5.12 Significance History Skills Activity to consider the reasons for having a coat of arms.

### How will students demonstrate their understanding?

**Task 2:** Students should complete Work activities **1** to **4**. To support them in Work question **4**, they could use 5.12 Shield Worksheet to create their own heraldic shield.

## Plenary suggestions

- Exit note: Students could copy and complete the following sentences: 'One thing I learned about heraldry is…'; 'One thing I enjoyed doing is…'.

## Differentiation suggestions

### Support

- 5.12 Shield Worksheet helps students to create their heraldic shield.

### Extension: Hungry for more?

- Students could research the coats of arms of the following familiar names: King John; Richard the Lionheart; Henry VIII; Richard III; Henry II. What can they learn about these men from their coats of arms?

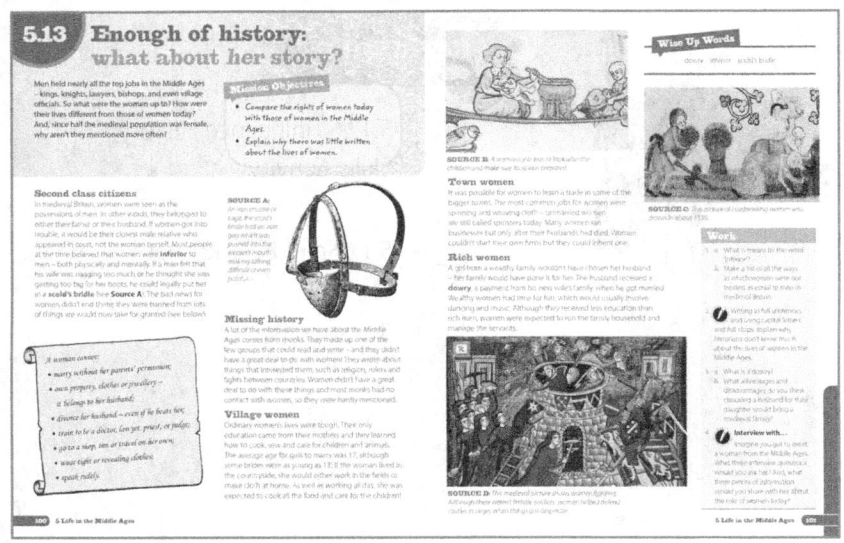

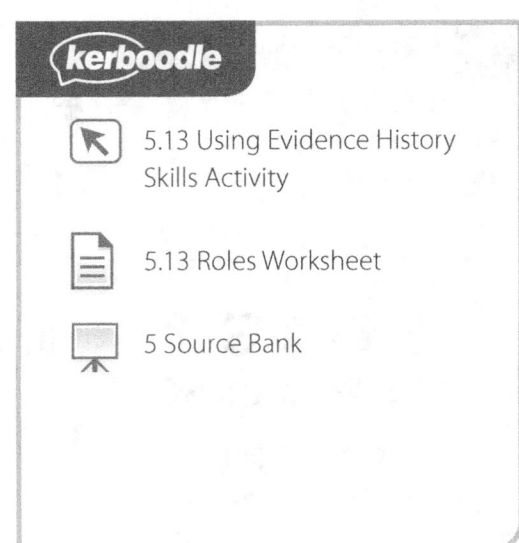

Invasion, Plague and Murder pages 100–101

## Lesson summary

Students will gain an understanding of how women were treated in England during the Middle Ages.

### What are the lesson outcomes?

**All** students will be able to identify some of the jobs that medieval women did in European society.

**Most** students will be able to describe similarities and differences between the lives of women today and those living in the Middle Ages.

**Some** students will be able to explain whether they believed medieval English society was tolerant towards women.

## Starter suggestion

- Students could be given access to **Source D**, either as a photocopied sheet or on a whiteboard. Ask them to work out answers to the following questions: What is going on in this source? Are you surprised by this source? Why? This works best as a class discussion, asking students to offer their ideas.

## Main learning suggestions and assessment

### What activities will take place?

**Task 1:** Students should read the information on pages 100–101, and create a list of as many examples as they can of medieval society being intolerant to women.

**Task 2:** Students should complete 5.13 Using Evidence History Skills Activity on **Sources B** and **D** to develop their understanding of the roles that women had in medieval England.

### How will students demonstrate their understanding?

**Task 3:** Students could use 5.13 Roles Worksheet to rank whether they would like to have been a rich woman, a townswoman, or a peasant women. Encourage them to consider the advantages and disadvantages of each role.

## Plenary suggestions

- Different shoes: Students could imagine they are townswomen living in medieval England. They should list five ways in which their lives are different from today.

## Differentiation suggestions

### Support

- Ask students to discuss the definitions of the Wise Up Words, using the glossary at the back of the *Student Book* if they need more support. Then, ask them to write down a definition for each of the terms as part of their own mini glossary.

### Extension: Hungry for more?

- Higher ability students should complete Work activity **3** in the *Student Book*.

- Ask students to research the lives of the following medieval women: Eleanor of Aquitaine; Catherine de Valois; Christina of Markgate; Margaret Paston; Margery Kempe.

# 5.14 Matilda: the forgotten queen

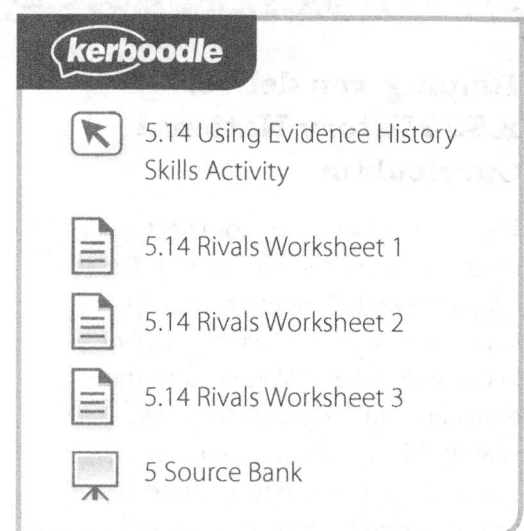

Invasion, Plague and Murder pages 102–103

## Lesson summary

Students will understand and organize the reasons why Matilda was not made Queen of England.

### What are the lesson outcomes?

**All** students will understand why Matilda thought she should have been crowned queen in 1135.

**Most** students will understand the reasons why she was not crowned queen.

**Some** students will decide who won in the struggle between Stephen and Matilda.

## Starter suggestion

- Split the class into two groups: girls and boys. The team with the most correct answers wins the game. The questions are:
  - What rights did medieval women have?
  - What job did women in medieval villages do?
  - What was a dowry?
  - What did women in medieval towns do?
  - What job did rich women do?

## Main learning suggestions and assessment

### What activities will take place?

**Task 1:** Students should read the information on pages 102–103 and complete 5.14 Using Evidence History Skills Activity to compare **Source A** and **Source B**. This will help them to understand two contemporary views of Stephen and Matilda.

### How will students demonstrate their understanding?

**Task 2:** Students should use 5.14 Rivals Worksheet 1, reading the cards written there. They should sort the cards into four columns: reasons why Matilda would have made a strong,

successful Queen of England; reasons why Matilda did not become Queen of England; reasons why Stephen became King of England; reasons why Stephen was a weak king.

**Task 3:** Students should use 5.14 Rivals Worksheet 2 to create a speech for either Matilda or Stephen, explaining why people should support them. Students should use the success criteria to organize their answers.

## Plenary suggestions

- Hot seat: Students could imagine that they are Matilda, and create answers for the following questions, either individually or in pairs:
  - Why are you expecting to be made queen?
  - Why do think the barons chose Stephen instead of you?
  - Were you happy with their decision?
  - Do you think you won the final battle of the sexes, now that your son is king?

## Differentiation suggestions

### Support

- You may wish to recap the rights of women in medieval England from the previous lesson in order to help students understand Matilda's struggle to become queen.

### Extension: Hungry for more?

- Students could create their own banners in support of either Matilda or Stephen, using 5.14 Rivals Worksheet 3. They should use the success criteria on the worksheet to create their banner, explaining their reasons for supporting their chosen contender.

- Higher ability students should read **Source A** and **Source B**. They should add to the four columns created in **Task 2** any quotations from these sources that they think support each argument.

# Overview:
# Chapter 6  Who rules?

## Helping you deliver KS3 History National Curriculum

This chapter focuses on some of the most significant cultural, political, and religious events in British history – the struggle between Church and Crown in the Middle Ages; Magna Carta; the emergence of Parliament; and the Peasants' Revolt. Through sources, storyboards, narrative text, cartoons, and well-structured and progressive tasks, the students will be required to think critically, weigh evidence, sift arguments, and develop their own opinions.

## The Big Picture

### Why are we teaching 'Who rules?'?

The shifting scales of power and the evolution of parliamentary democracy are obviously essential areas of study in any era of British history, and none more so than in the Middle Ages. The concept of the monarch's absolute authority will have been established in the students' minds from studying the Norman invasion and the feudal system. Students will also be aware that, although we still have a monarch today, society is no longer organized that way. This chapter allows students to chart the gradual shift in power by examining separate challenges to the king's authority – Henry II's struggles with the Church; King John's and Henry III's struggles with the barons; and Richard II's struggles with the peasants. These challenges, which came from different sections of society, make for a dramatic, exciting, and often gory narrative that will readily engage the students.

## Skills and processes covered in this chapter

| | | 6.1 | 6.2A | 6.2B | 6.3 | 6.4A | 6.4B | 6.5 | 6.6A | 6.6B |
|---|---|---|---|---|---|---|---|---|---|---|
| **History Skills** | Historical enquiry | ✓ | ✓ | ✓ | ✓ | ✓ | ✓ | ✓ | ✓ | ✓ |
| | Using evidence and source work | | ✓ | ✓ | | | ✓ | | ✓ | ✓ |
| | Chronological understanding | | ✓ | ✓ | | | | | ✓ | ✓ |
| | Understanding cultural, ethnic and religious diversity | ✓ | | | | | | | | |
| | Change and continuity | | | | | ✓ | ✓ | ✓ | ✓ | |
| | Cause and consequence | ✓ | ✓ | ✓ | | ✓ | | ✓ | ✓ | ✓ |
| | Significance | ✓ | ✓ | ✓ | ✓ | ✓ | ✓ | ✓ | ✓ | ✓ |
| | Interpretations | | ✓ | ✓ | ✓ | ✓ | | | | |
| | Making links/connections | ✓ | | | ✓ | ✓ | | ✓ | ✓ | ✓ |
| | Explores similarities and differences | | | | | ✓ | | | | ✓ |
| **Literacy and Numeracy** | Key words identified/deployed | ✓ | | | | | | | | |
| | Extended writing | | | ✓ | ✓ | | | ✓ | ✓ | ✓ |
| | Encourages reading for meaning | | | | | | ✓ | | | |
| | Focuses on structuring writing | | | ✓ | ✓ | | | ✓ | | |
| | Asks students to use writing to explore and develop ideas | ✓ | ✓ | ✓ | | ✓ | ✓ | ✓ | ✓ | |
| | Learn through talk/discussion | | | | ✓ | ✓ | ✓ | | | |
| | Numeracy opportunities | | | | | | | | | |
| **Activity types** | Creative task | | | | | | | ✓ | ✓ | ✓ |
| | Emphasizes role of individual | ✓ | | ✓ | ✓ | ✓ | | | | ✓ |
| | Group work | | ✓ | | ✓ | | | ✓ | | |
| | Independent research | | | ✓ | ✓ | | ✓ | | | ✓ |
| | Develops study skills | | | ✓ | ✓ | ✓ | | | | |

# Lesson sequence

| Lesson title | NC references | Objectives | Outcomes |
|---|---|---|---|
| **6.1 Crown versus Church: the story of Henry II and Thomas Becket pp104–105** | The struggle between Church and crown | • Summarize the events in the quarrel between Henry II nd Becket in the correct chronological order.<br>• Evaluate King Henry's motives in making Becket Archbishop of Canterbury. | **All** students will be able to understand why Henry II and Thomas Becket were friends and why they fell out.<br>**Most** students will be able to explain how the relationship between Henry II and Thomas Becket affected the relations between the Crown and the Church.<br>**Some** students will be able to justify who they think won the power struggle, and why. |
| **6.2A Newsflash: murder in the cathedral pp106–107**<br><br>**6.2B Newsflash: murder in the cathedral pp108–109** | The struggle between Church and crown | • Discover how Thomas Becket was murdered and by whom.<br>• Investigate the consequences of the murder. | **All** students will be able to describe the story of how Thomas Becket was murdered and by whom.<br>**Most** students will be able to explain the consequences of the murder.<br>**Some** students will be able to explain whether the Church or the Crown had the most power in medieval England. |
| **6.3 King John: Magna Carta man pp110–111** | Magna Carta and the emergence of Parliament | • Analyse the consequences of King John's mistakes.<br>• Explain the importance of Magna Carta. | **All** students will be able to describe the mistakes made by King John that upset the barons.<br>**Most** students will be able to explain why the Magna Carta was created.<br>**Some** students will be able to understand the effects the Magna Carta still has in the world today. |
| **6.4A Where did our Parliament come from? pp112–113**<br><br>**6.4B Where did our Parliament come from? pp114–115** | Magna Carta and the emergence of Parliament | • Examine why King Henry III argued with the barons.<br>• Discover the origins of Britain's Parliament. | **All** students will be able to identify at least three mistakes made by King Henry III.<br>**Most** students will be able to explain how Henry's mistakes led to the creation of Parliament.<br>**Some** students will be able to explain what the most important thing about de Montfort's Parliament was. |
| **6.5 Why were peasants so angry in 1381? pp116–117** | The Peasants' Revolt | • Examine why peasants were so angry in 1381.<br>• Link some of the causes of the peasants' anger together. | **All** students will be able to describe what the Peasants' Revolt was.<br>**Most** students will be able describe at least one reason why the poorest people in England argued with the king.<br>**Some** students will be able to explain at least one reason why the poorest people in England argued with the king. |
| **6.6A Power to the people pp118–119**<br><br>**6.6B Power to the people pp120–121** | The Peasants' Revolt | • Discover what happened to the angry peasants when they took their revolt to London.<br>• Examine evidence and identify similarities and differences. | **All** students will be able to describe at least one reason why the poorest people in England argued with the king.<br>**Most** students will be able to describe the causes, events, and consequences of the Peasant's Revolt.<br>**Some** students will be able to explain the causes, events, and consequences of the Peasants' Revolt. |
| **Assessing Your Learning 2 pp122–123** | Magna Carta and the emergence of Parliament | • Interrogate sources in order to judge how different interpretations of King John were created and changed over time | **Good:** Students will describe some different interpretations of King John.<br>**Better:** Students will suggest some reasons for different interpretations of King John.<br>**Best:** Students will explain how and why different interpretations of the past have arisen or been constructed. |

## Ideas for enrichment

Students could be set up with a scenario. For example, they could imagine that a bypass, airport extension, or similar is planned for the local area. Pose the question: What could or can ordinary people do to protest? Ask them to research methods that ordinary people have used to protest about these sorts of things in the past. Ask them to come back to the classroom with real examples.

A further research option might be to look at the origins of the main political parties. This will help with their studies later on in History, and follows neatly on from the 'first Parliament' of De Montford's time. A school trip to the Houses of Parliament could be ideal too, of course!

Why not 'go global'? Ask students to look for examples of how people in other countries have reacted, protested, or rebelled against their leaders in the past. The 2011 'Arab Spring', the 1968 'Prague Spring', the 1789 French Revolution, or the American War of Independence are obvious areas of focus.

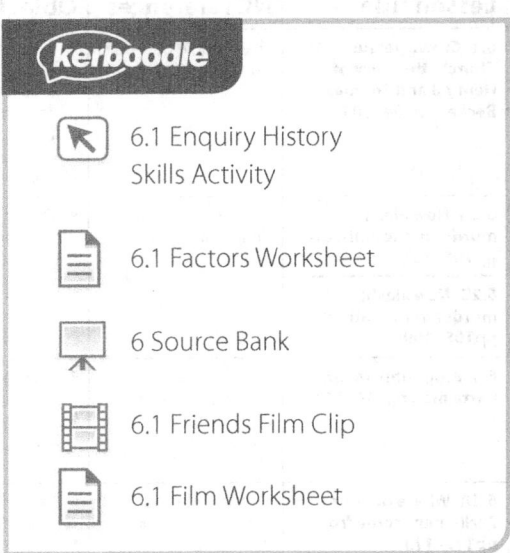

Invasion, Plague and Murder pages 104–105

## Lesson summary

Students will be able to identify the reasons why Henry II and Thomas Becket fell out and the impact this had on the relationship between the Crown and the Church.

### What are the lesson outcomes?

**All** students will be able to understand why Henry II and Thomas Becket were friends and why they fell out.

**Most** students will be able to explain how the relationship between Henry II and Thomas Becket affected the relations between the Crown and the Church.

**Some** students will be able to justify who they think won the power struggle, and why.

## Starter suggestion

- Why do people fall out?: Ask students to think of reasons why they might have fallen out with their friends in the past. Did their anger last? Do they regret anything they said or did whilst they had fallen out? Explain to students that there were two great friends in the Middle Ages that faced this very problem!

## Main learning suggestions and assessment

### What activities will take place?

**Task 1:** Students should read the information on pages 104–105. This should develop their understanding of how the relations between the Church and the Crown changed. They should also watch 6.1 Friends Film Clip, in which a knight discusses the relationship between Henry and Becket, and complete the accompanying film worksheet.

### How will students demonstrate their understanding?

**Task 2:** Students should complete 6.1 Enquiry History Skills Activity, which asks them to debate whether Henry or Becket was most at fault.

**Task 3:** Students should complete 6.1 Factors Worksheet. This asks them to organize the causes of the murder of Thomas Becket chronologically and into causes and consequences.

## Plenary suggestions

- Different shoes: Students could work in pairs. One should take on the role of Thomas Becket and the other should take on the role of Henry II. They should come up with as many reasons as possible why they have fallen out with each other.

## Differentiation suggestions

### Support

- It may be difficult for some students to grasp the meanings of the Wise Up Words in this lesson. Make sure to explain the meaning of 'excommunicated' clearly, and direct students' attention to the glossary at the back of the *Student Book*.

### Extension: Hungry for more?

- Write status updates for both Henry II and Thomas Becket on the following days:
  - the day Henry became king
  - the day Becket became archbishop
  - after Henry asked Becket to change the Church courts
  - when Becket went to France
  - when Becket returned to England
  - when Becket excommunicated those who helped Henry.

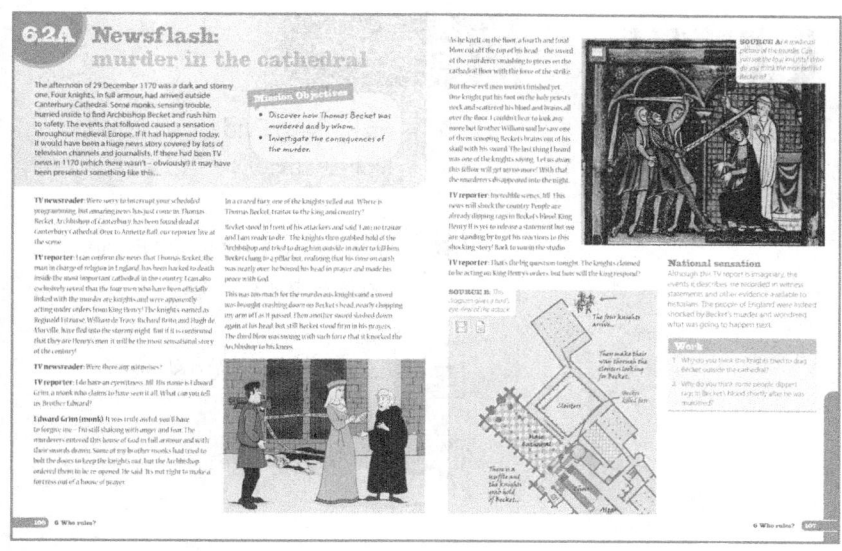

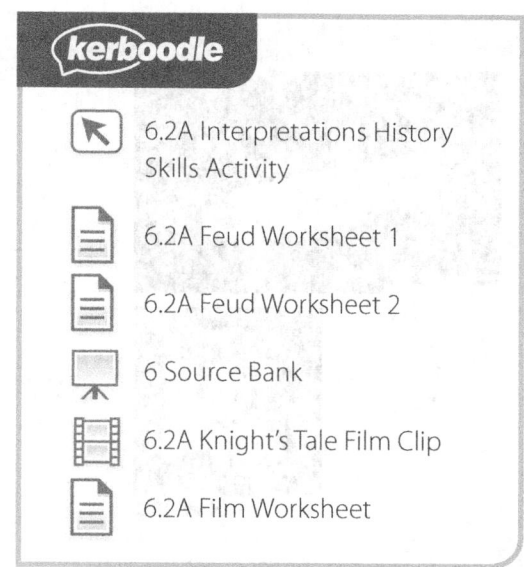

Invasion, Plague and Murder pages 106–107

## Lesson summary

Students will be able to explain the causes, events, and consequences of Thomas Becket's murder.

### What are the lesson outcomes?

**All** students will be able to describe the story of how Thomas Becket was murdered and by whom.

**Most** students will be able to explain the consequences of the murder.

**Some** students will be able to explain whether the Church or the Crown had the most power in medieval England.

## Starter suggestion

- Tell your neighbour: Students could tell their neighbour at least one reason why Henry II fell out with Thomas Becket, and at least one reason why Thomas Becket fell out with Henry II.

## Main learning suggestions and assessment

### What activities will take place?

**Task 1:** Students should read the information on pages 106–107, then complete 6.2A Interpretations History Skills Activity to judge who was most and least responsible for Becket's death. They should also watch 6.2A Knight's Tale Film Clip, which features the same knight from the film clip in the previous lesson. Completing 6.2A Film Worksheet will aid their understanding of the murder.

### How will students demonstrate their understanding?

**Task 2:** Students should complete 6.2A Feud Worksheet 1. They will create their own newspaper front page for the events of 29 December 1170. Students should use the success criteria on the worksheet to organize their work, making sure it has an eye-catching headline, a

chronological understanding of the events, and quotes from eyewitnesses. It could also have a picture of the crime scene and an interview with King Henry II explaining his reaction to the death of Becket. Students should also complete Work activity **1**.

**Task 3:** Students should use 6.2A Feud Worksheet 2 to create social networking pages for Henry and Becket, highlighting each person's job and describing them, their religion, their interests, and their friends.

## Plenary suggestions

- Today's headline: Students could create a headline story for this lesson. Encourage them to consider the names of key people and events in the story.

## Differentiation suggestions

### Support

- 6.2A Feud Worksheet 1 includes success criteria to help support lower ability students in creating their newspaper article.

- Encourage lower ability students to keep a graphic organizer to help them with reading long texts. For each paragraph ask them to draw an image summarizing what they have learned.

### Extension: Hungry for more?

- You could ask students to consider why the knights tried to drag Becket outside the cathedral. Why do they think some people dipped rags in Becket's blood shortly after he was murdered?

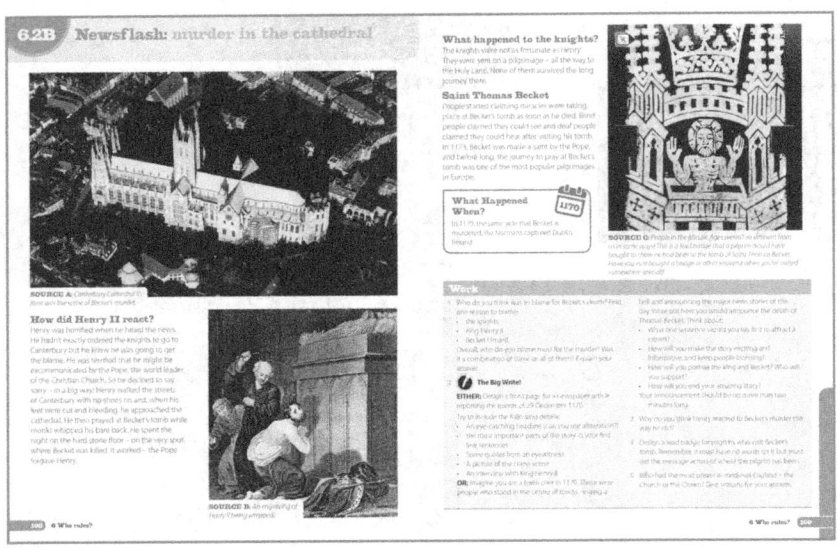

Invasion, Plague and Murder pages 108–109

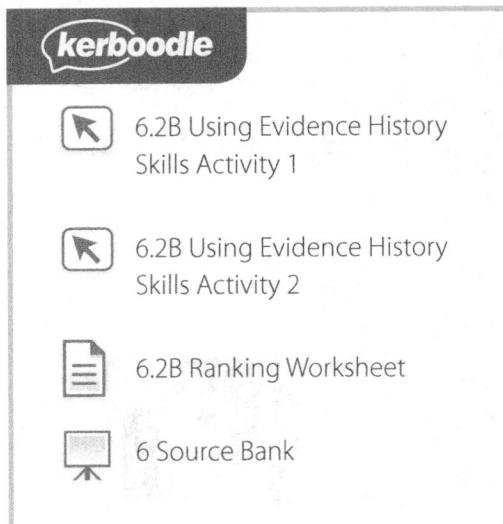

## Lesson summary
Students will be able to explain the causes, events, and consequences of Thomas Becket's murder.

### What are the lesson outcomes?
**All** students will be able to describe the story of how Thomas Becket was murdered and by whom.

**Most** students will be able to explain the consequences of the murder.

**Some** students will be able to explain whether the Church or the Crown had the most power in medieval England.

## Starter suggestion
- Key questions: Ask students to consider three key questions to unlock the lesson, giving one reason for each:
  - Why did Henry II fall out with Thomas Becket?
  - Why did Thomas Becket fall out with Henry II?
  - Why did the knights go to kill Thomas Becket?

## Main learning suggestions and assessment
### What activities will take place?
**Task 1:** Students should read the information on pages 108–109 and complete 6.2B Using Evidence History Skills Activity 1, where they must consider whether they think Henry regretted what happened to Thomas Becket.

### How will students demonstrate their understanding?
**Task 2:** Students should complete 6.2B Ranking Worksheet. In this worksheet, students must decide who was most to blame for Becket's death – Becket himself, King Henry or the knights – and explain their reasoning.

**Task 3:** Students could also complete 6.2B Using Evidence History Skills Activity 2, which encourages them to consider the importance of a pilgrim badge.

## Plenary suggestions
- Washing line: Identify a place in the classroom where students can display their ideas under the following headings: Causes; Events; Consequences. Students should work in teams to come up with a sticky note to go in each area, using their knowledge from this lesson.

## Differentiation suggestions
### Support
- Some students may find the meaning of the Wise Up Words in this lesson difficult to grasp. Ensure they understand what 'excommunicate' means and the significance being excommiunicated would have had. You may wish to direct their attention to the glossary at the back of the *Student Book*.

### Extension: Hungry for more?
- Students could design their own pilgrim badge for Thomas Becket. Remind students that they cannot use words. They must get the message across regarding where the pilgrim has been and why they chose to visit Thomas Becket.

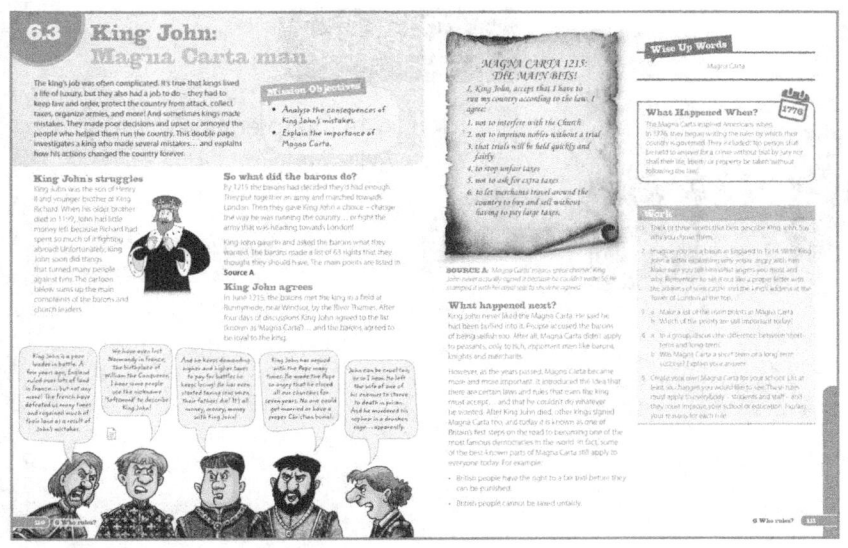

Invasion, Plague and Murder pages 110–111

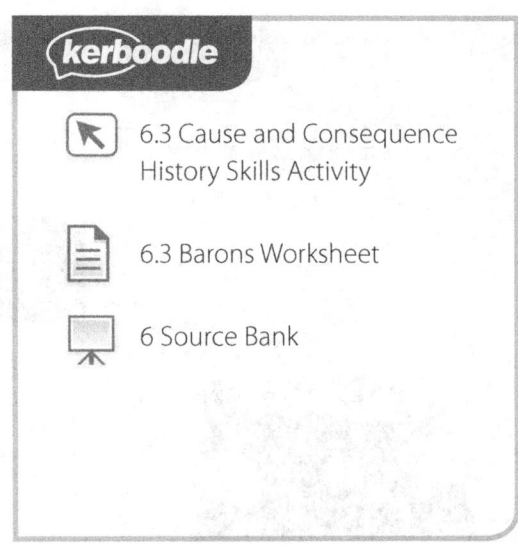

6.3 Cause and Consequence History Skills Activity

6.3 Barons Worksheet

6 Source Bank

## Lesson summary

Students will develop an understanding of how the mistakes King John made led to the creation of the Magna Carta and the effect it still has on life today.

### What are the lesson outcomes?

**All** students will be able to describe the mistakes made by King John that upset the barons.

**Most** students will be able to explain why the Magna Carta was created.

**Some** students will be able to understand the effects the Magna Carta still has in the world today.

## Starter suggestion

- How is our school run?: Ask students to work with a partner to come up with the five most important rules in the school. Encourage them to explain why these rules are in place. For example, do they make the school safer? Ask the students if they agree with these rules, and if they would change them, given the chance. To provide a link to this lesson, explain to students that in medieval England there were rules and decisions made by the king that the barons didn't agree with.

## Main learning suggestions and assessment

### What activities will take place?

**Task 1:** Students should read the information on pages 110–111 and complete 6.3 Cause and Consequence History Skills Activity to decide what they think was the biggest mistake made by King John.

### How will students demonstrate their understanding?

**Task 2:** Students should imagine that they are barons in England in 1214. They should write a letter to King John explaining why they are angry with him. They can use the framework on 6.3 Barons Worksheet to set out their letter.

**Task 3:** Students should work in groups of four. They should spend ten minutes creating their own version of the Magna Carta for their school, listing at least six changes they would like to see. Remind them that these rules must apply to both students and staff, and that they must improve their school or education. This activity works best with students writing their ideas on A3 sheets of paper, which can then be displayed in the classroom for the entire class to see. Each group should nominate one person to act as spokesperson to explain their ideas. Open up a class discussion to decide on the six best new rules for their school.

## Plenary suggestions

- Just a minute!: Students could have one minute each to tell the class or a partner everything they have learned about the Magna Carta and King John in this lesson.

## Differentiation suggestions

### Support

- 6.3 Barons Worksheet includes sentence starters to help lower ability students to write their letter.

### Extension: Hungry for more?

- Students could carry out research to find out where the Magna Carta is currently located. Ask them to consider why sources like the Magna Carta are important to modern historians.

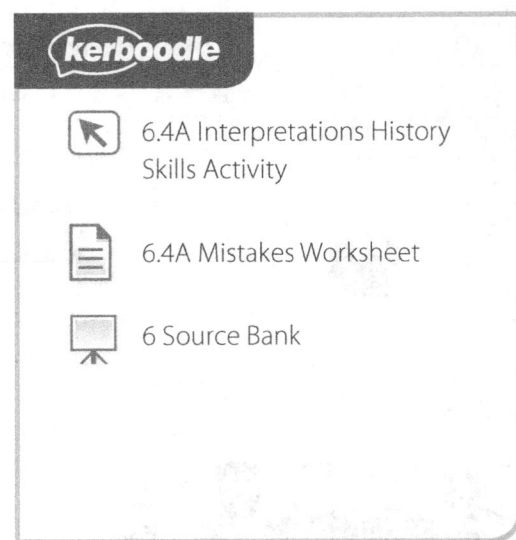

Invasion, Plague and Murder pages 112–113

## Lesson summary

Students will develop an understanding of how the mistakes made by King Henry III led to the creation of Parliament and the effect of this on our lives today. Students should be able to develop an understanding of the systems in place to run the country.

### What are the lesson outcomes?

**All** students will be able to identify at least three mistakes made by King Henry III.

**Most** students will be able to explain how Henry's mistakes led to the creation of Parliament.

**Some** students will be able to explain what the most important thing about de Montfort's Parliament was.

## Starter suggestion

● How is our country run?: Ask students if they know how the UK is run today and how power is shared out. Students should be able to explain the role of the Queen and Parliament. Encourage students to consider why we have a Parliament. Ask students if they know when the monarch began to share power with Parliament.

## Main learning suggestions and assessment

### What activities will take place?

**Task 1:** Students should read the information on pages 112–113 and complete Work activity **1**.

### How will students demonstrate their understanding?

**Task 2:** Students should complete 6.4A Interpretations History Skills Activity to judge the reasons for Henry's unpopularity with the barons. They should then complete Work activity **2**.

**Task 3:** Students should complete 6.4A Mistakes Worksheet, ranking the severity of Henry's mistakes.

## Plenary suggestions

● Exit note: Students should copy and complete the sentence: 'Before this lesson I could already… Now I can also…'

## Differentiation suggestions

### Support

● You may wish to draw students' attention to the glossary at the back of the *Student Book* to help them understand the political terms used in this lesson. These are also marked out as Wise Up Words.

### Extension: Hungry for more?

● Higher ability students could choose one of the barons' complaints on page 112 and research it in more detail to find out exactly what it was that Henry III did and how events unfolded.

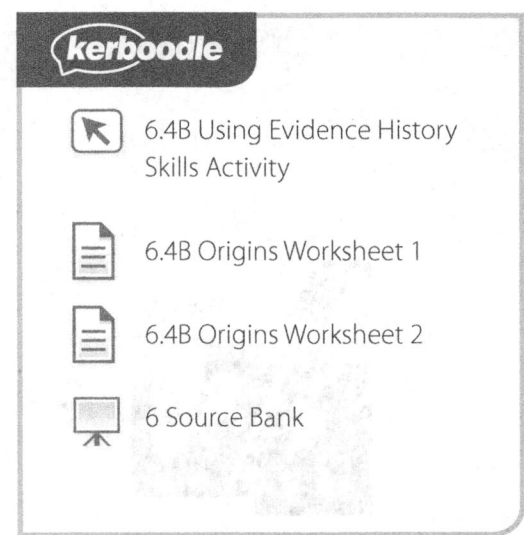

Invasion, Plague and Murder pages 114–115

## Lesson summary

Students will develop an understanding of how the mistakes made by King Henry III led to the creation of Parliament and the effect of this on our lives today. Students should be able to develop an understanding of the systems in place to run the country.

### What are the lesson outcomes?

**All** students will be able to identify at least three mistakes made by King Henry III.

**Most** students will be able to explain how Henry's mistakes led to the creation of Parliament.

**Some** students will be able to explain what the most important thing about de Montfort's Parliament was.

## Starter suggestion

- Think, pair, share: Students could think of one fact they have learned about Parliament in the Middle Ages. Ask them to go into pairs and discuss their ideas, and then share their ideas with the rest of the class.

## Main learning suggestions and assessment

### What activities will take place?

**Task 1:** Students should read the information on pages 114–115 and then complete 6.4B Using Evidence History Skills Activity, which encourages them to analyse **Source B** in detail.

### How will students demonstrate their understanding?

**Task 2:** Students should complete Work activities **1** to **5**. They can also complete 6.4B Origins Worksheet 1, comparing Parliament in 1350 with today's Parliament, and 6.4B Origins Worksheet 2, which assesses their understanding of de Montfort's Parliament.

## Plenary suggestions

- Learning triangle: Students could identify three things that they have learned in this lesson and two questions that they would like to ask another student or research further.

## Differentiation suggestions

### Support

- In order to help students complete 6.4B Origins Worksheet 1, it could be useful to conduct a 'hands up' exercise, where students share what they know about today's Parliament. This information could be recorded in a spider diagram on the board for students to refer to when making comparisons.

### Extension: Hungry for more?

- Students could create their own leaflets about the history of the Houses of Parliament. They could research when the Palace of Westminster was first built, which famous architects were involved in designing it, and how it has changed and developed. They could list the 'top five' events in its history, and identify how its use has changed from the Middle Ages to today.

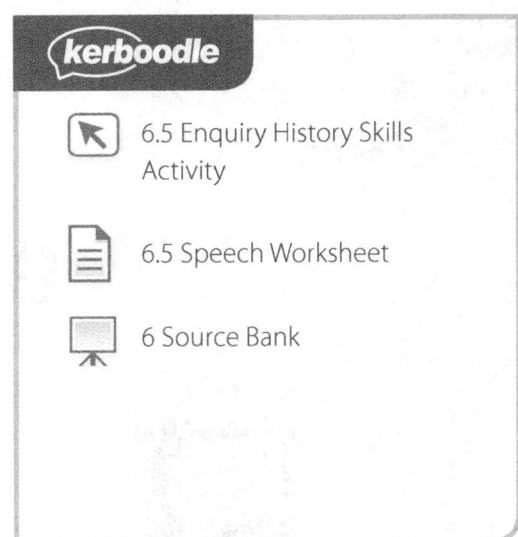

Invasion, Plague and Murder pages 116–117

## Lesson summary
Students will be able to identify the causes of the Peasants' Revolt.

### What are the lesson outcomes?
**All** students will be able to describe what the Peasants' Revolt was.

**Most** students will be able describe at least one reason why the poorest people in England argued with the king.

**Some** students will be able to explain at least one reason why the poorest people in England argued with the king.

## Starter suggestion
● Goal setting: Students could set themselves two targets for this lesson. Encourage them to set one target based around knowledge and one based on learning a skill.

## Main learning suggestions and assessment

### What activities will take place?
**Task 1:** Students should read the information on pages 116–117 and complete 6.5 Enquiry History Skills to debate the causes of the Peasants' Revolt.

**Task 2:** Students should complete Work activity **1**.

### How will students demonstrate their understanding?
**Task 3:** Students should create a campaign to convince people in their medieval village to join the Peasants' Revolt and march to London. They should create a speech, a poster, and slogans for their campaign. 6.5 Speech Worksheet includes sentence starters to help students organize their speeches.

## Plenary suggestions
● Muddiest point: Students could work in pairs or in small groups to identify any misconceptions that they have and try to solve them. Any that cannot be solved should be referred to the class, and as a last resort to the teacher.

## Differentiation suggestions

### Support
● 6.5 Speech Worksheet includes sentence starters to help students organize their speeches.

### Extension: Hungry for more?
● Ask students if they can think of any protests that have taken place recently, either in the UK or in other countries. Do they know what the protest was about?

Invasion, Plague and Murder pages 118–119

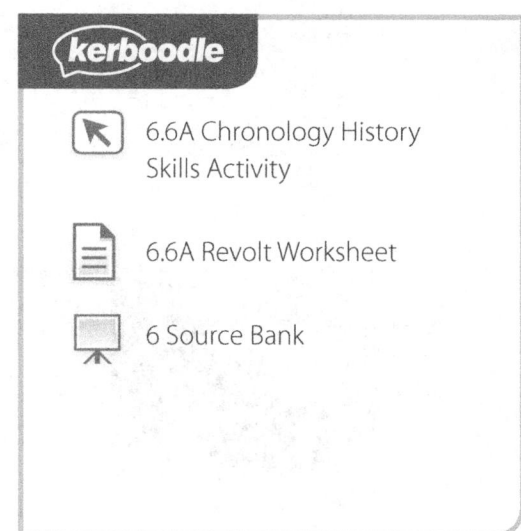

6.6A Chronology History Skills Activity

6.6A Revolt Worksheet

6 Source Bank

## Lesson summary

Students will be able to identify the causes and events of the Peasants' Revolt.

### What are the lesson outcomes?

**All** students will be able to describe at least one reason why the poorest people in England argued with the king.

**Most** students will be able to describe the causes, events, and consequences of the Peasant's Revolt.

**Some** students will be able to explain the causes, events, and consequences of the Peasants' Revolt.

## Starter suggestion

- Different shoes: Ask students to imagine that they are peasants in medieval England. Can they tell their neighbours what they are so angry about? Compile a class list of reasons for the peasants' anger.

## Main learning suggestions and assessment

### What activities will take place?

**Task 1:** Students should read the information on pages 118–119 and complete 6.6A Chronology History Skills Activity to order the events of the Peasants' Revolt.

### How will students demonstrate their understanding?

**Task 2:** Students should complete 6.6A Revolt Worksheet, which involves analysing what options Wat Tyler had during the revolt and encourages students to consider which option they would have chosen.

## Plenary suggestions

- One more thing: Students could copy and complete the following sentence: 'One thing I have learned is…'

## Differentiation suggestions

### Support

- You could assign roles (including a narrator) and ask students to read through the cartoon in the *Student Book* out loud. They could even act it out! This will help the story stay in their minds so students will become more familiar with the chronological sequence of events.

### Extension: Hungry for more?

- Students could pick one person from pages 118–119 and write their diary entry for the night the king has asked for the Poll Tax. Students should identify and explain why they are so upset. Encourage them to develop the use of emotive language to help their writing.

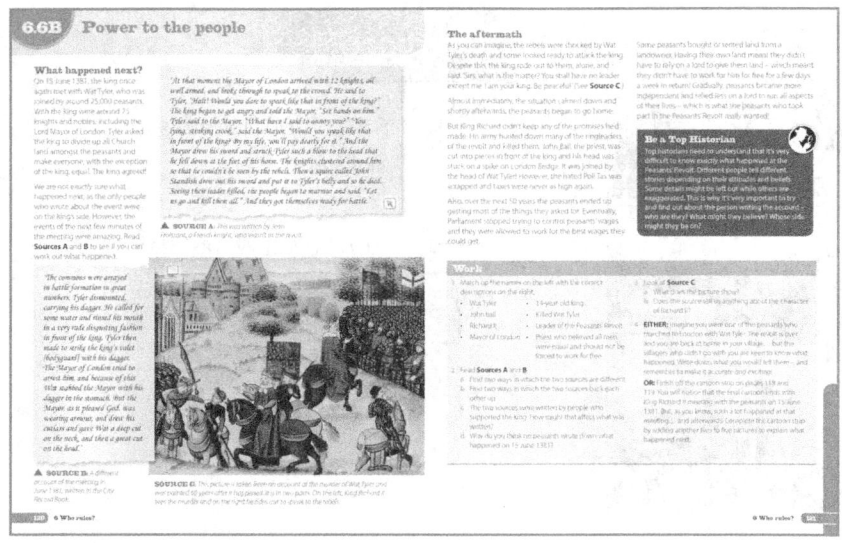

Invasion, Plague and Murder pages 120–121

6.6B Using Evidence History Skills Activity

6.6B Cause and Consequence History Skills Activity

6.6B Accounts Worksheet

6 Source Bank

6.6B Executioner Film Clip

6.6B Film Worksheet

## Lesson summary

Students will be able to identify the events and consequences of the Peasants' Revolt.

### What are the lesson outcomes?

**All** students will be able to describe at least one reason why the poorest people in England argued with the king.

**Most** students will be able to describe the causes, events, and consequences of the Peasant's Revolt.

**Some** students will be able to explain the causes, events, and consequences of the Peasants' Revolt.

## Starter suggestion

- Hangman!: Students could play hangman with the names of key people from the story of the Peasants' Revolt. They could choose from: Wat Tyler; John Ball; Richard II; the Mayor of London. Students can only guess the correct answer if they can describe the person's role.

## Main learning suggestions and assessment

### What activities will take place?

**Task 1:** Students should read the information on pages 120–121 and complete Work activities **1** to **3**. They should then complete 6.6B Accounts Worksheet, which encourages them to consider different interpretations in accounts of the death of Wat Tyler. They should also watch and complete the film worksheet for 6.6B Executioner Film Clip, where the hangman discusses the outcome of the Revolt.

### How will students demonstrate their understanding?

**Task 2:** Students should complete 6.6B Using Evidence History Skills Activity and 6.6B Cause and Consequence History Skills Activity.

**Task 3:** Students should create either an account of the Peasants' Revolt or complete the cartoon strip found on pages 118 and 119 of the *Student Book*.

## Plenary suggestions

- Students should be able to summarize their knowledge about this topic. This activity works well as a class discussion with mini whiteboards, allowing all students the chance to participate. The tasks are:
  - Give three reasons why the peasants became so angry in 1831.
  - Describe and explain how the peasants behaved on the way to London.
  - State how the revolt ended for Wat Tyler, John Ball, and the king.
  - Can you explain exactly what happened on 15 June 1381? Can anyone?

## Differentiation suggestions

### Support

- The two textual sources in this lesson are quite long, so you might want to analyse them in small chunks, or highlight key words or phrases.

### Extension: Hungry for more?

- Students could write an obituary for Wat Tyler. Explain that an obituary describes the recent death of a person, and includes an account of important events in the person's life. The obituary should be no longer than 250 words.

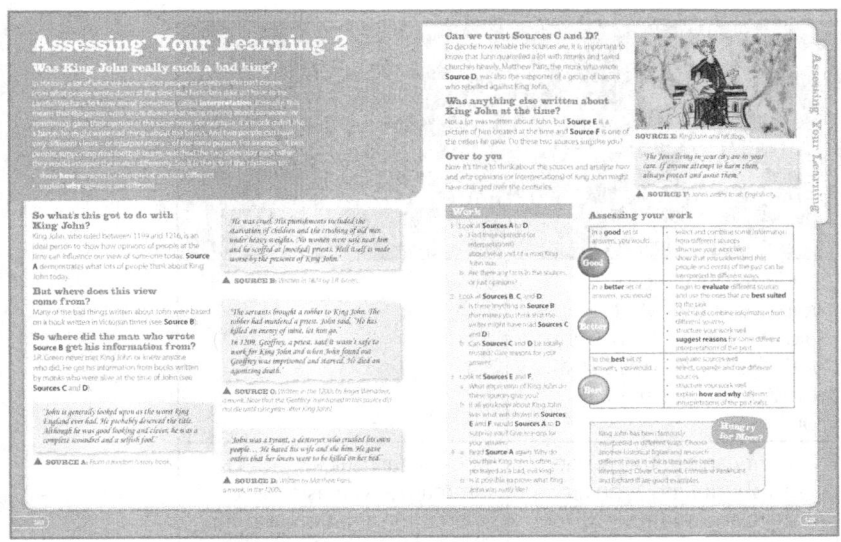

Invasion, Plague and Murder, Student Book pages 122–123

## Assessment in the *Student Book*

In this assessment task, students are asked to complete a series of source analysis questions in order to form an opinion on King John and assess the reliability of historical sources. 'Interpretations' is a key history skill mentioned in the 2014 National Curriculum. As such, this assessent encourages students to consider why different opinions of historical figures or events might exist.

In the *Student Book* (and on the supporting worksheets), you'll find guidance on success criteria that you can use to help your students understand what their work should include. You could ask them to use these criteria for self- or peer-assessment once they've completed the task.

## Chapter 6 Who rules? task

Think about the sources presented in the *Student Book* and analyse *how* and *why* opinions (or interpretations) of King John might have changed over the centuries.

Why do you think King John is often portrayed as a bad, evil king?

Is it possible to prove what King John was *really* like?

### Student Book
- Assessment task
- Student 'Assessing your work' grid

### kerboodle

Assessment Task Presentation 2

Assessment Worksheet 2

Success Criteria Teacher Grid 2

### Teacher Handbook
- Success Criteria Teacher Grid 2

> **Hungry for More?**
>
> King John has been famously interpreted in different ways. Choose another historical figure and research different ways in which they have been interpreted. Oliver Cromwell, Emmeline Pankhurst and Richard III are good examples.

## Assessing your work

| In a **good** response, you would… | <ul><li>select and combine some information from different sources</li><li>structure your work well</li><li>show that you understand that people and events of the past can be interpreted in different ways.</li></ul> |
|---|---|
| In a **better** response, you would… | <ul><li>begin to **evaluate** different sources and use the ones that are **best suited** to the task</li><li>select and combine information from different sources</li><li>structure your work well</li><li>**suggest reasons** for some different interpretations of the past.</li></ul> |
| **In the best** response, you would… | <ul><li>evaluate sources well</li><li>select, organize and use different sources</li><li>structure your work well</li><li>explain [bold] how and why [end bold] different interpretations of the past exist.</li></ul> |

## Success criteria teacher grid

| Assessment criteria | Beginning/ Developing | Securing | Extending |
|---|---|---|---|
| | Current NC Level 3/4 | Current NC Level 5/6 | Current NC Level 7/8 |
| | GCSE Grade Indicator E/D | GCSE Grade Indicator C/B | GCSE Grade Indicator A/A* |
| **Remembering** | Student can list some opinions about what people said about King John | Student can list some opinions about what people said about King John, using both their own words and some quotes from the sources | |
| **Understanding** | Student demonstrates that they know that people have different opinions about King John | Student can see that some views about King John are positive and some views are negative<br><br>Student knows that the statements about King John are mainly interpretations, rather than facts | Student can quickly summarize what is meant by an 'interpretation' and can classify each source in the spread into ones that show King John in a positive or a negative way |
| **Applying** | Students can select some sources that they might use to answer a particular question | Student can select and combine information from different sources to produce structured work | Students can use their knowledge of the sources to construct answers to different questions |
| **Analyzing** | Student can categorise the sources into those that support King John and those that don't | Student can suggest reasons why some of the people in the sources might have portrayed King John as a bad king | Student can critically consider each source when considering its origin, nature and purpose |
| **Evaluating** | Student can describe how a source is portraying King John | Student can explain how different interpretations of King John have arisen over time | Student can explain how and why different interpretations of King John have arisen or been constructed |
| **Creating** | | | Student produces a coherent, supported and wide-ranging analysis of the range of interpretations and begin to ask their own questions about the sources |

# Overview:
# Chapter 7 Health and medicine

## Helping you deliver KS3 History National Curriculum

'The Black Death and its social and economic impact' is specifically mentioned in the 2014 National Curriculum. Each spread asks students to rigorously analyse this significant event in British (and world) history. Students will be required to examine historical concepts such as continuity and change, and cause and consequence. They will also need to interrogate sources accurately in order to find answers and to support their ideas and writing.

### The Big Picture

## Why are we teaching 'Health and medicine'?

The catastrophe that was the Black Death is the headline story of health and medicine in the Middle Ages and provides a dramatic entry to the subject area. By portraying the arrival of the plague through the eyes of medieval villagers, students can both identify the symptoms and observe the impact of the disease on medieval village life.

Once the horror of the plague has been established, the modern understanding of the biology behind it is covered. The gruesome details glue students to the page and provide an ideal opportunity to create curriculum links with the Science department. The spread of the Black Death is also covered in this chapter. Students are encouraged to dissect contemporary sources to chart the reach of the plague across the world.

Obviously, the Black Death was not the only threat to life in the Middle Ages. Students tend to believe that modern medical beliefs (such as knowledge of

## Skills and processes covered in this chapter

| | | 7.1A | 7.1B | 7.2 | 7.3A | 7.3B | 7.4 |
|---|---|---|---|---|---|---|---|
| **History Skills** | Historical enquiry | ✓ | ✓ | ✓ | ✓ | ✓ | ✓ |
| | Using evidence and source work | | ✓ | ✓ | ✓ | ✓ | |
| | Chronological understanding | | | | | | ✓ |
| | Understanding cultural, ethnic and religious diversity | | | | | ✓ | |
| | Change and continuity | | | | ✓ | ✓ | ✓ |
| | Cause and consequence | ✓ | ✓ | ✓ | | | |
| | Significance | | | | | ✓ | |
| | Interpretations | | | | | ✓ | |
| | Making links/connections | ✓ | ✓ | ✓ | | | |
| | Explores similarities and differences | | | | | | ✓ |
| **Literacy and Numeracy** | Key words identified/deployed | ✓ | ✓ | ✓ | ✓ | ✓ | ✓ |
| | Extended writing | | ✓ | ✓ | | | |
| | Encourages reading for meaning | ✓ | | | | ✓ | |
| | Focuses on structuring writing | ✓ | | | | | |
| | Asks students to use writing to explore and develop ideas | ✓ | ✓ | ✓ | ✓ | ✓ | ✓ |
| | Learn through talk/discussion | ✓ | ✓ | ✓ | | | |
| | Numeracy opportunities | | | | | | ✓ |
| **Activity types** | Creative task | ✓ | ✓ | ✓ | ✓ | | |
| | Emphasizes role of individual | | | | ✓ | | |
| | Group work | | | | | ✓ | ✓ |
| | Independent research | ✓ | | ✓ | | | ✓ |
| | Develops study skills | | | | | | ✓ |

germs) and techniques have always existed and are amazed to conceive of a world without doctors and hospitals. The spreads towards the end of the chapter covering blood, bodily functions, excreta, and drilling holes in skulls instantly grab students' attention.

The final spread looks at the health of the most privileged members of medieval society – the monarchs. The timeline not only provides an overall chronology of England's kings between 1066 and 1509, it also enables the horrific, hilarious, unbelievable (and often mundane) ends of their lives to be recounted. Students undertake some statistical analysis of the deaths – requiring them to draw on their numeracy skills – and this results in a breakdown of the most prevalent 'king killers' of the Middle Ages.

### Ideas for enrichment

You could set a research project that looks at modern epidemics, such as the Spanish 'flu of 1919, foot-and-mouth disease in Britain in the 21st century, avian influenza, and the AIDS pandemic in modern Africa. This would provide excellent opportunities for links with the Science department.

We would also strongly recommend sourcing the 2013 BBC series from Lucy Worsley – *Fit to Rule: How Royal Illness Changed History*. Whilst this series focuses on the Tudor period and beyond, it is still a brilliant series and relates very well to the spread in the chapter 'Was it dangerous to be the king?'.

## Lesson sequence

| Lesson title | NC references | Objectives | Outcomes |
|---|---|---|---|
| 7.1A We're all going to die! pp124–125 <br><br> 7.1B We're all going to die! pp126–127 | The Black Death and its social and economic impact | • Define the main symptoms of the Black Death. <br> • Discover what people thought caused the disease at the time and how they tried to protect against it. <br> • Create a Black Death warning leaflet. | **All** students will be able to describe the causes and symptoms of Black Death. <br> **Most** students will be able to describe the causes, symptoms, and methods used to try and cure Black Death. <br> **Some** students will be able to explain the causes, symptoms, and methods used to try and cure Black Death. |
| 7.2 How deadly was Black Death? pp128–129 | The Black Death and its social and economic impact | • Discover how the plague spread throughout the world. <br> • Analyse the spread of the disease. | **All** students will be able to describe the spread of Black Death. <br> **Most** students will be able to describe the spread and consequences of Black Death. <br> **Some** students will be able to explain the spread and consequences of Black Death. |
| 7.3A Who healed the sick in the Middle Ages? pp130–131 <br><br> 7.3B Who healed the sick in the Middle Ages? pp132–133 | Society, economy and culture 1066–1509 | • Investigate the theories behind different treatments in the Middle Ages. <br> • Evaluate ways in which doctors diagnose illness in the Middle Ages. | **All** students will be able to describe how some illnesses were treated in the Middle Ages. <br> **Most** students will be able to evaluate the ways in which doctors diagnosed illnesses in the Middle Ages. <br> **Some** students will be able to use sources to support their writing. |
| 7.4 Was it dangerous to be the king? pp134–135 | Society, economy and culture 1066–1509 | • Develop an opinion – do you think England's kings were a particularly healthy bunch? | **All** students will be able to categorize the deaths of English kings. <br> **Most** students will be able to identify whether they think English kings were healthy or not. <br> **Some** students will be able to explain their opinions using historical examples. |
| Assessing Your Learning 3 pp136–137 | The Black Death and its social and economic impact | • Interrogate sources in order to assess the impact of Black Death on the medieval world. | **Good:** Students will identify and select relevant information from sources. <br> **Better:** Students will include quotations and use correct historical terms and dates. <br> **Best:** Students will explain the effects of Black Death and judge which were more important. |

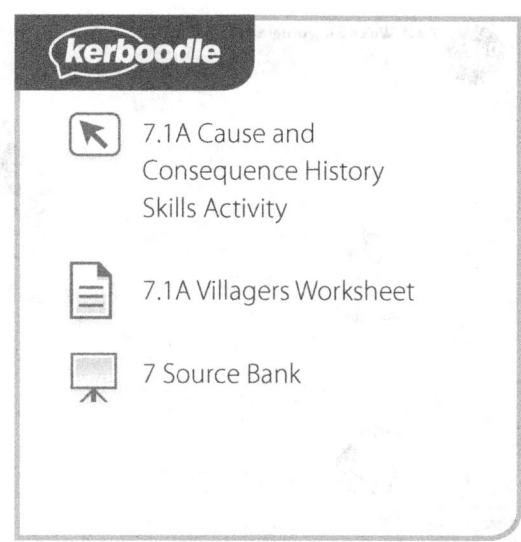

Invasion, Plague and Murder pages 124–125

## Lesson summary

Students will complete a research task to find out about the symptoms of Black Death.

### What are the lesson outcomes?

**All** students will be able to describe the causes and symptoms of Black Death.

**Most** students will be able to describe the causes, symptoms, and methods used to try and cure Black Death.

**Some** students will be able to explain the causes, symptoms, and methods used to try and cure Black Death.

## Starter suggestion

- You could ask students, individually or in pairs, to use sticky notes to identify one thing that they already know and one thing that they would like to know about this topic. For example: 'I know that Black Death killed lots of people during the Middle Ages'; 'I want to know what caused Black Death to spread'.

## Main learning suggestions and assessment

### What activities will take place?

**Task 1:** Students should read the information on pages 124–125 and complete Work activities **1** to **3**. Students should complete 7.1A Cause and Consequence History Skills Activity, filling the gaps in a passage of text to gain a greater understanding of the symptoms and causes of Black Death.

### How will students demonstrate their understanding?

**Task 2:** Students should complete 7.1A Villagers Worksheet to understand the symptoms of Black Death. This involves reading for meaning to answer questions on the villagers'

accounts of the start of Black Death and writing a diary entry for a family who lived through Black Death.

## Plenary suggestions

- High five!: Students could identify five symptoms of the Black Death that they have learned about during this lesson.

## Differentiation suggestions

### Support

- In order to get students to engage with the characters' accounts and draw out the key facts, create a bullet point list for each character on the board. Symptoms and other key points can be recorded for reference throughout the lesson.

### Extension: Hungry for more?

- Students could create a diary for an imaginary family who lived through Black Death in their town. They could write entries for one week, showing how life changed after Black Death arrived in the town.

- Encourage higher ability students to use evidence from the sources available to support their writing.

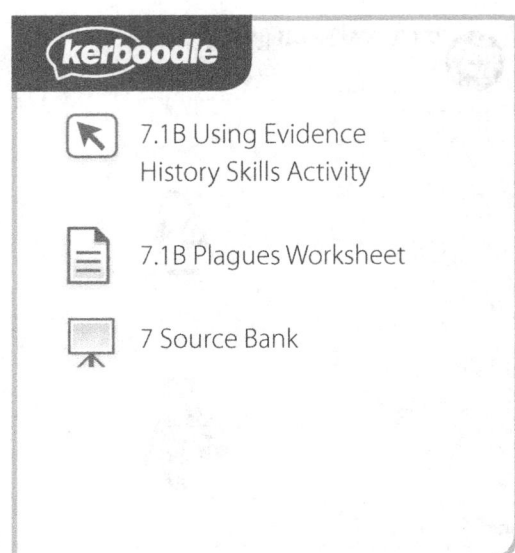

Invasion, Plague and Murder pages 126–127

## Lesson summary

Students will complete a research task to find out about the symptoms of Black Death.

### What are the lesson outcomes?

**All** students will be able to describe the causes and symptoms of the Black Death.

**Most** students will be able to describe the causes, symptoms, and methods used to try and cure Black Death.

**Some** students will be able to explain the causes, symptoms, and methods used to try and cure Black Death.

## Starter suggestion

- Ask students, either individually or in pairs, to look back at the sticky note questions they came up with at the start of the last lesson. Can they answer any of these questions now? Encourage them to record their answers to their questions on the post-it notes.

## Main learning suggestions and assessment

### What activities will take place?

**Task 1:** Students should read the information on pages 126–127 and complete Work tasks **1** and **2**.

**Task 2:** Complete 7.1B Using Evidence History Skills Activity with the class; this activity encourages students to consider the reasons for various medieval attitudes and reactions to Black Death.

### How will students demonstrate their understanding?

**Task 3:** Students can either complete Work activity **3** or use 7.1B Plagues Worksheet to write a letter imagining that they are the king's royal physician. They need to imagine that they have been asked to research possible causes of Black Death, identify the symptoms of the disease, and study cures for it. They need to write their findings in a letter and present it to the king.

## Plenary suggestions

- Students could write one more sticky note to complete the sentence 'During this lesson I have learned …'. You may wish to get students to share their thoughts with each other or the whole class.

## Differentiation suggestions

### Support

- 7.1B Plagues Worksheet includes sentence starters to help support lower ability students.

### Extension: Hungry for more?

- Students could design a poster displaying the most bizarre medieval cure for Black Death.

# 7.2 How deadly was Black Death?

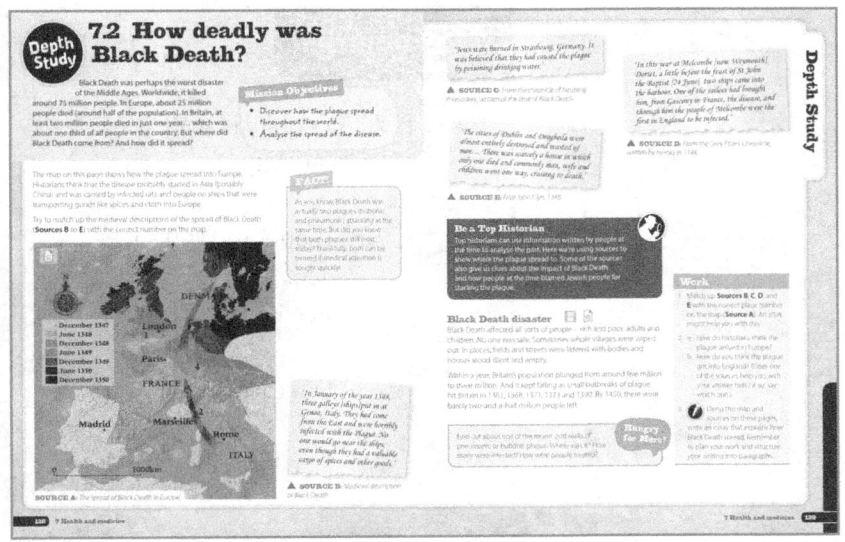

Invasion, Plague and Murder pages 128–129

## Lesson summary

Students will complete a research task about the ways in which the plague spread through Europe.

### What are the lesson outcomes?

**All** students will be able to describe the spread of Black Death.

**Most** students will be able to describe the spread and consequences of Black Death.

**Some** students will be able to explain the spread and consequences of Black Death.

## Starter suggestion

●  Hangman: Students could use the keywords from last lesson to complete a game of hangman. The key words are: bubonic; pneumonic; plague.

## Main learning suggestions and assessment

### What activities will take place?

**Task 1:** Students should read the information on pages 128–129 and complete 7.2 Spread Worksheet. Students are encouraged to use sources to support their writing. This worksheet includes sentence starters.

**Task 2:** Students should complete Work activity **1** using the map on 7.2 Spread Worksheet. They should write each source letter in the correct area of the map according to the places mentioned in the source.

**Task 3:** Watch 7.2 Plague Film Clips 1 and 2 with the class. In the first clip, an archer describes how he saw Black Death spread through Europe, and in the second, he outlines some of the cures people tried. The accompanying film worksheet encourages students to consolidate their learning.

## kerboodle

- ▶ 7.2 Using Evidence History Skills Activity 1
- ▶ 7.2 Using Evidence History Skills Activity 2
- 7.2 Spread Worksheet
- 7 Source Bank
- 7.2 Plague Film Clip 1
- 7.2 Plague Film Clip 2
- 7.2 Film Worksheet

### How will students demonstrate their understanding?

**Task 4:** Students should complete 7.2 Using Evidence History Skills Activities 1 and 2 to gain a greater understanding of how Black Death changed life in Britain.

**Task 5:** Students should create an extended piece of writing entitled 'How Black Death spread.'

## Plenary suggestions

● Exit note: Students could complete the following sentences: 'Before this lesson I could already …'; 'Now I can also …'.

## Differentiation suggestions

### Support

● Worksheet 7.2 Spread Worksheet includes sentence starters to help support lower ability students.

### Extension: Hungry for more?

● Students could carry out some research into a recent outbreak of pneumonic or bubonic plague. Where was it? How many people were infected? How many were treated? What treatment did they receive?

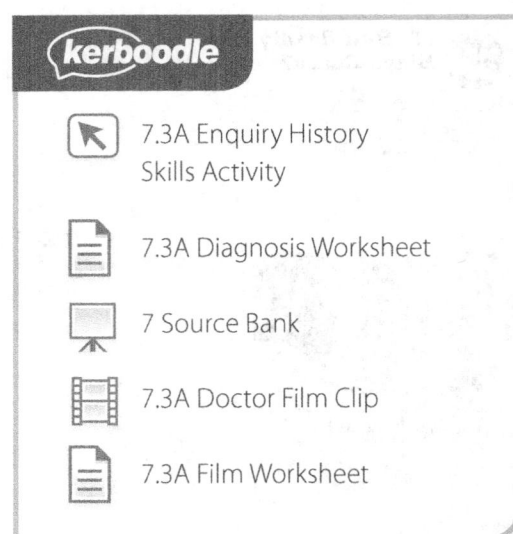

Invasion, Plague and Murder pages 130–131

## Lesson summary

Students should develop an understanding of how illnesses in the Middle Ages were diagnosed and treated.

### What are the lesson outcomes?

**All** students will be able to describe how some illnesses were treated in the Middle Ages.

**Most** students will be able to evaluate the ways in which doctors diagnosed illnesses in the Middle Ages.

**Some** students will be able to use sources to support their writing.

## Starter suggestion

- Student as the teacher!: Ask students to look at the key words on page 131. Challenge them to do some research and then teach a partner what one of these words means.

## Main learning suggestions and assessment

### What activities will take place?

**Task 1:** Students should read the information on pages 130–131 and complete 7.3A Enquiry History Skills Activity to gain a greater understanding of the skills required of a medieval doctor.

### How will students demonstrate their understanding?

**Task 2:** Students should complete the activities on 7.3A Diagnosis Worksheet.

## Plenary suggestions

- Watch 7.3A Doctor Film Clip with the class. Then, ask students to write and role-play their own script between a doctor and a patient, using the information

they've learned in the lesson. 7.3A Film Worksheet could be set as homework.

## Differentiation suggestions

### Support

- As there are quite a few new and difficult words in this topic, you may wish to ask students to look up the Wise Up Words in a dictionary or the glossary in the back of the *Student Book*. You should then go over the correct definitions as a class before explaining how they relate to medieval medical thinking.

### Extension: Hungry for more?

- Encourage higher ability students to use evidence from sources to support their writing on Worksheet 7.3A Diagnosis Worksheet.

- Ask students to read **Source B**. They could write an application for the job of a medieval doctor. Ask them to consider the skills and qualifications that they would need.

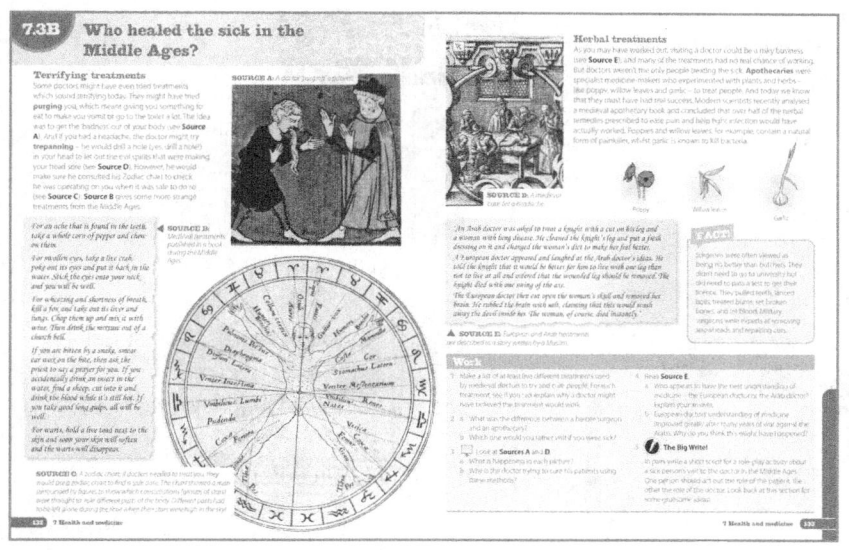

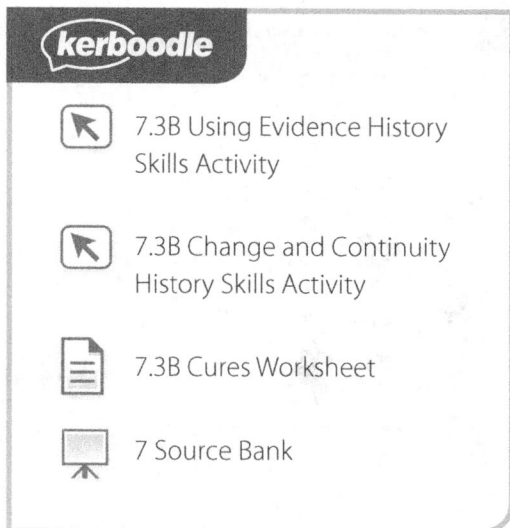

Invasion, Plague and Murder pages 132–133

## Lesson summary

Students should develop an understanding of how illnesses in the Middle Ages were diagnosed and treated.

### What are the lesson outcomes?

**All** students will be able to describe how some illnesses were treated in the Middle Ages.

**Most** students will be able to evaluate the ways in which doctors diagnosed illnesses in the Middle Ages.

**Some** students will be able to use sources to support their writing.

## Starter suggestion

- 3, 5, 7: Students could identify three things that they already know about medieval cures. They could then share their ideas in pairs and come up with five things that they know about medieval cures. Finally they could share their ideas in a group and come up with the top seven things that they know about medieval cures. This should feedback into a class discussion

## Main learning suggestions and assessment

### What activities will take place?

**Task 1:** Students should read the information on pages 132–133 and complete 7.3B Using Evidence History Skills Activity and 7.3B Change and Continuity History Skills Activity to gain a greater understanding of medieval and modern cures.

**Task 2:** Students should complete the activities on 7.3B Cures Worksheet. This worksheet asks students to look at medieval cures and complete investigation questions on the sources across this spread.

### How will students demonstrate their understanding?

**Task 3:** Students should complete Work activities **1** to **5** on page 133. Students are asked to investigate **Sources D** and **E** on the spread to understand what trepanning was, and how Western and Middle Eastern medicine differed in the Middle Ages.

## Plenary suggestions

- Learning triangle: Students could identify three things that they have learned about medieval medicines and two questions that they would like to research or have answered.

## Differentiation suggestions

### Support

- You may wish to recap the ideas covered in the last lesson by replaying 7.3A Doctor Film Clip at the beginning of this lesson.

### Extension: Hungry for more?

- Students could design their own TV advert for a medieval cure for an illness of their choosing. They should consider how they would sell it to people in the Middle Ages.

- Encourage higher ability students to use evidence from sources to support their writing on 7.3B Cures Worksheet.

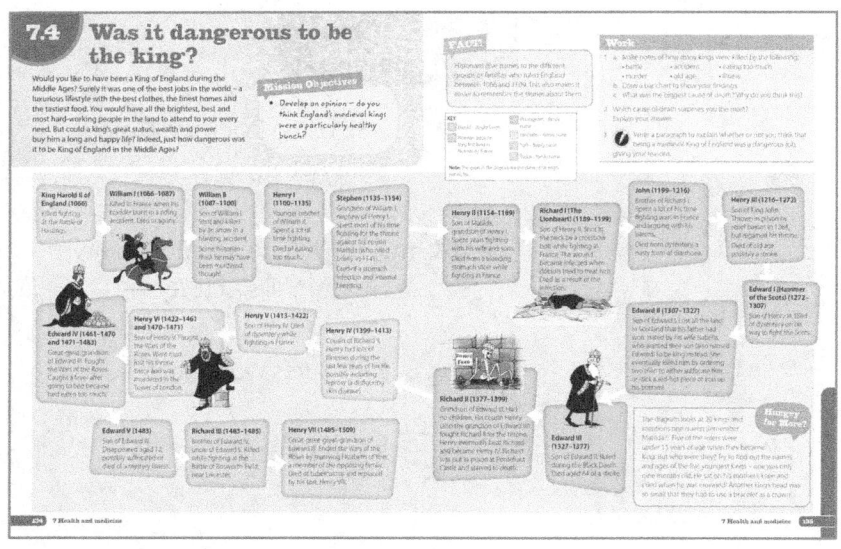

Invasion, Plague and Murder pages 134–135

## Lesson summary

Students will create a timeline and judge how healthy English kings were. This activity includes cross-curricular numeracy skills.

### What are the lesson outcomes?

**All** students will be able to categorize the deaths of English kings.

**Most** students will be able to identify whether they think English kings were healthy or not.

**Some** students will be able to explain their opinions using historical examples.

## Starter suggestion

- Ask students to consider how healthy they think medieval English people were during the Middle Ages. Can they give any examples to support their reasoning? You could encourage them to consider rich versus poor people. Do they think English kings would have been more or less healthy than other people? You could run this as a class vote, which you could return to at the end of the lesson.

## Main learning suggestions and assessment

### What activities will take place?

**Task 1:** Students should read the information on pages 134–135 and complete 7.4 Royal Deaths Worksheet 1. Completing the activities will develop their understanding of how dangerous it was to be a medieval king.

**Task 2:** Students should complete Work tasks **1** and **2**. They could also complete 7.4 Enquiry History Skills Activity, which includes sorting kings by how they died, and 7.4 Chronology

History Skills Activity, where students must order medieval royal families.

### How will students demonstrate their understanding?

**Task 3:** Students should complete 7.4 Royal Deaths Worksheet 2. Students should complete their timeline and colour code each king depending on the type of death.

## Plenary suggestions

- Today's headline!: Students could write the headline for a king of their choice on the night that he died. What has happened? How has he died? Students should use no more than 50 words.

## Differentiation suggestions

### Support

- 7.4 Royal Deaths Worksheet 1 supports lower ability students as they complete Work activities **4** and **5** in the *Student Book*.

### Extension: Hungry for more?

- Students could research the names and ages of the five youngest kings in the Middle Ages.

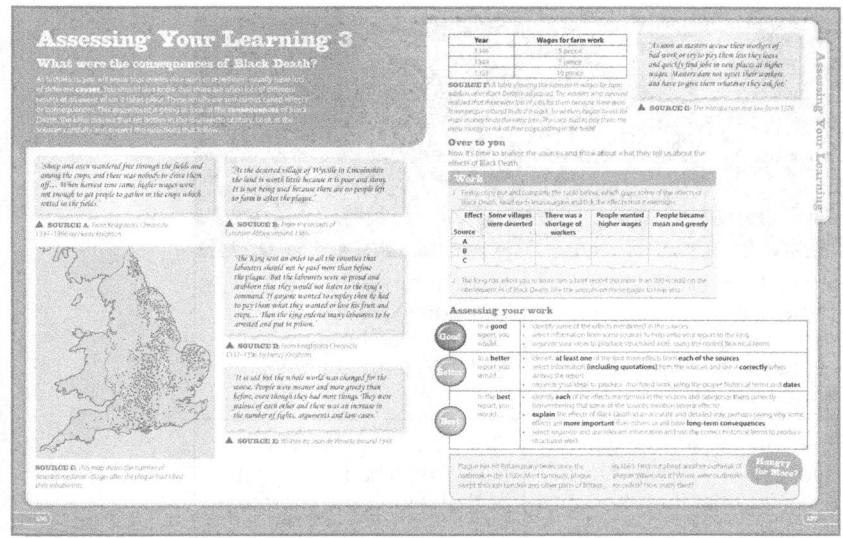

Invasion, Plague and Murder, Student Book pages 136–137

## Assessment in the *Student Book*

In this assessment task, students are asked to investigate various sources in order to write a report on the consequences of Black Death. Since 'the Black Death and its social and economic impact' is specifically mentioned in the 2014 National Curriculum, this assessment encourages students to rigorously analyse this pivotal event in British history. This assessment also allows students to further develop their understanding of causes and consequences in history.

In the *Student Book* (and on the supporting worksheets), you'll find guidance on success criteria that you can use to help your students understand what their work should include. You could ask them to use these criteria for self- or peer-assessment once they've completed the task.

## Chapter 7 Health and medicine task

1 Copy out the table in the *Student Book*, which gives some of the effects of Black Death. Read each of the sources in the *Student Book* and tick the effects that it mentions.

2 The king has asked you to write him a brief report (no more than 200 words) on the consequences of Black Death. Use the sources in the *Student Book* to help you.

### Student Book
- Assessment task
- Student 'Assessing your work' grid

### kerboodle
 Assessment Task Presentation 3

 Assessment Worksheet 3

 Success Criteria Teacher Grid 3

### Teacher Handbook
- Success Criteria Teacher Grid 3

> **Hungry for More?**
>
> Plague has hit Britain many times since the outbreak in the 1300s. Most famously, plague swept through London and other part of Britain in 1665. Find out about another outbreak of plague. When was it? Where were outbreaks recorded? How many died?

## Assessing your work

| In a **good** report, you would… | • identify some of the effect mentioned in the sources<br>• select information from some sources to help write your report to the king<br>• organize your ideas to produce structured work, using the correct historical terms. |
|---|---|
| In a **better** report, you would… | • identify **at least one** of the four main effects from **each of the sources**<br>• select information (**including quotations**) from the sources and use it **correctly** when writing the report<br>• organize your ideas to produce structured work, using the proper historical terms and **dates**. |
| In the **best** report, you would… | • identify **each** of the effects mentioned in the sources and categorize them correctly (remembering that some of the sources mention several effects)<br>• **explain** the effects of Black Death in an accurate and detailed way, perhaps saying why some effects are **more important** than others, or will have **long-term consequences**<br>• select, organize and use relevant information and use the correct historical terms to produce structured work. |

## Success criteria teacher grid

| Assessment criteria | Beginning/ Developing | Securing | Extending |
|---|---|---|---|
| | Current NC Level 3/4 | Current NC Level 5/6 | Current NC Level 7/8 |
| | GCSE Grade Indicator E/D | GCSE Grade Indicator C/B | GCSE Grade Indicator A/A* |
| **Remembering** | Student can understand what is meant by the term 'Black Death', including describing symptoms | Student can explain the cause of Black Death, and show awareness of how people at the time believed it was spread | Student can identify the consequences of Black Death, including short term and long term examples |
| **Understanding** | Student can understand the basic order of Black Death symptoms, or can arrange them chronologically | Students can explain why people in the Middle Ages believed what they thought about the spread of Black Death and its causes | Student can explain why Black Death had an impact in both the long and short term |
| **Applying** | Student can identify causes of Black Death from sources | Student can explain causes of Black Death with support from sources | Student can pick relevant quotes from sources to support their answers in task **2** |
| **Analyzing** | Student can identify some effects of Black Death | Student will explain each consequence of Black Death, with support from sources | Student can justify why some consequences of Black Death are more important than others |
| **Evaluating** | Student use sources of information in ways that go beyond simple observations to answer questions about Black Death | Student selects and deploys a range of evidence which are used appropriately to support their report | Student can evaluate sources to establish relevant evidence for consequences of Black Death |
| **Creating** | Student produces a structured piece of work, using the correct historical terms | Student organizes ideas to produce structured work, using the proper historical terms and dates | Student can select, organize and use relevant information and use the correct historical terms to produce structured work |

## Helping you deliver KS3 History National Curriculum

'Could you get justice in the Middle Ages?' is an historical enquiry that challenges students to delve into the weird and wonderful world of medieval crime and punishment. Through evaluating sources, making connections, drawing contrasts, and creating their own structured account, students are also given the opportunity to judge how 'fair' the whole criminal justice system really was in the Middle Ages.

Students will be required to use historical terminology accurately and appropriately in this chapter. They will need to interrogate sources to discover their meanings. They will also investigate the origins of a particular aspect of British culture, namely 'trial by jury'.

## The Big Picture

### Why are we teaching 'Could you get justice in the Middle Ages?'?

The whole topic of crime, punishment, and justice is very relevant to the students through its inherently topical nature. Students are constantly exposed to crime, criminal investigations, and the prosecution of suspects through films, TV series, and news reports. There may well be a major real life crime trial, manhunt, or TV show based around the criminal justice system when you teach this chapter, which will provide you with an easy 'in' to the topic. The fact that crime and punishment is always so topical will provide numerous opportunities to reinforce the relevance of studying medieval crime and punishment!

## Skills and processes covered in this chapter

| | | 8.1 | 8.2 |
|---|---|:---:|:---:|
| **History Skills** | Historical enquiry | ✓ | ✓ |
| | Using evidence and source work | ✓ | ✓ |
| | Chronological understanding | | |
| | Understanding cultural, ethnic and religious diversity | | |
| | Change and continuity | ✓ | |
| | Cause and consequence | ✓ | ✓ |
| | Significance | | |
| | Interpretations | | |
| | Making links/connections | ✓ | |
| | Explores similarities and differences | | ✓ |
| **Literacy and Numeracy** | Key words identified/deployed | ✓ | |
| | Extended writing | | |
| | Encourages reading for meaning | | ✓ |
| | Focuses on structuring writing | | ✓ |
| | Asks students to use writing to explore and develop ideas | ✓ | ✓ |
| | Learn through talk/discussion | ✓ | ✓ |
| | Numeracy opportunities | ✓ | |
| **Activity types** | Creative task | | ✓ |
| | Emphasizes role of individual | | |
| | Group work | | ✓ |
| | Independent research | ✓ | |
| | Develops study skills | | |

When delving into the curious world of medieval crime detection and trials, most students find the idea of a world without a police force quite incredible. They can be utterly engaged by the bizarre nature of trials by ordeal. Studying this helps to reinforce their knowledge of the importance of God in the medieval world, due to the fact that whole concept of 'trial by ordeal' was linked to the idea of God as the supreme judge.

The chapter closes by detailing the blood, guts, and gore that typified medieval punishments. It then briefly looks at the introduction of 'trial by jury', a concept that students will be particularly familiar with.

## Lesson sequence

| Lesson title | NC references | Objectives | Outcomes |
|---|---|---|---|
| **8.1 Keeping law and order pp138–139** | Society, economy and culture 1066–1509 | • Recall how towns and villages tried to keep law and order in the Middle Ages.<br>• Compare medieval types of punishment with modern methods. | **All** students will be able to describe at least three crimes and their punishments in the Middle Ages.<br>**Most** students will be able to explain how criminals were captured in the Middle Ages.<br>**Some** students will begin to explain why punishments were so harsh in the Middle Ages. |
| **8.2 Trial and punishment pp140–141** | Society, economy and culture 1066–1509 | • Investigate the medieval trial system.<br>• Judge the effectiveness of 'trial by ordeal'. | **All** students will be able to describe at least three serious crimes and their punishments in the Middle Ages.<br>**Most** students will be able to explain how criminals were tried in the Middle Ages.<br>**Some** students will be able to explain why punishments for serious crimes were so harsh in the Middle Ages. |

### Ideas for enrichment

You could set up a mock medieval trial as a class activity, which would catch the imaginations of students as they take on different roles. You could ask each student to write a 'script' that they will act out in class in front of the 'judge'. The script will detail the crime of which they are accused. The judge (which could be the class voting together) will decide on an appropriate – and historically accurate – punishment.

A school trip to a real court would be a fantastic way of enriching the chapter, and would allow the students to put their learning in the History classroom into a modern context.

Further, you might recommend watching Tony Robinson's excellent series *Crime and Punishment*. The episode *Guilty as charged* charts the establishment of the three key elements of the modern legal system – independent judges, trial by jury, and English Common Law.

# 8.1 Keeping law and order

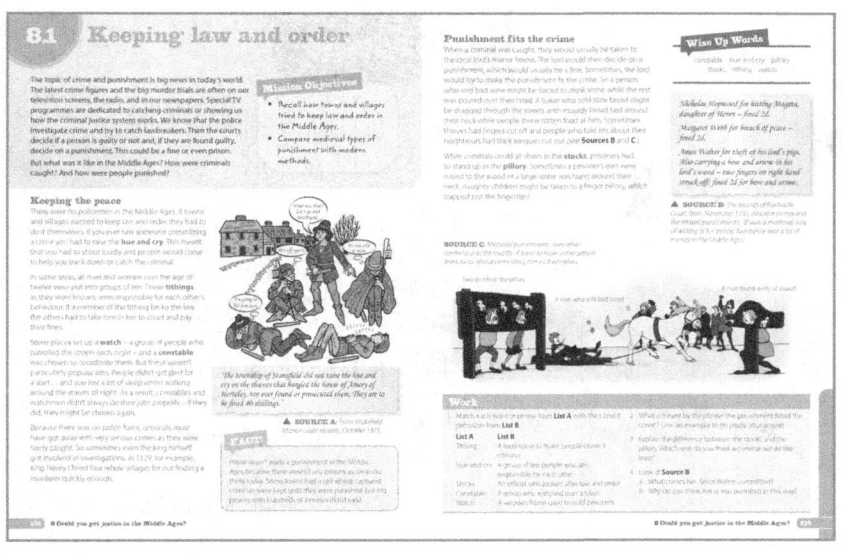

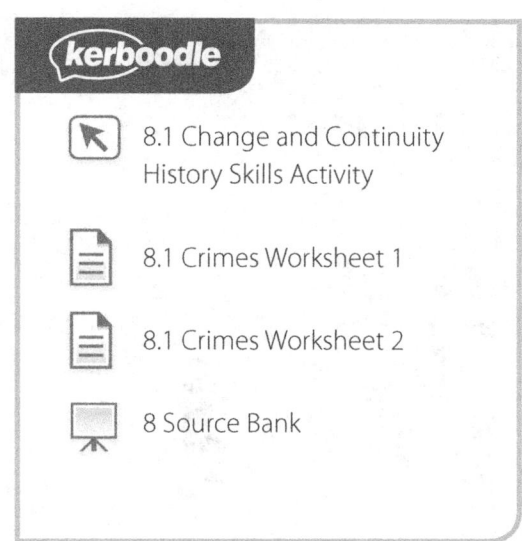

Invasion, Plague and Murder pages 138–139

## Lesson summary

Students will develop an understanding of how criminals in the Middle Ages were tried and punished, depending on their crimes.

### What are the lesson outcomes?

**All** students will be able to describe at least three crimes and their punishments in the Middle Ages.

**Most** students will be able to explain how criminals were captured in the Middle Ages.

**Some** students will begin to explain why punishments were so harsh in the Middle Ages.

## Starter suggestion

- How do we catch criminals today? Allow students 30 seconds to write a list of all the ways in which criminals are caught today. Allow them a further ten seconds to underline those that they think would have been available in the Middle Ages. Can they underline many? Why is this? Can they identify any problems regarding catching criminals in the Middle Ages?

## Main learning suggestions and assessment

### What activities will take place?

**Task 1:** Students should read the information on pages 138–139 and complete Work activity **1**. They should use 8.1 Crimes Worksheet 1 to create a pie chart to show the proportion of the different types of crime committed in the Middle Ages.

### How will students demonstrate their understanding?

**Task 2:** Students should complete 8.1 Change and Continuity History Skills Activity to organize medieval and modern punishments and methods of law enforcement.

Students could then complete 8.1 Crimes Worksheet 2, creating a list of suggested punishments for the medieval crimes.

**Task 3:** Students should complete Work activities **2** to **4**.

## Plenary suggestions

- Three is the magic number!: Ask students if they can remember three matching crimes and punishments from this lesson.

## Differentiation suggestions

### Support

- 8.1 Crimes Worksheet 1 supports developing numeracy skills for all students.

### Extension: Hungry for more?

- Students could write an essay to answer the following question: Why do you think criminals in medieval England were so harshly punished? They should write no more than 150 words, and should try to use evidence from sources to support their writing.

# 8.2 Trial and punishment

Invasion, Plague and Murder pages 140–141

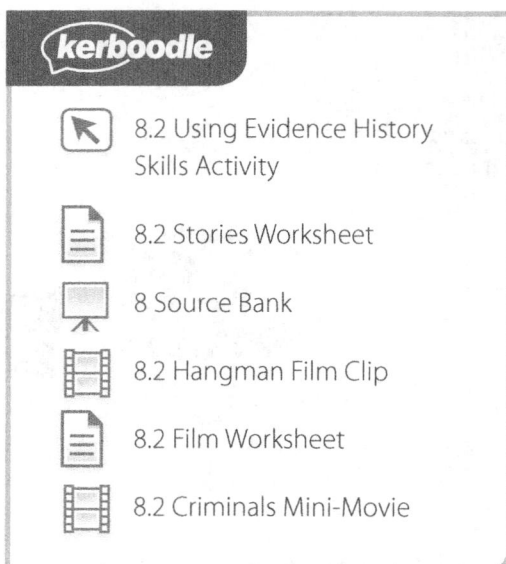

**kerboodle**

- 8.2 Using Evidence History Skills Activity
- 8.2 Stories Worksheet
- 8 Source Bank
- 8.2 Hangman Film Clip
- 8.2 Film Worksheet
- 8.2 Criminals Mini-Movie

## Lesson summary
Students will develop an understanding of how more serious crimes in the Middle Ages were tried and punished.

### What are the lesson outcomes?
**All** students will be able to describe at least three seroius crimes and their punishments in the Middle Ages.

**Most** students will be able to explain how criminals were tried in the Middle Ages.

**Some** students will be able to explain why punishments for serious crimes were so harsh in the Middle Ages.

## Starter suggestion
- Tell your neighbour: Students could tell their neighbour about any medieval crime and its punishment that they know of. They should then watch 8.2 Criminals Mini-Movie to see how many they got right.

## Main learning suggestions and assessment
### What activities will take place?

**Task 1:** Students should read the information on pages 140–141 and complete Work activities **1** and **2**. They could also watch 8.2 Hangman Clip, where an executioner discusses how criminals are punished. They could complete 8.2 Film Worksheet during or after viewing the clip.

### How will students demonstrate their understanding?
**Task 2:** Students should complete 8.2 Using Evidence History Skills Activity to gain a greater understanding of trial by ordeal in the Middle Ages.

**Task 3:** Students should complete 8.2 Stories Worksheet, investigating two sources on medieval punishments.

**Task 4:** Students should complete Work activity **3**.

## Plenary suggestions
- Debate stations: You could pose the question: Were punishments in the Middle Ages fair? Run a class discussion, allowing students to answer the question. Designate three areas around the classroom: one area for 'Yes, punishments were fair!'; one for 'No, punishments were not fair!'; and one for 'Don't know yet!'. Remind students that if they stand in the 'Don't know yet!' area they must be able to explain their final decision by the end of the debate.

## Differentiation suggestions
### Support
- 8.2 Stories Worksheet encourages higher ability students to support their writing by using examples from sources.

### Extension: Hungry for more?
- Encourage students to find three current news stories of different crimes that have been committed. Ask them to research the punishments that might have been handed out if the crimes had been committed in the Middle Ages.

# Overview: Chapter 9 England at war

## Helping you deliver KS3 History National Curriculum

This chapter covers a series of significant events that shaped the history of the British Isles. The English campaigns to conquer Wales and Scotland up to 1314, the Hundred Years War, the Wars of the Roses, and the reign of Henry VII are expressly mentioned in the 2014 National Curriculum. This chapter covers all these topics, and more. Students are asked to make connections and draw contrasts between different events. They are also asked to show how one event or change could lead to another. They are required to focus on key individuals and judge the impact they had. They are also asked to select and combine information from sources to help with their enquiries as well as evaluate the strengths and weaknesses of those sources.

## The Big Picture

### Why are we teaching 'England at war'?

The 2014 National Curriculum specifically mentions a number of pivotal wars which took place in the Middle Ages and this chapter covers two of them in considerable detail – the English campaigns to conquer Wales and Scotland up to 1314, and the Hundred Years War. England's relationships with its immediate neighbours – Wales, Scotland, Ireland, and France – are both intriguing and engaging.

Some spreads focus on war and the struggle for power within England itself. The Wars of the Roses (also specifically mentioned in the 2014 National Curriculum) are presented in a chronological framework that charts the twists and turns of the English throne. There is an extended source-based exercise on the famous mystery of the Princes in the Tower, and a spread

## Skills and processes covered in this chapter

| | | 9.1 | 9.2 | 9.3 | 9.4A | 9.4B | 9.5 | 9.6 | 9.7A | 9.7B | 9.8A | 9.8B | 9.9 |
|---|---|---|---|---|---|---|---|---|---|---|---|---|---|
| **History Skills** | Historical enquiry | ✓ | ✓ | ✓ | ✓ | ✓ | ✓ | ✓ | ✓ | ✓ | ✓ | ✓ | ✓ |
| | Using evidence and source work | ✓ | ✓ | | ✓ | ✓ | ✓ | | | | ✓ | ✓ | ✓ | |
| | Chronological understanding | | | ✓ | | ✓ | ✓ | | ✓ | ✓ | | | |
| | Understanding cultural, ethnic and religious diversity | | | | | | ✓ | | | | | | |
| | Change and continuity | ✓ | | ✓ | | | | ✓ | ✓ | ✓ | ✓ | | |
| | Cause and consequence | | | | ✓ | ✓ | | | ✓ | | | | |
| | Significance | ✓ | ✓ | ✓ | ✓ | | ✓ | | | | ✓ | ✓ | ✓ |
| | Interpretations | ✓ | | ✓ | ✓ | | | | | | ✓ | ✓ | ✓ |
| | Making links/connections | | | ✓ | | | ✓ | ✓ | | | | | ✓ |
| | Explores similarities and differences | | | | | | | | | | | | ✓ |
| **Literacy and Numeracy** | Key words identified/deployed | ✓ | ✓ | | ✓ | ✓ | | ✓ | | ✓ | | | ✓ |
| | Extended writing | | ✓ | | | ✓ | | | | ✓ | | ✓ | |
| | Encourages reading for meaning | ✓ | | | | | | | | | ✓ | ✓ | ✓ |
| | Focuses on structuring writing | | ✓ | | | | | ✓ | ✓ | | | | |
| | Asks students to use writing to explore and develop ideas | ✓ | ✓ | ✓ | ✓ | | | ✓ | ✓ | ✓ | ✓ | ✓ | ✓ |
| | Learn through talk/discussion | ✓ | | | ✓ | ✓ | | ✓ | | | | ✓ | ✓ |
| | Numeracy opportunities | | ✓ | | | | | | | | | | |
| **Activity types** | Creative task | | ✓ | | | | | ✓ | ✓ | | | | |
| | Emphasizes role of individual | ✓ | ✓ | ✓ | ✓ | ✓ | ✓ | | | | ✓ | ✓ | ✓ | ✓ |
| | Group work | | | | | | | ✓ | | | ✓ | ✓ | ✓ |
| | Independent research | | | ✓ | ✓ | | ✓ | | | | ✓ | ✓ | ✓ |
| | Develops study skills | | | | ✓ | | | | | ✓ | | ✓ | ✓ |

looking at the man who emerged at the end of the Wars of the Roses as England's monarch, Henry VII. His journey from battlefield victor in 1485 to supreme ruler of England in 1509 is investigated in a unique way – by comparing him to a gangster!

The spread 'Choose your weapons' provides students with a chronological route through the significant developments in military technology in the Middle Ages.

## Lesson sequence

| Lesson title | NC references | Objectives | Outcomes |
|---|---|---|---|
| 9.1 England and its neighbours: Wales pp142–143 | The English campaigns to conquer Wales and Scotland up to 1314 | • Identify how and why England tried to conquer Wales.<br>• Judge how successful these attempts were. | **All** students will be able to describe how Edward I tried to control Wales.<br>**Most** students will be able to explain how Edward I tried to control Wales.<br>**Some** students will be able to explain why Edward felt the need to control Wales. |
| 9.2 England and its neighbours: Scotland pp144–145 | The English campaigns to conquer Wales and Scotland up to 1314 | • Identify how and why England tried to conquer Scotland.<br>• Judge how successful these attempts were. | **All** students will be able to describe reasons why Edward I invaded Scotland.<br>**Most** students will be able to describe one historical figure who fought against Edward I.<br>**Some** students will be able to explain whether they think Edward I deserved the title of 'The Hammer of the Scots'. |
| 9.3 England and its neighbours: Ireland pp146–147 | | • Analyse how the English tried to control Ireland.<br>• Assess why medieval kings failed to conquer Ireland. | **All** students will be able to identify at least three English kings who tried to control Ireland.<br>**Most** students will be able to analyse how the English tried to control Ireland.<br>**Some** students will be able to assess why medieval kings failed to conquer Ireland. |
| 9.4A Why do we give the 'V sign' as an insult? pp148–149 | The Hundred Years War | • Summarize the key events of the Hundred Years War.<br>• Relate a modern-day insult to a historical event. | **All** students will be able to describe the chronological story of the Hundred Years War.<br>**Most** students will be able to identify reasons why England and France went to war.<br>**Some** students will be able to explain which was the most important reason why England and France went to war. |
| 9.4B Why do we give the 'V sign' as an insult? pp150–151 | | | |
| 9.5 Joan of Arc – the teenage girl who led an army pp152–153 | The Hundred Years War | • Recall who Joan of Arc was and how she affected the outcome of the Hundred Years War.<br>• Examine why she is still a national hero in France today. | **All** students will be able to describe the story of Joan of Arc.<br>**Most** students will be able to explain why Joan of Arc was different from most medieval women.<br>**Some** students will be able to identify reasons why Joan of Arc should be remembered. |
| 9.6 Choose your weapons! pp154–155 | The Hundred Years War | • Identify different weapons that were used in medieval warfare.<br>• Judge which weapons were the most effective and explain why. | **All** students will be able to name five medieval weapons.<br>**Most** students will be able to describe at least three medieval weapons.<br>**Some** students will be able to explain which weapons were most effective for different types of soldiers. |
| 9.7A What were the Wars of the Roses? pp156–157 | The Wars of the Roses | • Recall why England went to war with itself in the fifteenth century.<br>• Discover why England came to be ruled by Henry Tudor. | **All** students will be able to identify which families were involved in the Wars of the Roses and who won.<br>**Most** students will be able to describe in detail the story of the Wars of the Roses.<br>**Some** students will be able to explain the reasons why England went to war. |
| 9.7B What were the Wars of the Roses? pp158–159 | | | |
| 9.8A History Mystery: the Princes in the Tower pp160–161 | The Wars of the Roses | • Explain why Edward V was never crowned king.<br>• Evaluate what happened to Edward and his brother and justify the decision you have made. | **All** students will be able to state who they think was responsible for the princes' deaths.<br>**Most** students will be able to explain who they believe was responsible for the princes' deaths and will be able to provide evidence to support their judgement.<br>**Some** students will be able to judge which evidence is the most reliable. |
| 9.8B History Mystery: the Princes in the Tower pp162–163 | | | |
| 9.9 Was King Henry VII a gangster? pp164–165 | Henry VII and his attempts to restore stability | • Investigate the life of Henry VII.<br>• Assess the tactics Henry VII used to become more powerful. | **All** students will identify at least three problems that Henry VII faced.<br>**Most** students will be able to explain how Henry VII solved the problems he faced.<br>**Some** students will be able to identify what characteristics Henry VII displayed to solve his problems. |

## Ideas for enrichment

The spreads covering the English campaigns to conquer Wales and Scotland could be broadened to encompass devolution, nationalist parties, and other current issues.

'Should Scotland and Wales be totally independent from England?' is an excellent topic for a class debate where students can showcase their historical knowledge in a contemporary context.

There are other research possibilities. The Battle of Agincourt (which is a keystone of the English self-image) has been re-interpreted by modern historians. You could ask students to research these new interpretations.

Another great research possibility is the controversy over the Princes in the Tower. You could ask students to watch the Channel 4 programme *Richard III: The King in the Car Park* and look for their own answers to the mystery.

# 9.1 England and its neighbours: Wales

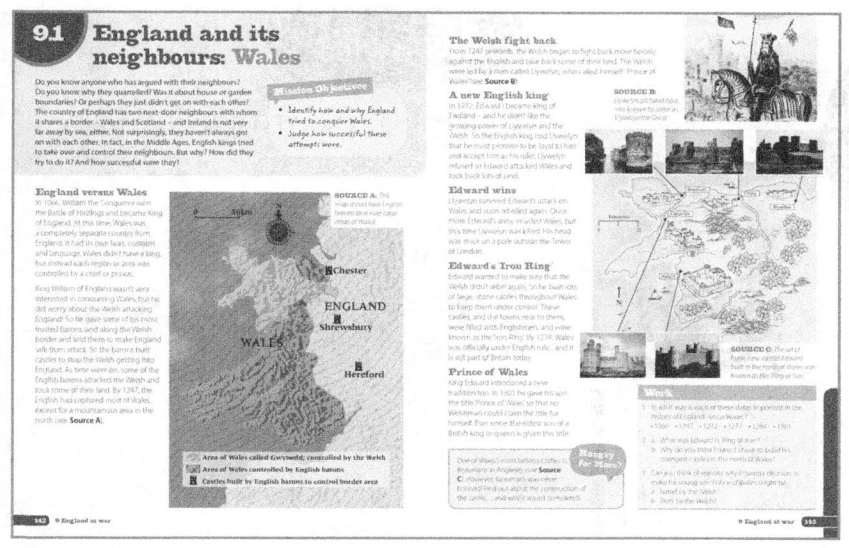

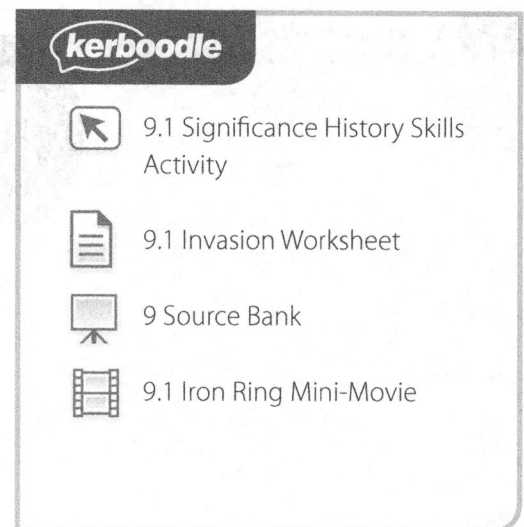

## Lesson summary
Students will develop an understanding of how and why Edward I tried to control Wales.

### What are the lesson outcomes?
**All** students will be able to describe how Edward I tried to control Wales.

**Most** students will be able to explain how Edward I tried to control Wales.

**Some** students will be able to explain why Edward felt the need to control Wales.

## Starter suggestion
- 3, 5, 7: Explain to students that they have 30 seconds to think of three reasons why castles were important in medieval England. Then give them one minute to discuss their reasons with a partner and come up with five good reasons between them. Students should then work in small groups to come up with the seven best reasons why castles were important in medieval England.

## Main learning suggestions and assessment
### What activities will take place?
**Task 1:** Students should read the information on pages 142–143 and complete 9.1 Significance History Skills Activity to examine why Edward I played an important role in Welsh history.

**Task 2:** Students should complete Work activity **1** and then watch 9.1 Iron Ring Mini-Movie to learn more about Edward's set of castles in Wales.

### How will students demonstrate their understanding?
**Task 3:** Students should complete the two activities on 9.1 Invasion Worksheet, firstly explaining the reasons why Edward invaded and then labelling a diagram of Edward's castles.

**Task 4:** Students should complete Work activities **2** and **3**.

## Plenary suggestions
- True or false: Students could guess whether the following statements are true or false:
  - Edward I became King of England and Scotland in 1272 (false – he was only King of England)
  - Llywelyn's head was put on a pole outside the Tower of London (true)
  - Edward built many motte and bailey castles in Wales (false – he built stone castles)
  - Edward eventually gave his son the title Prince of Wales (true)
  - Harlech was not a castle in the Ring of Iron (false).

## Differentiation suggestions
### Support
- Students may wish to use the highlighting tool on the *Kerboodle Book* as they read, to highlight reasons why Edward invaded. This will help them to complete the tasks throughout the lesson.

### Extension: Hungry for more?
- Higher ability students could write a speech for Edward I explaining to the people of Wales why they should pay homage to him. Their letter should explain how Edward is controlling Wales and how he has got rid of his enemies in Wales.

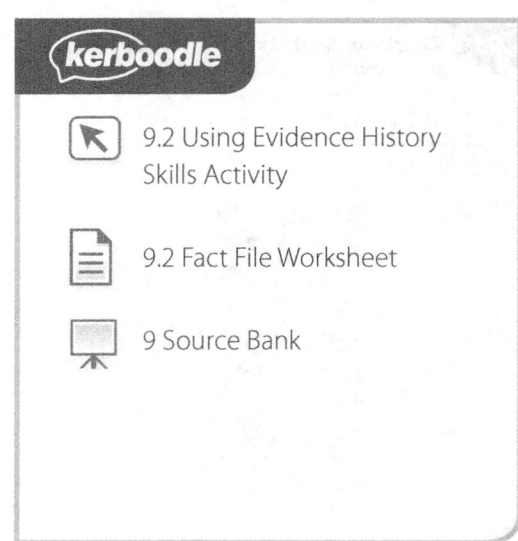

Invasion, Plague and Murder pages 144–145

## Lesson summary

Students will develop an understanding of the reasons why Edward I invaded Scotland and develop a fact file for one historical figure studied in the lesson.

### What are the lesson outcomes?

**All** students will be able to describe reasons why Edward I invaded Scotland.

**Most** students will be able to describe one historical figure who fought against Edward I.

**Some** students will be able to explain whether they think Edward I deserved the title of 'The Hammer of the Scots'.

## Starter suggestion

- Let's recap!: Students could try to explain how Edward I has tried to control people in and around Britain so far. Can students imagine how they think Edward will try to control the Scots?

## Main learning suggestions and assessment

### What activities will take place?

**Task 1:** Students should read the information on pages 144–145 and complete 9.2 Using Evidence History Skills Activity, comparing two sources on why England invaded Scotland.

**Task 2:** Students should complete Work activities **1** and **2**. Activity **2** asks students to create a timeline with the key events in the relationship between England and Scotland at this time.

### How will students demonstrate their understanding?

**Task 3:** Students should use 9.2 Fact File Worksheet to create a fact file on one of the following: John Balliol; William

Wallace; Robert the Bruce. They should explain the person's role in Scottish history and what happened to them. They should give them a thistle rating – either 'Highland legend' or 'Lowland loser'.

## Plenary suggestions

- Learning triangle: Students could complete a learning triangle, explaining two things they have learned and three questions they would like to ask to complete their understanding of Edward I.

## Differentiation suggestions

### Support

- You may wish to draw attention to the Fact! box on page 144, which gives a brief explanation as to why so many kings shared the same name.

### Extension: Hungry for more?

- Mel Gibson played William Wallace in the film *Braveheart*. Some historians criticized the film because they said it wasn't true to life. Students could research what parts of the story were changed and what parts were added.

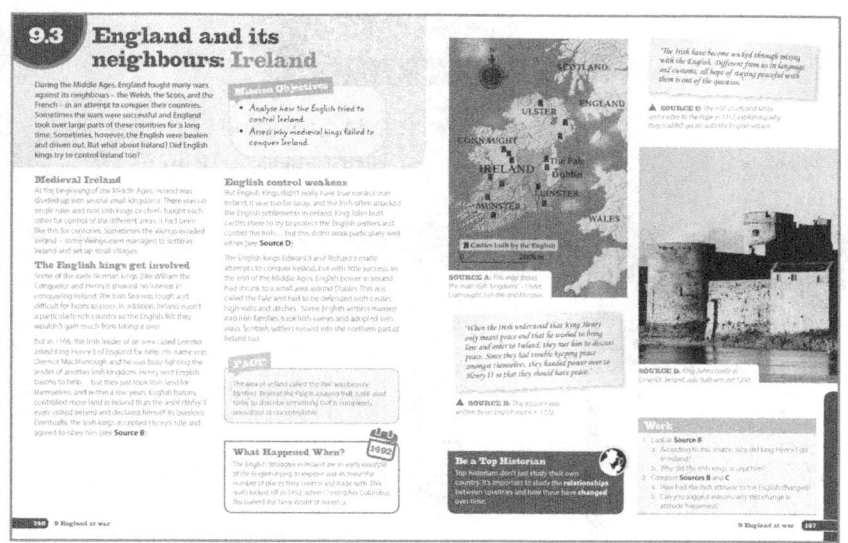

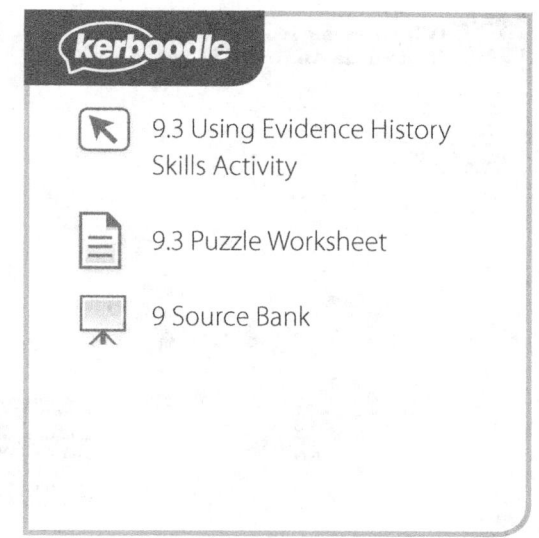

Invasion, Plague and Murder pages 146–147

## Lesson summary
Students should investigate how the English tried to control Ireland in the Middle Ages.

### What are the lesson outcomes?
**All** students will be able to identify at least three English kings who tried to control Ireland.

**Most** students will be able to analyse how the English tried to control Ireland.

**Some** students will be able to assess why medieval kings failed to conquer Ireland.

## Starter suggestion
- 3 is the magic number!: Students could work in pairs to think of three reasons why English kings might have wanted to control Ireland in the Middle Ages.

## Main learning suggestions and assessment
### What activities will take place?
**Task 1**: Students should read the information on pages 146–147 and complete 9.3 Puzzle Worksheet, which will help develop literacy skills.

### How will students demonstrate their understanding?
**Task 2**: Students should complete 9.3 Using Evidence History Skills Activity on **Sources B** and **C**. This activity encourages students to think about the effect English settlers had in Ireland.

**Task 3**: Students should complete Work activities **1** and **2**.

## Plenary suggestions
- One more thing…!: Students could complete the following sentence to state what they have learned today: 'One thing I have learned is…' You can either pick students to tell the class one thing they have learned, or they can write on sticky notes which they can hand in at the end of the lesson.

## Differentiation suggestions
### Support
- Using **Source A** in the *Student Book*, ask students to list the Irish Kingdoms, then write three facts about the Irish leader of one of those kingdoms (Dermot MacMurrough of Leinster, for example). Then ask students to try and link the actions of Dermot MacMurrough to the actions of King Henry (cause and consequence).

### Extension: Hungry for more?
- Encourage higher ability students to use evidence from activities **1** and **2**.

- Ask students to research the history of Carrickfergus Castle in County Antrim. Which important historical events have occurred there? What role did it play while the English were trying to control Ireland?

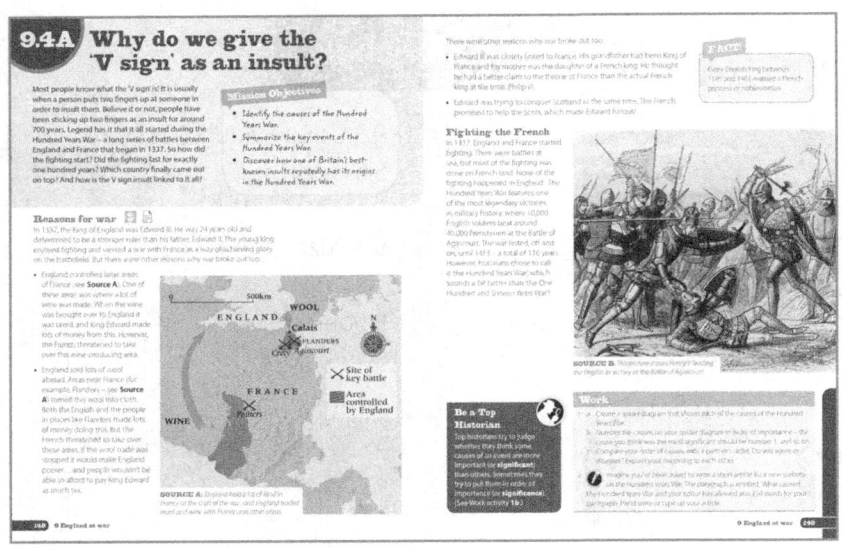

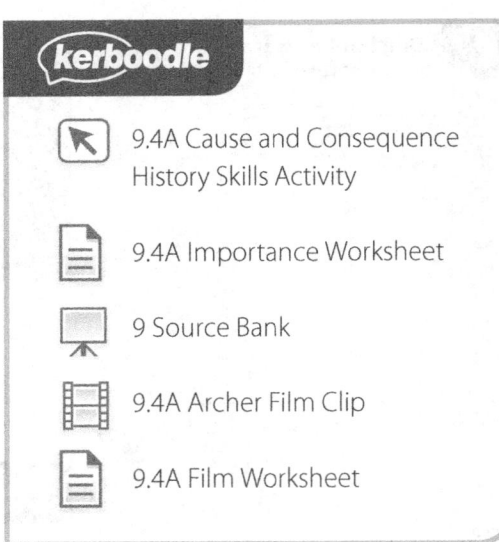

Invasion, Plague and Murder pages 148–149

## Lesson summary

Students will develop an understanding of why Henry V was so successful at fighting the French, and the weapons and tactics he used in fighting.

### What are the lesson outcomes?

**All** students will be able to describe the chronological story of the Hundred Years War.

**Most** students will be able to identify reasons why England and France went to war.

**Some** students will be able to explain which was the most important reason why England and France went to war.

## Starter suggestion

- Think, pair, share: Ask students to think of reasons why people went to war in the Middle Ages. They should then work in pairs to discuss their reasons. Finally they should share their reasons with the rest of the class. You could carry out a class vote to decide which reason is the most important.

## Main learning suggestions and assessment

### What activities will take place?

**Task 1:** Students should read the information on pages 148–149 and complete 9.4A Cause and Consequence History Skills Activity.

**Task 2:** Watch 9.4A Archer Film Clip, where a soldier discusses why war broke out, and ask students to complete 9.4A Film Worksheet. Students should then complete Work activity **1** to create a spider diagram about the causes of the Hundred Years War.

### How will students demonstrate their understanding?

**Task 3:** Students should complete 9.4A Importance Worksheet, which asks students to rank the causes of war with France in order of importance.

**Task 4:** Students should complete Work activity **2**.

## Plenary suggestions

- Exit note: Students could complete the following sentence: 'One thing I learned or enjoyed is…'.

## Differentiation suggestions

### Support

- For Work activity **1**, through careful questioning, create a template mind-map that gives headings for each of the causes/reasons behind the outbreak of war e.g. Edward's love of fighting, the French threats to England's wool trade and so on. Then ask students to bullet point the detail beneath the headings. These notes will inform their article (Work activity **2**).

### Extension: Hungry for more?

- Ask students to research and write a brief 'battle commentary' on the Battle of Agincourt.

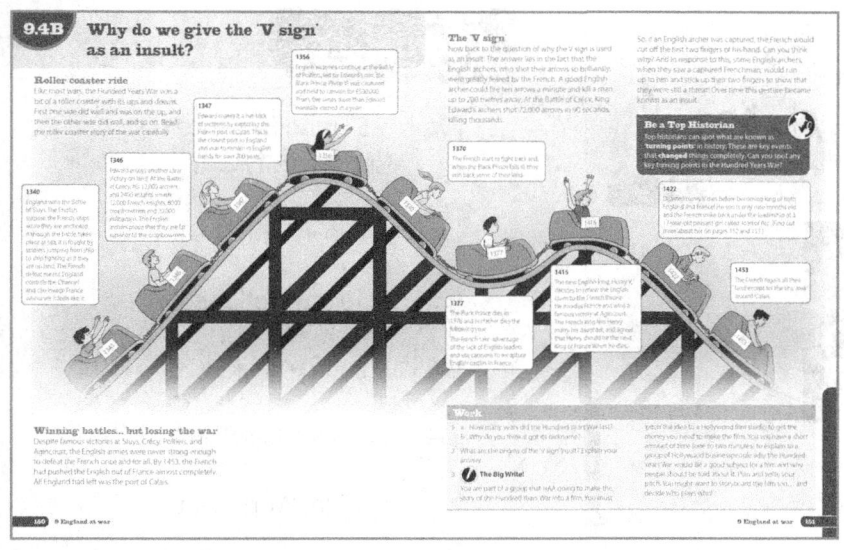

Invasion, Plague and Murder pages 150–151

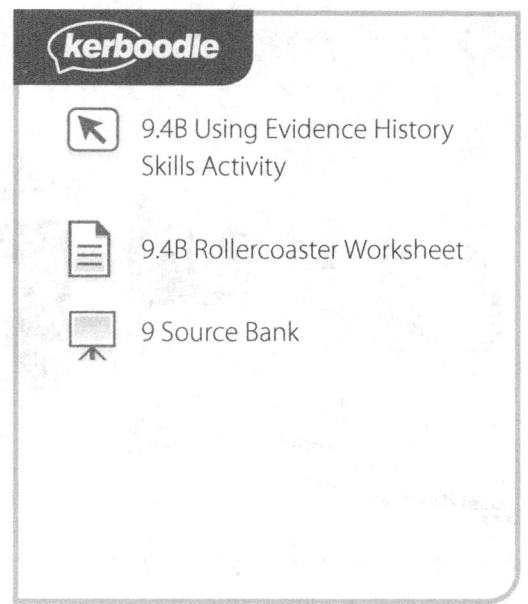

**kerboodle**

9.4B Using Evidence History Skills Activity

9.4B Rollercoaster Worksheet

9 Source Bank

## Lesson summary

Students will develop an understanding of why Henry V was so successful at fighting the French, and the weapons and tactics he used in fighting.

### What are the lesson outcomes?

**All** students will be able to describe the chronological story of the Hundred Years War.

**Most** students will be able to identify reasons why England and France went to war.

**Some** students will be able to explain which was the most important reason why England and France went to war.

## Starter suggestion

- Students could complete two post-it notes; one containing a statement they already know about the Hundred Years War, and one with a question they would like to have answered in this lesson.

## Main learning suggestions and assessment

### What activities will take place?

**Task 1:** Students should read the information on pages 150–115 and complete 9.4B Using Evidence History Skills Activity. Encourage students to read the excerpt from Shakespeare to understand the role that his play, *Henry V*, had in keeping the battle in the memories of the English people.

### How will students demonstrate their understanding?

**Task 2:** Students should complete 9.4B Rollercoaster Worksheet to create their own timeline, explaining what happened on each date.

**Task 3:** Students should complete Work activities **1** to **3**.

## Plenary suggestions

- Students should write one sticky note to show what they have learned in this lesson.

## Differentiation suggestions

### Support

- For the Big Write activity in the *Student Book*, you may want to organize students into mixed ability groups to discuss and plan their film pitch.

### Extension: Hungry for more?

- Students could answer the following question: What do you think were the key turning points during the Hundred Years War?

- After completing 9.4B Using Evidence History Skills Activity students could answer the following question: How has Shakespeare helped to make Henry V a well-known and popular king?

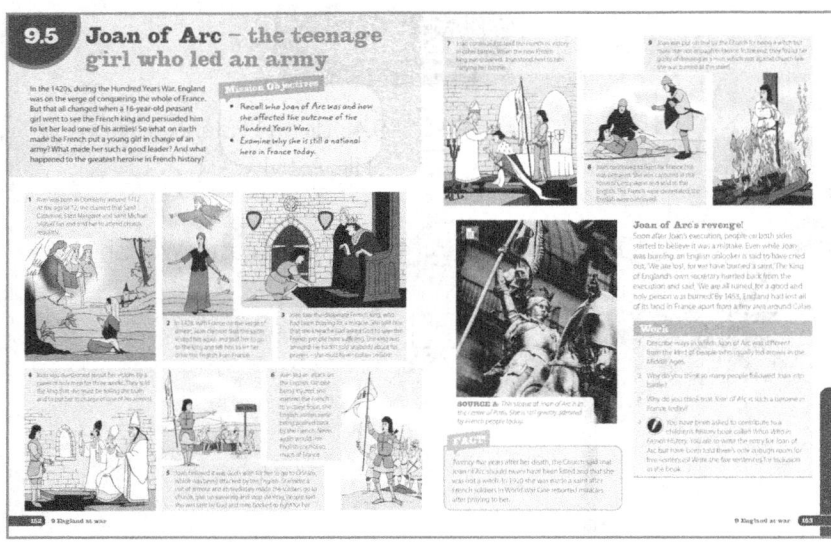

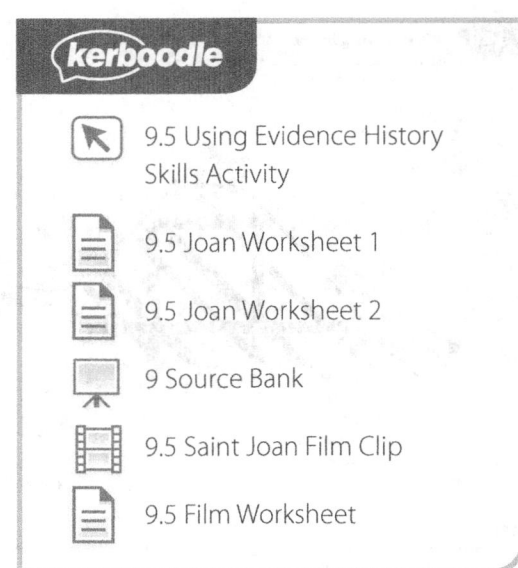

Invasion, Plague and Murder pages 152–153

## Lesson summary

Students will develop an understanding of how Joan of Arc affected the outcome of the Hundred Years War.

### What are the lesson outcomes?

**All** students will be able to describe the story of Joan of Arc.

**Most** students will be able to explain why Joan of Arc was different from most medieval women.

**Some** students will be able to identify reasons why Joan of Arc should be remembered.

## Starter suggestion

- Who do you think it is?: Read out the following five facts about Joan of Arc. Don't tell the students who these facts refer to! Ask the students to guess who this lesson is about, from these facts: she was born around 1412; she is French; she fought the English in the Hundred Years War; she was burned to death by the English; she is a saint.

## Main learning suggestions and assessment

### What activities will take place?

**Task 1:** Students should read the information on pages 152–153 and complete 9.5 Using Evidence History Skills Activity, debating the importance of Joan of Arc.

**Task 2:** Students should watch 9.5 Saint Joan Film Clip, in which an archer who witnessed her execution describes the influence she had on both the French and English people. Students should then complete 9.5 Film Worksheet to encourage them to think about what they have just seen.

### How will students demonstrate their understanding?

**Task 3:** Students should complete Work activities **1** to **3**.

**Task 4:** Students should either complete Work activity **4** or complete 9.5 Joan Worksheet 1 to create a storyboard of the life of Joan of Arc. For each image students should create their own captions of no more than ten words.

## Plenary suggestions

- Be a DJ!: Students could pick their top five facts about Joan of Arc from this lesson.

## Differentiation suggestions

### Support

- **Task 4** is differentiated. Lower ability students can test their chronology skills through the timeline tasks whilst higher ability students can look at the importance of Joan of Arc.

### Extension: Hungry for more?

- Students could design a memorial to immortalize Joan of Arc. It should remind the people of France what she is famous for and why she is still a heroine in France today. Students could use 9.5 Joan Worksheet 2 to help them with this.

# 9.6 Choose your weapons!

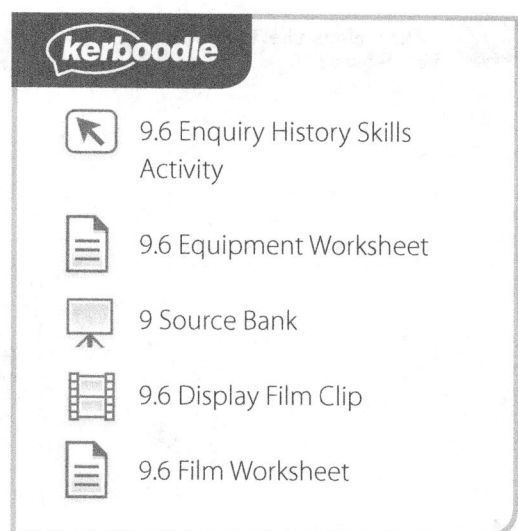

nvasion, Plague and Murder pages 154–155

## Lesson summary

Students will develop an understanding of how soldiers fought in the Middle Ages and how effective weapons were by the Tudor period.

### What are the lesson outcomes?

**All** students will be able to name five medieval weapons.

**Most** students will be able to describe at least three medieval weapons.

**Some** students will be able to explain which weapons were most effective for different types of soldiers.

## Starter suggestion

- Goal setting: Students could set themselves two targets for the lessons on the Wars of the Roses. Encourage them to focus one target on knowledge and one target on improving a skill.

## Main learning suggestions and assessment

### What activities will take place?

**Task 1:** Students should read the information on pages 154–155 and complete Work activity **1**, explaining which weapons they would take into battle. In order to help them with this choice, you might like to show the students 9.6 Display Film Clip, in which the powerful longbow is demonstrated. Students could complete 9.6 Film Worksheet after viewing the clip.

### How will students demonstrate their understanding?

**Task 2:** Students should complete 9.6 Enquiry History Skills Activity, completing a literacy puzzle and then considering how modern weapons are different from medieval ones.

**Task 3:** Students should use 9.6 Equipment Worksheet to complete a drawing of a fully equipped knight, showing what weapons they would choose to take into battle and explain why. There are also questions that will test their understanding of medieval combat.

## Plenary suggestions

- Different shoes: Ask students to imagine being a Tudor soldier about to go into battle. Tell them they can carry only three weapons. Which ones would they choose to take with them? Why?

## Differentiation suggestions

### Support

- **Task 3** is well suited to lower ability students.

### Extension: Hungry for more?

- Students could research one battle from the Wars of the Roses. Ask them to write a 150-word summary explaining: where the battle was fought; how long it lasted; which kings were fighting. They should also include one interesting fact.

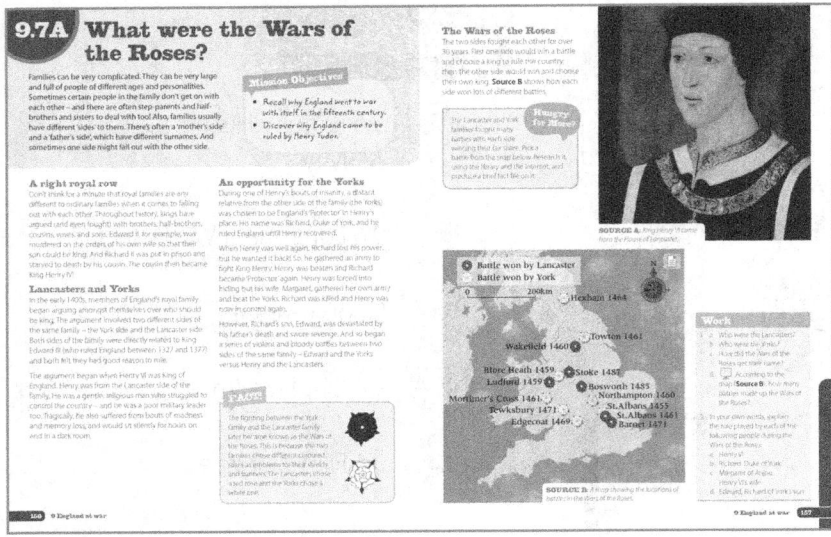

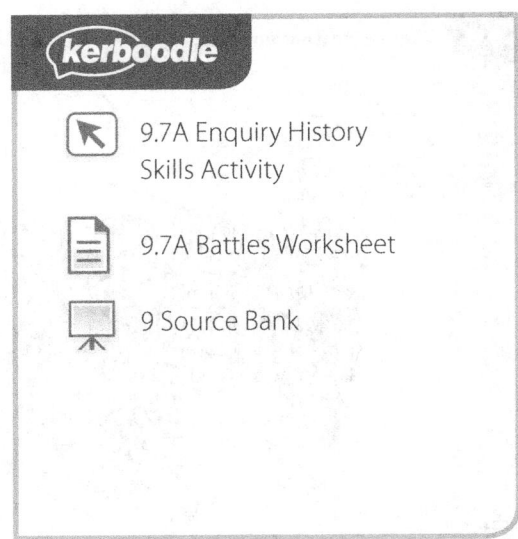

Invasion, Plague and Murder pages 156–157

## Lesson summary

Students will develop an understanding of how the Tudors became the new royal family and how they ended the fight for the English crown.

### What are the lesson outcomes?

**All** students will be able to identify which families were involved in the Wars of the Roses and who won.

**Most** students will be able to describe in detail the story of the Wars of the Roses.

**Some** students will be able to explain the reasons why England went to war.

## Starter suggestion

- Just a minute!: Students could tell a partner everything that they have learned so far about the Wars of the Roses. They each have one minute to complete this task. Can they easily fill their minutes?

## Main learning suggestions and assessment

### What activities will take place?

**Task 1:** Students should read the information on pages 156–157 and complete Work activities **1** and **2**.

### How will students demonstrate their understanding?

**Task 2:** Students should complete 9.7A Enquiry History Skills Activity about the Wars of the Roses.

**Task 3:** Students should complete 9.7A Battles Worksheet, creating a timeline of the Wars of the Roses. They should show the battles that were fought and colour the rose to show who won the battle.

## Plenary suggestions

- Show me the answer!: Students could use mini whiteboards to answer the following questions:
  - Why was there a civil war in England in the fifteenth century?
  - What were the names of the families that were fighting each other?
  - How did these wars get their name?
  - Which family won the Wars of the Roses?
  - What was the symbol that the two families created to show peace?

## Differentiation suggestions

### Support

- 9.7A Enquiry History Skills Activity provides an accessible way in to the topic using a literacy-based puzzle.

### Extension: Hungry for more?

- 9.7A Battles Worksheet includes an extension task (Hungry for More?).

- Ask students to imagine that the year is 1475. They need to write a report to send back to court. In the report they should explain to people who they think is on course to win the Wars of the Roses. They should refer to battles that have been fought already.

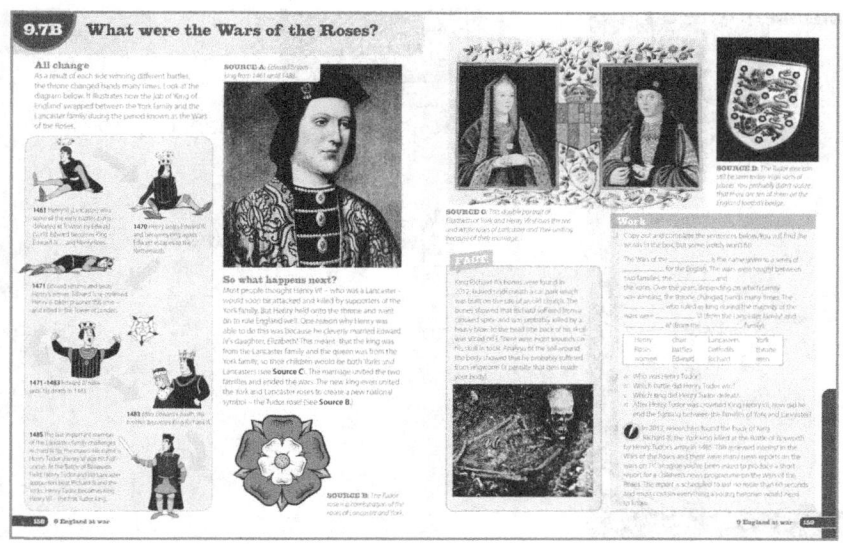

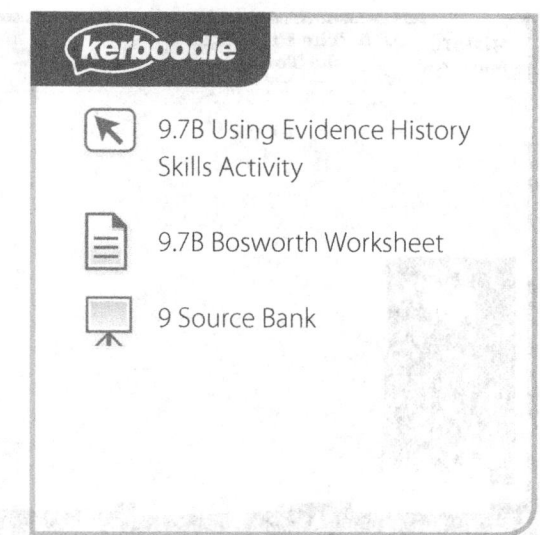

Invasion, Plague and Murder pages 158–159

## Lesson summary

Students will develop an understanding of how the Tudors became the new royal family and how they ended the fight for the English crown.

### What are the lesson outcomes?

**All** students will be able to identify which families were involved in the Wars of the Roses, and who won.

**Most** students will be able to describe in detail the story of the Wars of the Roses.

**Some** students will be able to explain the reasons why England went to war.

## Starter suggestion

- Key questions: Ask students three key questions to unlock the lesson:
  - Which two families fought in the Wars of the Roses?
  - How long did the war last?
  - By 1485, who is likely to win the struggle? Why?

## Main learning suggestions and assessment

### What activities will take place?

**Task 1:** Students should read the information on pages 158–159 and complete Work activities **1** and **2**.

### How will students demonstrate their understanding?

**Task 2:** Students should complete 9.7B Using Evidence History Skills Activity, investigating the coats of arms of Henry VII and Elizabeth of York.

**Task 3:** Students should complete 9.7B Bosworth Worksheet, investigating sources to understand the Battle of Bosworth.

 **Task 4:** Students should complete Work activity **3**, investigating Richard III.

## Plenary suggestions

- Learning triangle: Students could identify three things that they have learned in this lesson and two questions they would like to ask another student or research further.

## Differentiation suggestions

### Support

- Lower ability students will find using the timeline from lesson 9.7A helpful in answering Work activities **1** to **3**.

### Extension: Hungry for more?

- Work activity **3**, The Big Write, is an extended piece of writing to stretch higher ability students.

- Students could use the Internet to find a picture of Bosworth Field today. In their opinion, would a visit to the site of the battle be useful in working out what happened? They should explain their answers.

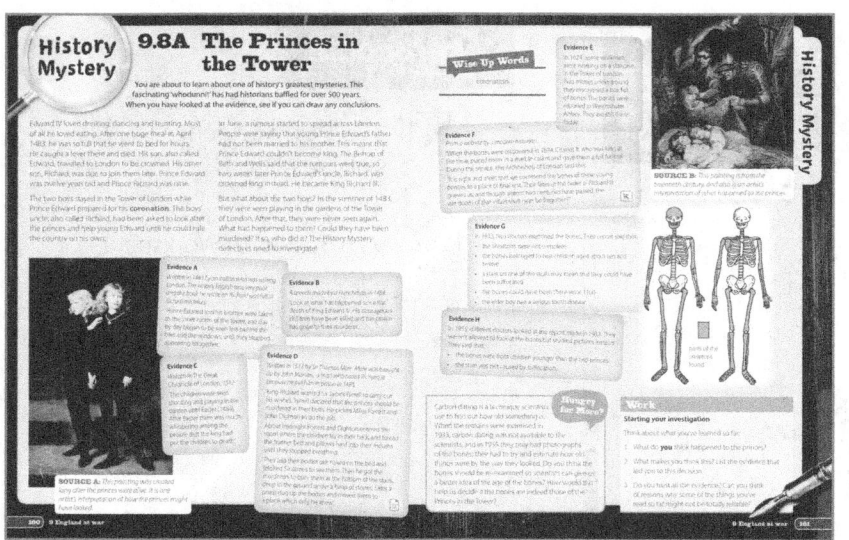

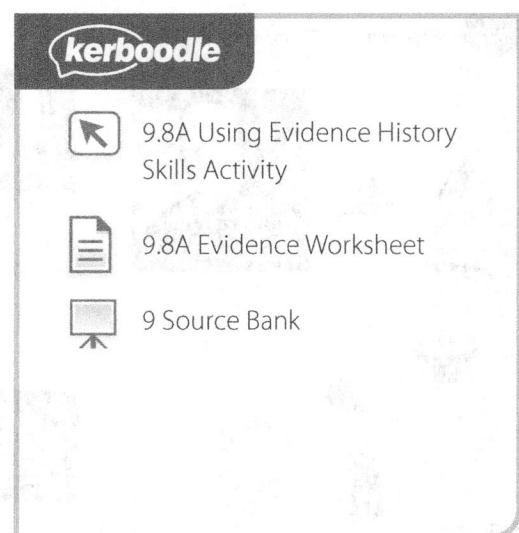

Invasion, Plague and Murder pages 160–161

## Lesson summary

Students will complete an investigation into who might have killed the Princes in the Tower.

### What are the lesson outcomes?

**All** students will be able to state who they think was responsible for the princes' deaths.

**Most** students will be able to explain who they believe was responsible for the princes' deaths and will be able to provide evidence to support their judgement.

**Some** students will be able to judge which evidence is the most reliable.

## Starter suggestion

- You could start by reading the following statement to students: 'Detectives, you have a new case to investigate. Two princes – one of them being Edward V, the next King of England – have disappeared and you need to solve the mystery to find out what has happened to them. Use pieces of evidence A to L to help you complete your report, but remember to ask yourself, can I trust each piece of evidence?' Students should work in pairs to come up with three questions that they are going to investigate over the next two lessons.

## Main learning suggestions and assessment

### What activities will take place?

**Task 1:** Students should read the information on pages 160–161 and complete 9.8A Using Evidence History Skills Activity, comparing **Evidence D** and **Evidence F** to investigate what happened to the two princes.

### How will students demonstrate their understanding?

**Task 2:** Students should investigate **Evidence D** using 9.8A Evidence Worksheet.

**Task 3:** Students should complete Work activities **1** to **3**.

## Plenary suggestions

- Exit note: Students could complete the following sentence: 'One thing I need to remember from this lesson is that…'

## Differentiation suggestions

### Support

- As there are a lot of textual sources in this lesson, it might be a good idea to list key bullet points for each piece of evidence as a class, or highlight them using the tools in the *Kerboodle Book*.

### Extension: Hungry for more?

- Students could investigate modern methods that could be used to find out who the bones belonged to.

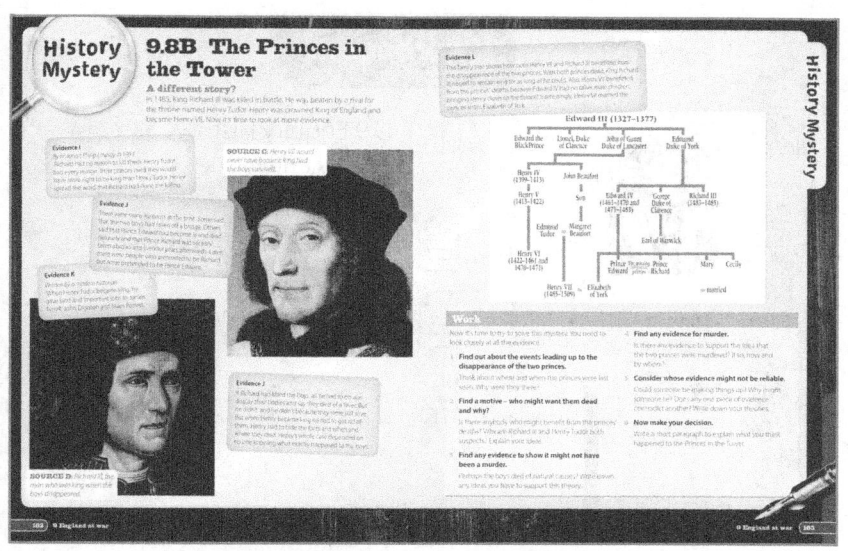

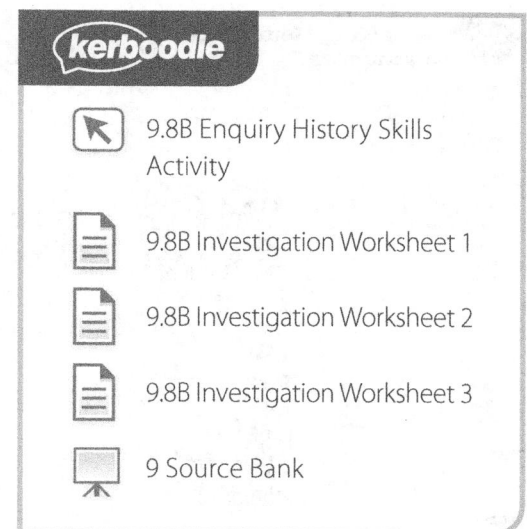

Invasion, Plague and Murder pages 162–163

## Lesson summary

Students will complete an investigation into who might have killed the Princes in the Tower.

### What are the lesson outcomes?

**All** students will be able to state who they think was responsible for the princes' deaths.

**Most** students will be able to explain who they believe was responsible for the princes' deaths and will be able to provide evidence to support their judgement.

**Some** students will be able to judge which evidence is the most reliable.

## Starter suggestion

- Today's headline: Students could write a headline for a news report on the death of the princes. What do they already know about their deaths? These can be shared with the class.

## Main learning suggestions and assessment

### What activities will take place?

**Task 1:** Students should read the information on 162–163 and complete 9.8B Enquiry History Skills Activity, deciding which sources suggest Richard might have killed the princes and which suggest it might not have been murder. During this task students should be recording their findings using 9.8B Investigtion Worksheet 1.

### How will students demonstrate their understanding?

**Task 2:** Students should complete 9.8B Investigation Worksheet 2 or 9.8B Investigation Worksheet 3, writing a report into who they think killed the princes. For higher ability students, Worksheet 2 contains a basic structure to help them to organize their report into paragraphs. For lower ability students, Worksheet 3 includes a writing frame to help them develop their answers.

## Plenary suggestions

- Debate stations: Allocate two areas within the classroom, one for students who believe that the princes were murdered and one are for students who believe that the princes were not murdered. Students should spend five minutes in their groups to create a statement to read to the other group. Each group should encourage the opposing group to question their evidence and hypothesis.

## Differentiation suggestions

### Support

- 9.8B Investigation Worksheet 3 includes a writing frame to support lower ability students.

### Extension: Hungry for more?

- In groups, students could film a historical reconstruction of the princes' murder, based on what they think happened. Ask them to imagine that the reconstruction will be televised and shown to a modern audience, so one of the students should be a narrator who will explain what evidence led them to their conclusion.

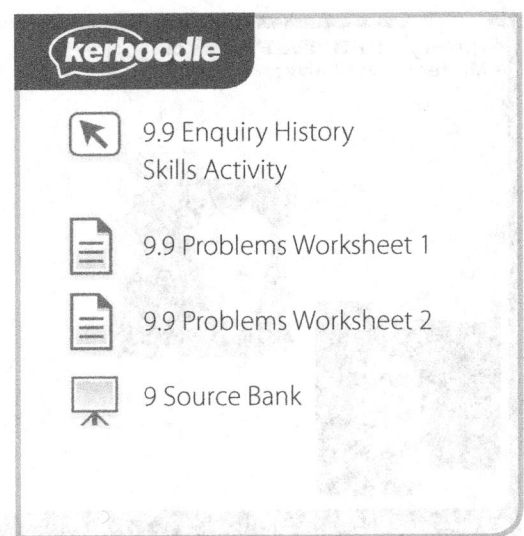

Invasion, Plague and Murder pages 164–165

## Lesson summary

Students should understand what problems Henry VII had to deal with when he became King of England and how he dealt with each of these issues.

### What are the lesson outcomes?

**All** students will identify at least three problems that Henry VII faced.

**Most** students will be able to explain how Henry VII solved the problems he faced.

**Some** students will be able to identify what characteristics Henry VII displayed to solve his problems.

## Starter suggestion

- Think, pair, share: Give students 30 seconds to consider what characteristics a gangster might possess. They should then be given one minute to discuss their ideas with a partner. This should feed into a class discussion where each pair shares their ideas with the class in order to create a list of characteristics a gangster might have. Encourage students to discuss throughout this lesson whether Henry VII displays any of these characteristics.

## Main learning suggestions and assessment

### What activities will take place?

**Task 1:** Students should read the information on pages 164–165 and complete 9.9 Problems Worksheet 1. They need to sort out the cards to match Henry's problems with the correct solution.

### How will students demonstrate their understanding?

**Task 2:** Students should complete 9.9 Problems Worksheet 2 to write a letter imagining that they are Henry VII, and detailing how they solved their problems.

**Task 3:** Was Henry VII a gangster? Students should look back at the gangster characteristics they created at the beginning of the lesson. Run a class debate using 9.9 Enquiry History Skills Activity to decide if Henry VII was a gangster. Encourage students to explain what characteristics Henry displayed whilst trying to solve his problems.

## Plenary suggestions

- Hot seat: Allocate each student a character from this list: a Viking; a Norman; Henry VII. They need to plan responses to the following questions:
  - Why will you make a good king?
  - What problems do you face?
  - How will you solve your problems?
  - Do you think you deserve the title of 'gangster'?

This can be run as a class discussion with students being invited to the front to answer. Other students can respond with questions. Alternatively, students can work in groups of three, discussing each response in turn.

## Differentiation suggestions

### Support

- 9.9 Problems Worksheet 2 includes detailed success criteria to support lower ability students.

### Extension: Hungry for more?

- Students could carry out research into **Source A**, the painting of Henry VII. Ask them to write a caption, of no more that 200 words, that could be used in an art gallery to tell visitors about the painting.

# Overview:
# Chapter 10 Medieval Britain: what changed?

## Helping you deliver KS3 History National Curriculum

This concluding chapter, set out in a chronological framework, challenges students to evaluate the historical concepts of change and continuity. The impact of new ideas and discoveries, both in Britain and the wider world, are covered here. Significant events are also highlighted. Together these show how Britain developed and changed during the medieval period. Students will also be asked to identify links between different events and/or discoveries, and show how one event and/or discovery led to another.

## The Big Picture

### Why are we teaching 'Medieval Britain: what changed?'?

This chapter aims to sum up how new ideas, theories, discoveries, and inventions changed Britain during the period 1066 to 1509. Firstly, the students are introduced to 'Edwin' from the year 1100. They are asked to consider what Edwin knows (or thinks he knows) about the world he lives in. The character then talks about his beliefs about the world, religion, health and medicine, the power of kings, and so on.

After establishing what a typical mindset of the Middle Ages might be, the students are then taken on a journey through over 400 years of invention, discovery, and development, up to 1509 (the year that the book closes on). The students are then introduced to 'John', a Tudor gentleman from the early 1500s. Dotted around John are some questions that the students need to think about, perhaps individually, with a partner, or as a class. These questions ask students to consider what has changed. Is the king still in

## Skills and processes covered in this chapter

| | | 10.1A | 10.1B |
|---|---|---|---|
| **History Skills** | Historical enquiry | ✓ | ✓ |
| | Using evidence and source work | | |
| | Chronological understanding | ✓ | ✓ |
| | Understanding cultural, ethnic and religious diversity | ✓ | ✓ |
| | Change and continuity | ✓ | ✓ |
| | Cause and consequence | ✓ | ✓ |
| | Significance | ✓ | ✓ |
| | Interpretations | | |
| | Making links/connections | ✓ | ✓ |
| | Explores similarities and differences | ✓ | ✓ |
| **Literacy and Numeracy** | Key words identified/deployed | | |
| | Extended writing | | ✓ |
| | Encourages reading for meaning | ✓ | ✓ |
| | Focuses on structuring writing | | ✓ |
| | Asks students to use writing to explore and develop ideas | ✓ | ✓ |
| | Learn through talk/discussion | ✓ | ✓ |
| | Numeracy opportunities | | |
| **Activity types** | Creative task | | |
| | Emphasizes role of individual | | ✓ |
| | Group work | | |
| | Independent research | | ✓ |
| | Develops study skills | ✓ | ✓ |

complete control of the country? Has weaponry altered? Has health and medicine moved on? Hopefully, by giving human faces to this chapter, the students will be able to put themselves into an early Tudor frame of mind. They should be able to identify that Tudor Britain was vastly different in many ways, but hadn't changed at all in others!

## Lesson sequence

| Lesson title | NC references | Objectives | Outcomes |
|---|---|---|---|
| **10.1A What does John know that Edwin didn't?** pp166–167 <br><br> **10.1B What does John know that Edwin didn't?** pp168–169 | Society economy and culture 1066–1509 | • Examine some of the key discoveries, theories, ideas, and inventions of the Middle Ages. <br> • Assess how new ideas, theories, discoveries, and inventions changed Britain. | **All** students will be able to identify three differences between life in 1066 and life in 1500. <br> **Most** students will be able to explain some of the key discoveries, theories, ideas, and inventions of the Middle Ages. <br> **Some** students will be able to assess how new ideas, theories, discoveries, and inventions changed Britain. |

### Ideas for enrichment

There is ample opportunity in this chapter for independent learning at home or in the school library. You could write each invention, discovery, or idea down and students could pick one out of a hat. This could become their personal research project, which could become a class project. Alternatively, each student could choose an invention or discovery themselves and research it carefully. Who invented it, for example? When? Where? How? What impact did it have? Was it an immediate impact, or did the importance of the invention or discovery take time to become apparent?

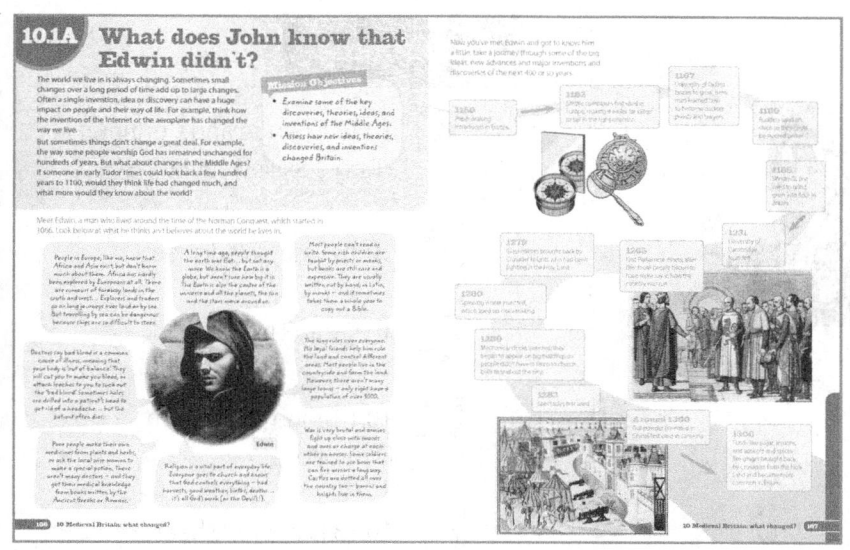

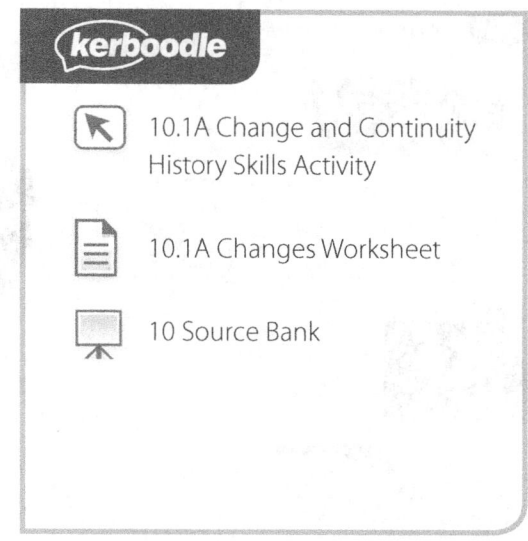

Invasion, Plague and Murder pages 166–167

## Lesson summary

Students should compare the lives of a man who lived in 1066 with a man who lived in 1500. How had life changed?

### What are the lesson outcomes?

**All** students will be able to identify three differences between life in 1066 and life in 1500.

**Most** students will be able to explain some of the key discoveries, theories, ideas, and inventions of the Middle Ages.

**Some** students will be able to assess how new ideas, theories, discoveries, and inventions changed Britain.

## Starter suggestion

- 3, 5, 7: Explain to students that they have 20 seconds to think of changes that happened between 1066 and 1500. Give them some prompts with the following headings: discoveries; theories; ideas; inventions. Then give them 30 seconds to discuss their ideas with a partner and come up with five good ideas between them. Students should then work in small groups to come up with the seven most significant changes during this period. Each group should share their ideas with the class.

## Main learning suggestions and assessment

### What activities will take place?

**Task 1:** Students should read the information on pages 166–167 and complete 10.1A Change and Continuity History Skills Activity to assess their understanding of the differences between life in 1066 and life in 1509.

### How will students demonstrate their understanding?

**Task 2:** Students should complete 10.1A Changes Worksheet to create a spider diagram showing what changed between 1066 and 1509, under the following headings: discovery; war; everyday life; inventions; science; medicine; religion; other.

**Task 3:** Students should write down at least five things that Edwin might have thought about Britain, the world, science, or medicine.

## Plenary suggestions

- Different shoes: Ask students to imagine being Edwin. They should make a list, with a partner, of the ways their lives as Edwin would be different from their lives today.

## Differentiation suggestions

### Support

- 10.1B John and Edwin can be played here or in the next lesson. The dialogue between the two characters makes it easier for students to grasp the main changes that took place in the Middle Ages.

### Extension: Hungry for more?

- Ask students to choose one of the events or inventions on page 167 of the *Student Book* and do some further research to produce a short fact file on it.

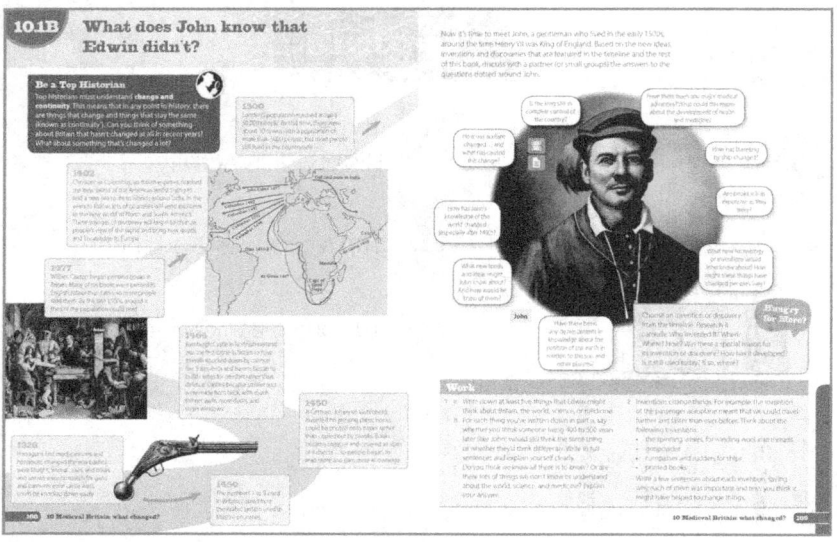
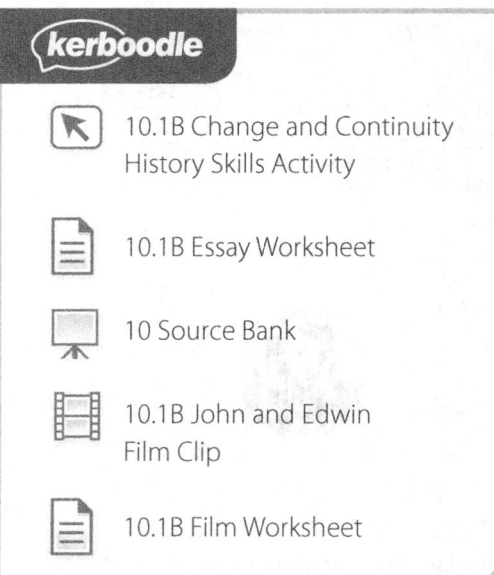

Invasion, Plague and Murder pages 168–169

## Lesson summary
Students should compare the lives of a man who lived in 1066 with a man who lived in 1500. How had life changed?

### What are the lesson outcomes?
**All** students will be able to identify three differences between life in 1066 and life in 1500.

**Most** students will be able to explain some of the key discoveries, theories, ideas, and inventions of the Middle Ages.

**Some** students will be able to assess how new ideas, theories, discoveries, and inventions changed Britain.

## Starter suggestion
● Let's get started!: Students could complete the following sentences: 'Before this lesson I could already…'; 'Today I would like to know…'.

## Main learning suggestions and assessment
### What activities will take place?
**Task 1:** Students should read the information on pages 168–169. They should create a spider diagram showing what John thinks and believes, under the following headings: discovery; war; everyday life; inventions; science; medicine; religion; other.

**Task 2:** Watch 10.1B John and Edwin Film Clip to see a villein from 1066 discussing everyday life with his descendant from 1509. Ask students to complete the accompanying film worksheet after viewing the clip. Students should then complete Work activities **1** and **2**.

### How will students demonstrate their understanding?
**Task 3:** Students should use 10.1B Change and Continuity History Skills Activity to debate how life changed from 1066 to 1509 in England, and what the driving forces for change were.

**Task 4:** Students should write an essay entitled 'How did life in England change from 1066 to 1509?'. They should pick four areas to discuss, and they can use 10.1B Essay Worksheet to help them organize their essays.

## Plenary suggestions
● Exit note: Students could consider everything they have learned in Chapter 10 and complete the following sentence: 'One thing I learned or enjoyed is…'.

## Differentiation suggestions
### Support
● 10.1B Essay Worksheet includes guidance to help students create their essay.

### Extension: Hungry for more?
● Students could choose an invention or discovery from the timeline, and carry out some research. Who invented it? When? Where? How? Was there a special reason for its invention or discovery? How has it developed? Is it still used today? If so, where?

### kerboodle
- 10.1B Change and Continuity History Skills Activity
- 10.1B Essay Worksheet
- 10 Source Bank
- 10.1B John and Edwin Film Clip
- 10.1B Film Worksheet

# Glossary

**Abbey**  A building where a community of monks or nuns lived

**AD**  'Anno domini'; used for dates after the birth of Jesus Christ

**Ale**  An alcoholic drink similar to beer

**Apothecary**  A person who prepared and sold medicines

**Barber-surgeon**  Men who performed surgery and dentistry as well as cutting hair

**Barbican**  The outer defensive tower of a castle, found above the drawbridge

**Battering ram**  A heavy beam swung or rammed against a door to break it down

**Battleaxe**  A large, broad-bladed weapon

**Battlements**  The top of a castle wall with openings for archers to shoot through

**BC**  'Before Christ'; used for dates before the birth of Jesus Christ

**Beaker people**  A European Bronze Age people who settled in Britain and made decorated pottery

**Black Death**  A killer disease that wiped out millions of people across Europe

**Bloodletting**  The practice of making someone bleed to help cure an illness

**British Isles**  The group of islands including Britain, Ireland, the Isle of Man, the Orkney Islands, and the Shetland Islands

**Bronze Age**  A period when weapons and tools were made of bronze; it came between the Stone Age and the Iron Age

**Bubonic**  One of the two types of plague in Black Death; carried by fleas

**Chain mail**  Flexible armour made of small metal rings linked together

**Chancellor**  The most important position in England after the king; it involved sending out royal letters and charters

**Charter**  A statement of a group of people's rights, written by the king or a lord

**Chivalry**  The moral and social code followed by medieval knights

**Chronicle**  A account of important historical events, most often written by a monk

**Chronology**  The arrangement of dates or events in the order they happened, starting with the earliest

**Church**  The collective name for Christians across England and the world

**Coat of arms**  A distinctive design belonging to a knight or family, often used on shields, flags and clothing

**Concentric castle**  A castle built with several walls of decreasing heights, so soldiers could shoot attackers more effectively

**Conqueror**  A person who takes over a place or people, often by invasion

**Consecrated**  When someone is officially given a position of religious responsibility and duty

**Constable**  A man in charge of a group of watchmen

**Coronation**  The ceremony of crowning a king or queen

**Crusades**  A series of journeys made by Europeans to take the Holy Land back from Muslims in the Middle Ages

**Curtain wall**  A strong wall around a castle that linked towers together

**Doom painting**  A painting in a church designed to show people images of heaven and hell

**Dowry**  Money that a bride's family give to her husband when she marries, or to a nunnery when she becomes a nun

**Dubbed**  When a man is touched on the shoulder with a sword and becomes a knight

**Dysentery**  A disease that causes terrible diarrhoea

**Earldom**  The piece of land that was controlled by an earl

**Evidence**  The facts or information that we have about a particular event, person or place

**Excommunicated**  When someone has been officially excluded from the Christian Church

**Export**  A product that is sold to another country

**Feudal system**  A system developed by King William where each group of people owed loyalty to the group above, starting with villeins, knights, barons and ending with the king

**Fyrd**  Warriors who fought for Harold at the battle of Hastings; they were numerous, but not very well trained

**Garderobe**  A toilet in a medieval building

**Great Council**  A group, including the king and his barons, that met to discuss how the country should be run

**Guild**  A group of a certain type of craftsmen, with their own rules

**Hauberk**  A full-length coat of chain mail

**Heir**  The person who is next in line to become king or queen

**Herald**  A person who supervised tournaments, made annoucements and carried messages

**Heraldry**  The way in which coats of arms were created and used to identify knights or families

**Housecarl**  A type of well trained warrior who used battleaxes and fought for Harold at the Battle of Hastings

**Hue and cry**  A loud cry calling for people to pursue and capture a criminal

**Humours**  The four main liquids in the body; illness was thought to be caused by them being out of balance

**Hundred Years War**  A series of battles between England and France that began in 1337

**Hunter-gatherer**  A person who lived mainly by hunting, fishing and harvesting wild plants

**Illuminated**  A manuscript that is decorated with gold, silver and coloured designs

**Immigrant**  Someone who has travelled from another country to settle

**Inferior**  A person who is lower in rank or status than someone else

**Infidel**  A person who has no religion or whose religion is not the same as that of another group of people

**Inhabited**  A place where people live

**Invasion**  Coming into another country, normally with an armed force, with the intention to take over

**Iron Age**  A period when weapons and tools were made of iron; it came after the Bronze Age

**Javelin**  A light spear thrown as a weapon

**Jury**  A group of people who decide whether someone is innocent or guilty of a crime

**Lance**  A long weapon with a pointed steel tip, used by warriors on horseback

**Leech**  Blood-sucking creatures used in medieval medicine

**Loyalty**  Staying true to someone, and being honest and helpful to them

**Mace**  A heavy club with a spiked metal head that could break armour

**Magna Carta**  A document setting out people's rights; the barons made King John sign it in 1215

**Mangonel**  A device used in sieges that could throw stones and other objects

**Manuscript**  A book that was written by hand, often by monks, and was sometimes illuminated

**Marshal**  A man responsible for supervising tournaments and making sure competitors didn't cheat

**Massacred**  When a large group of people has been brutally killed by someone else

**Merchant**  A person who is involved in the buying and selling of goods

**Minstrel**  A medieval singer or musician who often sang tales of heroic deeds

**Miracle play**  A popular medieval play based on biblical stories or the lives of the saints

**Monastery**  A building where a community of monks lived

**Monk**  A member of a community of men who lived under religious vows in a monastery

**Motive**  The reason that a person has for doing something

**Motte and bailey**  An early castle that featured a fort on a hill surrounded by a fence or wall

**Norman**  People from Normany, France, who invaded Britain in 1066 and were led by William of Normandy

**Norman Conquest**  The invasion and settlement of England by the Normans, starting with the Battle of Hastings in 1066

**Oubliette**  A secret dungeon in a castle

**Page**  A boy, in service to a knight, who is training to become a knight himself

**Parliament**  Controls the country and is made up of the monarch, the House of Lords and the House of Commons

**Paying homage**  When a man publicly shows respect and loyalty to his lord

**Peasants' Revolt**  An uprising where peasants, led by Wat Tyler, marched on London in 1381

**Pilgrim**  A person who travels to a holy place for religious reasons

**Pillory** A wooden frame with holes for head and hands that was used as a punishment

**Pneumonic** One of the two types of plague in Black Death; carried in the air

**Pope** The head of the Catholic Church

**Portcullis** A heavy, strong barrier that can be lowered to block a castle gateway

**Protest** An action that shows that someone is unhappy or angry about something

**Protestor** Someone who takes part in a protest

**Purging** Making someone sick or go to the toilet in the belief that this would cure their illness

**Rebellion** A violent protest

**Retreating** When an army pulls out from a battle because they are being defeated

**Revolt** Another word for a rebellion or uprising

**Sapper** Soldiers who mined under castles in order to collapse the walls

**Saracen** A name for a Muslim at the time of the Crusades

**Scavenger** A person employed to clean the streets

**Scold's bridle** An instrument of punishment for a scolding woman; it fitted over the head and made talking difficult or painful

**Scriptorium** A room in a monastery in which manuscripts were copied

**Scythe** A weapon with a long, curved blade at the end of a pole

**Shield-wall** A long line of shields used for defence in a battle

**Siege** A method of attack where an army surrounds a castle, cutting off essential supplies, until the enemy is forced to surrender

**Spear** A weapon with a pointed tip on the end of a pole

**Squire** A young man, in service to a knight, who is training to become a knight himself

**Stocks** A wooden frame with holes for feet that was used as a punishment

**Stone Age** A period when weapons and tools were made of stone; it came before the Bronze Age

**Tilt** The barrier between jousting knights that prevented a fallen knight being trampled by the horses

**Timeline** A diagram showing events or dates in chronological order

**Tithe** The tenth of the food peasants grew that had to be given to the Church

**Tithing** A group of ten people who were responsible for each other's behaviour

**Tournament** A medieval event in which knights mounted on horseback jousted with blunted weapons

**Trade** The buying and selling of materials

**Trebuchet** A machine used in siege warfare that could throw large stones or other objects

**Trencher** A thick slice of bread used as a plate

**Trepanning** Drilling a hole in a patient's head in the belief that this would cure their headache

**Trial by ordeal** A way of letting God decide whether someone is innocent or guilty; common trials were fire, water and combat

**Undermine** To dig beneath a castle's walls in order to make them collapse

**Vellum** Fine parchment made from animal skins

**Viking** People from Denmark, Norway and Sweden who invaded Britain after 800 AD

**Villein** A peasant who worked for a lord in return for land

**Wars of the Roses** A series of battles between the English houses of York and Lancaster

**Watch** A group of people who patrolled the streets at night

**Wattle and daub** A medieval building material made of interwoven sticks covered with mud or clay